Talismans

of the

Golden Dawn

Talismans & Evocations
of the
Golden Dawn

by
Pat Zalewski

THOTH PUBLICATIONS
Loughborough, Leicestershire

A CIP catalogue record for this book is available from the
British Library.

Cover design by Tabatha Cicero
Additional diagrams by Nick Farrell, Cass and Brian Thompson

Printed and bound in Great Britain

Published by Thoth Publications
64, Leopold Street, Loughborough, LE11 5DN

ISBN 1 870450 36 1
web address: www.thoth.co.uk
email: enquiries@thoth.co.uk

CONTENTS

Introduction

This book on talismans and evocation techniques is a further extension of my previous 'Z' works regarding the magical techniques used by the Golden Dawn. Although much has been written on the history and initiation ceremonies of the Order of the Golden Dawn and its successors, the Stella Matutina and Whare Ra, little has been presented on the practical magical workings of its Inner Order the Rosae Rubae Et Aureae Crucis. Many assume that the order members simply performed the rituals presented by Israel Regardie in his Golden Dawn book. However this is far from the case. A large body of teaching was presented to the new initiate about evocation and talisman manufacture and each adept was expected to use this information to write and perform his or her own rituals.

To the best of my knowledge only the evocation ritual has appeared in print and that was an edited version in Crowley's Equinox volume. Where I could I used original manuscript source and you will see this in the Evocation ritual where I have replaced text taken out of the original ritual. I am deeply indebted to my old friend Nick Farrell who, being based in England, waded through mountains of material for me to obtain the specific papers so that I could compare them with those I had in New Zealand.

Most personal rituals, such as the Z2, are an evolutionary process which change with the development of a personality. For example, when I spoke to Israel Regardie in 1983, he felt that it was unnecessary to use anything but planetary names of power during a talisman ritual. This meant omitting all the other Kabbalistic associations of the 0=0 ceremony and I disagreed with him. It was my view that the 0=0 ceremony, which is the template of the talisman making and evocation rituals must never be forgotten, and this employed a broad spectrum of names. But Regardie was in his seventies and felt they were unnecessary and perhaps I will think the same when I am that age. All people are different and they must evolve rituals to suit their nature.

In the old Golden Dawn, an adept was asked to do one of the Z2 rituals to prove that he or she had the ability to reach the next level. The most common Z2 rituals are that of the first two books of the Z2 paper known as formula Yod and Heh (evocation and talisman rituals). These two books have been included in a single volume in the Z2 series.

Included in this volume are Golden Dawn papers and some from the later Thoth-Hermes Temple that shed new light on talisman and evocation techniques. I have not included the other material, as this would make abook too large for present purposes. Other material has already been addressed in my book *Magical Tarot of the Golden Dawn*.

Personally I think that Mathers had a lot to answer for by putting the 'invisibility and transformation' rituals in the 5=6 grade. There is only one adept in ten million who could do either successfully. They should have been replaced with rituals for exorcism and healing as both these areas were neglected by the higher grades of the Golden Dawn.

In *Golden Dawn Enochian Magic* I showed how to manipulate the Z2 using a crystal for divination. In *Enochian Chess of the Golden Dawn* Chris Zalewski modified the Z2 Divination ritual to fit into an Enochian chess game. Z2 could be adapted to fit into other areas apart from those mentioned and I recommend that readers experiment in that direction.

I have to apologise to the reader for some previously published Golden Dawn material, but it is unavoidable if the whole package is going to be presented as a single unit, otherwise the reader will be going between books trying to piece it together. But there is also quite a bit of material that is new and shows some of the directions I have gone in my own research. If these are a help to readers then I have accomplished my task.

This was not a book I intended to publish. I had planned to hand it out to people who were members of my temple 10 years ago. However with a bit of arm-twisting on the part of friends and students I decided to give it a chance in the public domain. There is quite a bit of material in this book which I gave out in a lecture in Seattle in the United States of America during my last visit in 1996 for a serious of lectures for Laura Jennings and Peter Yorke's temple.

I wish to thank a number of people who helped in obtaining material for this book including Nick Farrell, who searched the Warburg manuscripts, Darcy Kuntz who provided two unpublished rituals of Bennett and his Talisman for Dr Felkin which was a real find. And lastly Tom Clarke of Thoth Publications. Without these three, this book would never have been published.

On a final note, I have returned to my native Australia after 30 years living in New Zealand and now live in the tropical city of Cairns on Australia's far North East Coast where the humidity is a life form of its own.

Pat Zalewski
Crocodile Country
Cairns 2002

BOOK ONE

YOD

EVOCATION

Chapter One

In 1896 a group of some of the finest adepts in Golden Dawn's history gathered in London to achieve the impossible, to make a spirit of Mercury physically appear before them.

The ritual to achieve this was written by Alan Bennett, who was later to became Aleister Crowley's teacher and it was conducted by one of the most senior members of the order, a former mistress of fellow Golden Dawn member WB Yeats, Florence Farr.

As Magus of the Art, she was dressed in a white robe and a yellow sash with an indigo nemyss. Around her neck was a seal of the being she hoped to make appear - Taphthartharath. In her left hand was an Egyptian symbol of immortality; in her right was the rainbow coloured lotus wand. In her belt was a dagger to banish evil.

Bennett was the assistant Magus, he was also dressed in a white robe but had a black nemyss and had a heavy black chain about his neck. He wore a snakeskin belt and a lamen with a symbol on the front that meant 'Spirit'. On the back of this lamen was a symbol that stood for the office of Heirus in the Golden Dawn. In his left hand Bennett held a whale oil candle that had been prepared in a separate ceremony. In his right a sword of exorcism - in case the ritual went wrong.

In front of them simmered a hell broth, a pot of magical substances designed to attract the spirit Taphthartharath.

The ritual was conducted within an octagram drawn in orange chalk on the floor of the temple. Outside the octagram was drawn a triangle in which the spirit was about to appear.

Inside the octagram were two other officers - the Magus of Fire, responsible for keeping a steady stream of perfumed smoke and the Magus of Water who had to keep the temple pure.

There was some nervousness in the participants. The ritual had been to be cancelled once because they had all developed mysterious illnesses. However, according to the diary notes of the participants, the ritual worked well. All four reported seeing an arm and a leg appear in the triangle of the art and gradually a grey human form emerged.

The effect was short lived, for within a few minutes the figure disappeared and all feeling of power left the room.

This ritual was declared a success.

Evocation techniques were introduced in the Golden Dawn to candidates hoping to attain the Theoricus Adeptus Minor grade. In the 19th century, evocation literature abounded in the British Museum and on dusty book shelves. But the Golden Dawn was more systematic, combining techniques with pertinent points from their Neophyte or initiation ritual to provide checks and balances. Adepts had to study what they were evoking and to what level they wanted to appear. It is possible to evoke a spirit or angel, a dead person (which comes under the heading Necromancy), or an elemental.

Evocation by a Golden Dawn magician had a definitive pattern which can be traced to a first century Greek text called the *The Testament of Solomon*.[1]

The text tells of how Solomon's favourite servant was enslaved by a demon during the building of the temple. The demon also appeared in the temple at night and knocked down the previous day's building work(other versions have the demon robbing Solomon daily).

Solomon called upon God's help and the Archangel Raphael (or Michael, depending on what version you read) appeared and handed him a ring[2] which was engraved with a magic five pointed

---

[1] Translated by Fleck from the Greek to the German around 1850, and then translated by Conybeare into English in the *Jewish Quarterly Review*, Vol. XI, London, 1899.

[2] This was said to be made of iron, a metal which demons cannot abide. Other stories say it was a diamond in a shamir stone, while other sources say it was made from the root of a mandrake plant (a plant which is said to have magical powers in exorcism).

star and with series of names.[3] Raphael told Solomon to use this ring to control all demons.

The first victim of the ring was the demon that enslaved his servant. Solomon commanded the demon to come before him and tell him his name. The demon appeared and said he was Ornais and he ruled over the sign of Aquarius. He could strangle people, change into human shape and seduce men in their sleep.

Solomon gave Ornais the ring and told him to bring other demons before the King. Ornais brought back Beelzeboul[4], King of the demons, who had all the demons under his control. Some of Beelzeboul's demonic officers mentioned in the text are Oneskelis[5], a succubus; Asmodeus, representing the constellation of the seven sisters or Wain's Wright, who prevents matrimony and inspires lust; Tephras the fire lighter, who governs a portion of the Moon; Akephalos and Obizuth the baby killer.

Solomon compiled a list of 32 demons and their areas of government, some of these areas being diseases. Solomon obtained the spells and words that rendered the demons' powers inoperative. These djin or demons of the decani of the zodiac and planets, appear to have their roots in Egyptian mythology.

Other *Clavicles of Solomon*[6] (or *Greater Key of Solomon* as it is sometimes called) appeared in Latin translations, around the mid 16th century[7]. MacGregor Mathers, one of the founders of the

---

[3] One version has the names SLYT, SPYLT, TRYKT, PPMRYT, HLPT, ALYPT, HLYPT. Another version has the names HQQPS, SHHLT, TWRSP, HSPT, BRWLHT, ALYLT, PTPNT, RHMT, QPYDT, SHPLT, HQYKT, PPAYSHNT, LMPS, WHLYMPT, DMPST, KTYBT, TRKLT, YSHRYET, DQST, LMSTMPS, MRYPT, PSYT, PPT, PSDMST, SHKLLT, PSYT, DMPS, PRYSHT, PLISHT.

[4] This Demon admitted that it was bound by the numbers 644 which translated into the name of Emanuel.

[5] Her opposite number, and whom she does combat with is the Angel Joel who represents the 'Wisdom of God'.

[6] Copies of this manuscript were distributed to Golden Dawn adepts (for those who could not afford to buy Mathers' book). Some of these are in the estate of Carr P. Collins and are Golden Dawn originals. At Whare Ra temple in New Zealand, I saw translations of this text in the estate of the late Euan Campbell (who reached the rank of 9=2 at Whare Ra) and who brought photos of each individual folio back from England and France in the late 1920's.

[7] British Museum (now library): Add. Mss 10,867, Tr. by Isau Abbraha, from the Hebrew.

Golden Dawn, translated different versions[8] of this manuscript into English in 1888.

Mathers' text has five major parts. The first is the purification of the items used in magic. The second is the process of evocation and the third is talismanic magic, by using pentacles. The fourth relates to the magical meanings of the biblical Psalms which bind a spirit to the operator's will. The magical use of the Psalms is something that most occultists overlook in favour of something more flamboyant. They are woven into the *Greater Key of Solomon* in such a way that their use is almost invisible.

The fifth part of the book relates to the use of planetary hours and seems to duplicate the work of the magician Peter Abano (though where he got his information is unknown to the writer). This is a sensible part of the manuscript and lists certain celestial patterns to be observed when performing rituals.

The text of the manuscript is well set out. It shows how to perform rituals correctly and safely. From studying of these texts, it is evident that the Mathers' version is incomplete, even if the missing sections found in other manuscripts are included. There may have been a master text that the present condensed versions were taken from.

The *Lesser Key of Solomon*[9] (or *Lemegeton*) is another manuscript used by Mathers for the Golden Dawn[10]. It is difficult to date, but there are elements in Agrippa's works that possibly came from this text or its original source. The *Lemegeton* is broken up into five parts.

---

[8] Taken from: Add.,10,862; Sloane Mss.,1307 & 3019; Harleian Mss.,3981; and King's Mss., 288; and Lansdowne Mss., 1202 & 1203. Additional titles (according to Waite) that can also be referred to on this Manuscript are at the French Library; *Les Clavicules de Rabbi Salomon*, 2346 (72SAF); *Livre de la Clavicule de Salomon, Roy des Hebreux* 2348(75SAF); Les Vrais Clavicules du Roy Salomon 2349(77SAF); *Les Secret des Secrets, autrement La Clavicule de Salomon, ou le veritable Gromoire* 2350(78SAF); *Livre Second de La Clavicule de Salomon* 2791 (76SAF).

[9] See 'Sloane 2731', & 'Sloane 3648' British Library, for an English translation of this text.

[10] The full manuscript was distributed to Golden Dawn adepts, Aleister Crowley published a part of it *The Goetia*. While some have considered that Crowley published this Mathers edition as his own work, the Mathers version was a direct copy of an English version in the British Museum.

The first part is called the *Goetia*[11] [12] and gives the names, sigils and functions of 72 spirits. These appear to be the mirror the angels of the Schemhamporesch whose names are based on the 72 lettered name of God.[13]. An example is the 31st spirit called Foras:[14]

'Foras, a great president who appears in the form of a strong man, and teaches the virtues of all herbs and precious stones, as well a logic and ethics; he makes men invisible, imparts wit, wisdom, and eloquence, discovers treasures and restores lost things.'

Both good and bad spirits, plus the entities of the cardinal points. The third part is called the *Pauline Art*[16] and is a treatise on the spirits of the hours of the days, nights and zodiac degrees. The Fourth part is the *Almadel*[17] and concerns angelic choirs and the spirits to the 360 degrees of the Zodiac. The Fifth part, a series of prayers that Solomon used in his Temple and is called the *Ars Notoria*[18] (Notary Art) and contains prayers and magical seals.

The second part is called the *Theurgia - Goetia*[15] which contains both good and bad spirits, plus the entities of the cardinal points. The third part is called the *Pauline Art*[16] and is a treatise on the spirits of the hours of the days, nights and zodiac degrees. The Fourth part is the *Almadel*[17] and concerns angelic choirs and the spirits to the 360 degrees of the Zodiac. The Fifth part, a series of prayers that Solomon used in his Temple and is called the *Ars Notoria*[18] (Notary Art) and contains prayers and magical seals.

---

[11] A Greek word meaning 'Witchcraft'.

[12] This is closely allied with a Latin work 'Psuedomonarchis Daemonum'(published as a part of the 'De Praestigiis Daemonum'by Johan Weir in 1563.

[13] See *Kabbalah of the Golden Dawn* by Pat Zalewski for a full discussion of these angels and their sigils.

[14] While playing the four handed game of Enochian chess, I invoked this spirit to prevent me losing. I needed additional logic and quickly. At the beginning of the game I invoked this spirit over the chess board and I won in only a couple of moves!

[15] See '*The first Book of the Steganographia* of Tithemius around 1500.

[16] See Bibliotheque Nationale (BN7170A).

[17] See *Florence II-iii:24*, a 15th century manuscript.

[18] The *Ars Notoria* is considered part of a memory treatise (attributed to Solomon), by Dame Francis Yates. It is found in *Archidoxes Magicae* of Paracelsus (Cracow 1569). Turner did a translation in 1657 *Ars Notoria: The Notary Art of Solomon*.

The *Grimorium Verum* is attributed to Solomon. There are indications it was first published by Alibeck in 1517.[19] To the best of my knowledge, no copy of the first publication has been found. It is like the *Greater Key* in its use of prayer, hierarchy, purification of items for evocation. The *Grimorium Verum* is in two main parts. The first concerns spirits for it says:

> "...is contained various dispositions of characters, by which the powers of the spirits, or, rather the devils are invoked, to make them, come when you will, each according to his power, and to bring whatever is asked: and that without any discomfort, providing that they are on their part content; for this sort of creature does not give anything for nothing."

The second part deals with the secrets of demons. There are instructions which could be considered a combination astral projection and divination:[20]

> "The two NN which you see in the second small circle mark the place where you put your name. To know what you will, write the names in the circle on virgin parchment, before sleeping, saying the following Orison...Having completed the Orison, lie down on your right side, and you will see in a dream that which you desire to know."

There are variations of this technique which are used today which in modern psychological jargon are called tapping into the 'Collective Unconscious'.

---

[19] Also called 'Most Approved Keys of Solomon the Hebrew Rabbin, wherein the most hidden secrets, both Natural and Supernatural, are immediately exhibited, but it is necessary that the Demons should be contended on their part. ' Translated the Hebrew (into French) by Plaingere, 'Jesiute Dominicaine'with a collection of Curious Secrets. The True Clavicles of Solomon. There are however, a later French edition ('Les Veritables Clavicules de Salomon. Tresor des Sciences Occultes, suives d'un Nombre des Secrets, et notamment de la Magie du papillionm Vert') and two editions published in Italian ('La Vera Clavicola del Re Salomone, Tesoro delle Scienze Occulte con Molti Altri Segreti e principalmonte La Cabala della Farfalla verde tradotte dalla Lingua Straniera alla Lingua Italiana da Bestetti. Milano 1868, and 1880 edition by Armato Muzzi) with the latter being more complete than the former.

[20] See 'Meditation and the Bible' by Rabbi Kaplan, (pages 90-91) who cites this prophetic technique from Isaiah 38:1 as being used by the Jews.

The *Grand Grimoire* is another important Solomonic text[21]. It is in two parts. The first is the evocation of Rofocale (Lucifer) while the second part is the 'how to' of making pacts with devils or spirits. The *Grand Grimoire* mixes black magic with alchemy, for some of its rituals may relate to uses of the Philosophers' Stone.

Another text is the *Grimoire of Honorius* which it is claimed to have been written by Pope Honorius III. This is unlikely since Pope Honorius III died about 900 years before this 17th Century text appeared. The author of this text introduced his work in the style of a Papal Bull giving priests the authority and techniques for controlling and directing good and evil spirits:

> "...But until the time of this Constitution, only the Ruling Pontificate has possessed the virtue and the power to command the spirits and invoking them. Now His Holiness, Honorius III, having become mellowed by his pastoral duties, has kindly decided to transmit the methods and ability of invoking and controlling spirits, to his brothers in Jesus Christ, the revered ones; and he has added the conjurations which are needed for this: and all is to be found in our Bull which follows...Servant of the Servants of God. To each and every one of our respected Brethren of the Holy Roman Church, the Cardinals, Archbishops, Bishops, and Abbots... Because, too, it is correct and right that those who minister at the Altar should be able to exercise power over the rebel spirits, we entrust them herewith the powers which have this far ours alone. And we command them, Papal Authority, to follow that which follows this utterly without change: otherwise through some omission they may attract upon them the anger of the All-Highest."

The *Three Books of Occult Philosophy*, by Henry Cornelius Agrippa', was studied intensely by Golden Dawn members.

Book One, first published in 1533 and was called *Natural Magic* and covered the properties of nature. Book Two was called *Celestial Magic* related to numerical structure and astronomy and astrology. Book Three was called *Ceremonial Magic* and covered angelic hierarchies, ritual and gematria[22].

The book that caused the most interest in the Golden Dawn

---

[21]   Its editor was purported to be Antino Venitiana del Rabina who is said to have copied it from the writings of Solomon.

[22]   These three books are available through Chthomios Books. Hastings, England.

was the so called *Fourth Book*, which was attributed to Agrippa. It was written in six parts, and was translated by Robert Turner. It was not written by Agrippa, though its text was often utilised by modern day occultists and is historically interesting.

The first part of the fourth Book is on Geomancy finishes with the word 'Gerard'. This may be Gerard of Sabbioneta[23] gave his geomantic framework to Agrippa to print in his Third Book. It is likely that Gerard may be the author of the Fourth book.

The second part[24] looks at astrology, astronomy, seals and sigils of good and evil spirits, planetary spirits and pentacles. It covers the consecration of magical implements, prayers, perfumes and oils to be used in ritual, and invocations and dream oracles.

The third part is the *Heptameron*[25] (magical elements) by Peter Abano. This examines the magical circle and tables of the hours of the ruling angels, consecrations and benedictions, construction of ritual garments and lamens.

The fourth part is called the *Isagoge*[26] (nature spirits) by Gerog Pictorius Villinganus. This is a treatise on the nature and function of spirits of the sublunary sphere. It covers illusions, names, powers and expulsions. The question and answer format distinguishes between spirits of the Church and Greek variety, which were considered negative. It is a compilation of different authors.

The fifth part is *Astronomical Geomancy* of Gerard Cremonensis. This departs from geomancy as a system of earth divination and aligns itself with astrology and the placement of geomantic symbols in the 12 astrological houses.

The sixth part is called the *Arbatel*[27]. This is a series of 49 aphorisms which explain the Olympic planetary spirits. There were to be nine sections or tomes of this book and this edition includes only one, with eight missing.

One of the most important figures in early occultism was that of Johannes Trithemius (1462-1516), who took magical concepts

---

[23]   I agree with Stephen Skinner, who first put forward this theory in his *Divination by Geomancy*.

[24]   There appears to be confusion as to Agrippa writing this, as his pupil Weir declared that this was not written by his master.

[25]   This text was printed in Latin in 1496.

[26]   Waite often accused Mathers of being too fond of the 'Isagoge'.

[27]   Printed at Basel in 1575.

and placed them on a scientific footing. He worked behind the scenes and advised his contemporary and friend, Agrippa[28],while still retaining his post as a Benedictine Abbot at Sponheim, in Germany. There are several works attributed to Trithemius, but the '*teganographia*[29] and '*Polygraphia* are the most important. The '*teganographia*' gives details on angels. It was from the *Steganographia*, that the alphabet used in mysterious Golden Dawn ciphers was based.

The *Secrets of Albert Magnus*[30] is another useful text. Whether this text is actually written by him is difficult to say. This Bishop of the Catholic Church was actually canonised in 1931. The first book of the *Secrets of Albert Magnus* discussed the virtue of magical plants and their use:

"Of the Healing power of the 13th herb.
     The 13th hearb is named of the Chaldees Olphantas, of the Greeks Hilirion, of the Latines Verbena, of the English men Vervin. This hearb (as witches say) gathered, the Sun being in the Signe of the ram, and put with graine or corne of piony of one yere old, heals them that are sick of the falling sickness."

The second book discusses the virtue of magical stones:

"If thou will burn any man's hand without fire.Take the stone which is called Fetipendamus which is of yellow colour, and if it be hanged upon the neck of any man it healeth Articum. Also, if this stone be griped straightly, it will burne the hand, and therefore it must be touched lightly and gently."

The third book discusses the virtues of certain beasts:

"Aquilla, the Eagle, is a bird very well known of the men of Chaldee.
It is called vorax, and of the Greeks Rimbicus.
Aaron and Euar say, that it hath marvelous nature of vertue.
For if the brain of it be turned into powder, and mixed with

---

[28]   Some occult historians claim that Agrippa's first three books were based on notes he took when he visited the Abbot around 1509. The written notes being different from the printed books of Agrippa.
[29]   A partial translation (Book II is missing) of this is published by *Magnum Opus Hermetic Sourceworks* 1982.
[30]   See *Book of Secrets* by Albert Magnus, also a Book of Marvels of the World.' edited by Best and Brightman, 1973.

the juice of Hemlocke, they that eat it shall take themselves by the haire, and shall not leave their hold, so long as they beare that they have received. The cause of this effect is, for that the braine is very colde insomuch that it engendereth fantastical vertue, shutting off the powers by smoke."

A favourite text that was consulted in the Golden Dawn was the Mathers' translation of *The Book of the Sacred Magic of Abra-Melin the Mage*. This was uncovered in the French Library Bibliotheque de l' Arsenal. This manuscript was said to have been delivered by Abraham the Jew to his son Lamech in 1458 A.D. Of all the magical manuscripts, this is the one that appears to have been the most effective.

Stories of its power and strength have abounded since its publication in the 1880's. One of the infamous instances was told in a letter to the *Occult Review* and subsequently appeared in Francis King's book *Ritual Magic in England*[31]. We will be looking at this incident later. The letter was written by a New Zealander, Hugh (Euan) Campbell[32]. Campbell was so troubled by the effects of a ritual using this book that Mrs. Felkin had to break him away from it. People who knew Campbell at the time of the problems say his letter was genuine.

Campbell had not done any preparation work before he used this system[33] and this was the cause of the problems. I have successfully used the Abra-Melin squares (after first doing the preparation work - modified from the manuscript instructions)[34].

One personal example of the effect of this system was when my neighbour wanted to destroy a garage which was supporting the bank on which our house sits. No amount of persuading would change my neighbour's mind and the workmen were to arrive the next day. That night, I made a magic square of Abra-Melin. On the

---

[31]   Pages 197-200.

[32]   Campbell was 6=5 at the time of the Abra-Melin problems.

[33]   Campbell was the highest ranking member of Whare Ra at the time of his death, in mid 1967. Mrs Felkin felt that the bad experience he had with this Abra - Melin system turned him into an alcoholic (one of the reasons he was never a Chief). He had opened certain chakras prematurely and when combined with certain forms of magic, the opened chakras lead to a pre-disposition towards possession.

[34]   See 'Sacred Magician' by Georges Chevalier who took the six month waiting process literally. My wife and I did a modified six month waiting process before

Saturday morning the workmen unloaded their equipment but as soon as the jack hammer started, the neighbour suddenly told them to stop. He could not give the reason for changing his mind and was out of pocket because of it.

The Abra-Melin book is in three parts, in Mathers' own words:

> "First Book:= Advice and autobiography; both addressed by the author to his son lamech.
> Second Book:= General and complete desperation of means of obtaining the magical powers desired.
> Third Book:= The application of these powers to produce an immense number of magical results."

Though the squares are often referred to as pentacles, I have included them in this evocation section of the Z2 (and not the talismanic section) because the entities are external forces. The 19th Chapter of *Sacred Magic* gives the clearest guidelines of angelic and demonic hierarchies.

Another Mathers translation in print recently is *The Grimiore of Armadel*[35]. The origin of this text is obscure and occult author Francis King (who gave the introduction to this text in the Weiser publication) cites it as belonging to the Faust School. Mathers commented (according to King) that one of the origins of this manuscript was the *Grimorium Verum*. Comparing both texts the *Armadel* is cleaned up in favour of a Christian slant. There is no doubt the *Armadel* is a compilation of a number of earlier texts such as the *Almadel*. If the Stella Matutina (with the strong Christian influences of its members behind it) had access to this manuscript[36] then more time would have been spent on the practical evocation. Another publication that greatly interested the Golden Dawn was the *Magus*[37] written by Francis Barrett. The effect of this book

---

attempting to use the Squares and neither of us have been troubled by use of the Abra-Melin system and have had a number of benefits through its use.

[35] Bibliotheque de l'Arsenal, Sc. st A. No.88.

[36] Euan Campbell was given a copy of this manuscript by Langford Garstin (a high ranking member of an A.O. temple in England) in the late 1920's and brought it back to New Zealand. Campbell kept the manuscript to himself though he did show it to a number of Whare Ra members, such as Taylor. When I showed Taylor the Weiser version of this manuscript, he mentioned the Mathers introduction (from Campbell's copy) was missing.

[37] First published in 1801.

on Western magic is so vast that it is difficult to gauge, save that it opened the door for real occult work to begin. Barrett was an editor rather than the author for the contents of the *Magus* are taken from Agrippa and other lesser known works.

Barrett pruned out useless information given in old books and texts and presented them so that anyone with a basic knowledge of magic could get started. His inclusion of Kabbalistic literature is presented clearly and concisely (even though some of the Hebrew may not be correct[38]). The Golden Dawn Kabbalistic text *Book of General Correspondences* drew a lot from Barrett's work. His editing genius presented the Golden Dawn with the bare bones of many subsystems of magic and only if one had some experience would the next layer open.

I also would refer readers to the texts of Dr. Rudd[39] which were widely read among Golden Dawn members.

THE HEBREW CONNECTION

Early texts of Hebrew evocation methods are difficult to find because of the fragmentation of some sects and their secrecy. Some did escape destruction. One of the earliest occult texts of Hebrew literature is the *Sword of Moses.*[40&41]

The origin of the *Sword* is difficult to pinpoint. From the letter of Haya Gaon (938-1038) it is evident that it must have been at least a few centuries older than his time (10th century).

> The Leyden Papyrus belongs to the third century, and those of the British Museum to the third or fourth century, we are justified in assigning to the first four centuries of the Christian era the origin of the Hebrew text.

---

[38]   Because of the blinds attributed to some magical texts it has been suggested to me that the errors were deliberately included and only the true student would find them and correct them. This is pure speculation.

[39]   Harley Mss 6481-6486, from the then British Museum.

[40]   Published in London in 1896 and translated and edited by Moses Gaster.

[41]   There is another text titled *The Sixth and Seventh Books of Moses* which is not to be confused with the *The Sword of Moses*. The original text of the *Sixth and Seventh Books of Moses* came from Ms. 2537, Darmstadt State Library. The date of origin of the work is 1540. There are a number of English copies available. I have not included an analysis because the names and symbols are corrupt.

The text is in three parts. The first tells of the books origin (from Moses) and gives the obligatory purification before it can be used effectively. A series of conjurations are given so that the underlying meaning given in the *Sword of Moses* is further revealed. There are hints that reading the text is not enough and to fully understand it the spirits that have the 'hidden meaning' have to be invoked before any work can begin.

The second part of the book consists of a list of 160 angelic names. The third part of the book gets into the subject of magical conjurations for all manner of purposes. It also refers back to Part Two, and brackets certain names with certain functions. Appendices I and II relate strongly with the third part of the book in composition.

Gaster translated a manuscript which he titled *The Wisdom of the Chaldeans: An old Hebrew Astrological Text.*[42] The date when this was written is obscure, but Gaster places it between the eighth and 14th centuries. The text is not long and gives a name of seven angels and the days they rule:

> On the sixth day rules Anael. His is appointed on all manner of love. This ruler is in the likeness of a woman... On her right arm serves an angel whose name is Arbiel, on the left one called Nininel, over her head one whose name is Lahabiel, and at her feet one called Ahabiel...

The text describes how to make a male or female follow you after a conjuration.

Another small book used by the Golden Dawn is a compilation of Hebrew Babylonian, Egyptian and European texts called *Ancient Jewish oil-magic*, translated by S. Daiches. This book is a revelation on what you can do with oils, especially when combining the magical uses of the Psalms and Talmudic passages.

THE GOLEM, A CONCEPT OF EVOCATION

One of the most interesting forms of evocation is that of evoking life into an inanimate form. In Hebrew mysticism this is the legend of the Golem. The Kabbalists consider that the legend goes back

---

[42]   First published in English in the *Proceedings of the Society of Biblical Archaeology* in 1900 (Dec).

to the First Adam where God created vessels, or pots, but when life was injected into them they shattered.[43&44]

One of the first Biblical references[45] to the Golem is in Psalm 139:15-16:

> My frame was not hidden from you when I was made in the secret place. When I was woven together in the depths of the earth. Your eyes saw my uniformed Golem[46].

Another early reference in traditional Judaism is in the Talmud:[47] Rabbi Ravi created a Golem or imitation man and sent him to Rabbi Zera who found that the Golem did not reply to his questions. He then realised that the man was not real and returned him to the dust from which he came.

There is no references as to how the Golem was made by Rabbi Ravi, though later researchers such as Rashi[48], say the Golem was formed from clay using the Sepher Yetzirah. They cite work of Rabbi Hananyah and Oshaya who made an animal Golem (a three year old calf) using the *Hecaloth* texts and the *Sepher Yetzirah* which was also cited in the same Talmudic section[49]. Rashi reasoned that if the Yetzirah was used for creating an animal Golem, then it could be also used to create a human form. Others maintain that if the Talmudic passage showed that Ravi knew the holy name of God which gave life to the dead if inserted in their mouth. This sounds like the Ankh in the *Egyptian Book of the Dead.*

---

[43]   See *Kabbalah Unveiled* by MacGregor Mathers for his translations of the Zohar books: *Book of Concealment, Great Holy Assembly, Lesser Holy Assembly*. Also the *Anatomy of God*, translated by Rosenberg also sheds new light on this formula.

[44]   See *Communications, Organisation and Science*. by J. Rothstein. Falcon Wing Press 1958. In the Introduction, American Physicist Charles A. Muses who realized the changes certain sounds or vibrations can be injected into inanimate objects and produce a magnetic field which in turn has an interaction on other substances. This is the same principle the occultists use in evocation and in ritual.

[45]   In Daniel 3: we are told of Nebuchadnezzar who brought to life a statue because it was beautiful with a stolen diamond from the High Priest.

[46]   The term body here in the translated versions of the Bible while in rabbinical literature some have considered that the word Golem relates to the vessel that is not filled with spirit or life and is analogous with the shell of the first Adam.

[47]   Babylonian Talmud, Sandhedrin 65b:

[48]   Who lived in the 12th century.

Within the Hecaloth texts one could include the *Book of Enoch* which gives a treatise on angelology. The *Lesser Hecaloth* describes the use of the letters of the Hebrew alphabet and is closely allied with the *Sepher Yetzirah*. Most occult historians will possibly agree that the use of the letters of the Hebrew Alphabet is vital to the creation of the Golem.

The history of the formation of the letters of the Hebrew alphabet from a rough cursive script to the letters of today makes it unlikely that they were written in Golem workings, but pronounced[50].

The work of Rabbi Ravi and the time of Golem creation in the Middle Ages shows that the letters of the Hebrew alphabet would be almost unrecognisable from the time of Ravi, to someone in the 15th century. The *Hecaloth* texts may produce a clue to the life giving essence of the Golem[51].

In the *Sepher Yetzirah*[52] we are told of the formation of the world through a three, seven and twelve stage system. The first three show the elements of Air, Water and Fire - Earth is missing. The next seven stages or letters are related to the seven planets of our solar system. While the third stage relates to the 12 constellations of the zodiac. The final chapter on the *Sepher Yetzirah* was where the Golden Dawn got its Dragon formula described in the *Convoluted Forces* manuscript[53]. In *The Book of Enoch* we are told of angels mating with humanity, and this may have something to do with the development of the Golem. This hints at the operator having to trap an entity and direct it into the body or form created for it. If this is so, then the Golem is not a creation, but a trapped

---

[49] In his *Kabbalah*, Scholem cites another passage of Golem creation.

[50] Hebrew pronunciation appears to be also a consistent factor through the ages as the early Jews might talk daily in Greek, Latin or Arabic, depending on their location. Their Hebrew pronunciation was considered holy and to be uttered in Temple and time of prayer only, and the likelihood of this being contaminated on any large scale is unlikely.

[51] See *Enoch 3* by Odeberg for an English translation of the Lesser Hecaloth texts.

[52] Westcott translation.

[53] For a detailed description of this formula that goes further into and simplifies it somewhat see *Complete Tarot of the Golden Dawn* by P.Zalewski.

spirit in matter which is the basis of talismanic work.

Around the 13th century, a number of Hebrew scholars started to comment on the formation of a Golem. Jewish Hasidim was a fertile field for the study of the Golem. Rabbi Eleazer[54] of Worms gives instructions in Golem creation though there is no evidence to support that he ever created one.

The method he suggested is simple. Create the shape out of clay with the first three Hebrew letters and letting life take form. Another method is to form the figure and then recite the first half of the letters of the Hebrew alphabet in different combinations.

One of the methods is to place half the alphabet over the other half and then recite the letters in pairs. In Golem creating, scholars refer back to the creation of man. Those who created Golems based their ritual on the heavenly creation of man - while God created man some of them thought that they might return the compliment, or at least try to emulate it.

Scholem cites the story of Jesus making birds from clay and giving them life by pronouncing the Holy name of God over them.[55]

If this story is true, then it appears that the vibration of Hebrew, uttered in a certain sequence is the paramount factor and not the actual inscription of the letters.

In his *Commentary on the Sepher Yetzirah*[56], Saadiyah Gaon[57]wrote on the formation of the Golem through the process of the 231 Gates[58]. This involves not only recitations of the 231 gates but also circumambulations around the clay figure. Importance was placed in the clockwise and anti-clockwise direction for if one goes clockwise, in the path of the sun, then life is given to the figure but if one reverses

---

[54]   Scholem, in his book *Kabbalah*, gets into an ideological debate over the meaning of Eleazer's reference to Abraham and Srah\Shem creating souls. He cites Saadya's *Commentary on the Book Yetzirah*, MS Munich, 40, Folio 77a., where Abraham actually created a human Golem as a demonstration.

[55]   Mentioned by Scholem in his *Kabbalah*, referring to the text 'Toledoth Yeshu.'

[56]   *Commentary of the Sepher Yetzirah*, Jerusalem 1965.

[57]   842-942 A.D.

[58]   The 231 Gates are a formulation of adding letters of the Hebrew alphabet together. For example match the letter A with every other letter of the Hebrew Alphabet and you have a total of 21 combinations. Match the letter B with the letter G then you have 20 combinations etc. No combinations are to be used twice.

the circumambulation then the figure returns to the returns to the earth.

While this part of the Commentary is enlightening, there is no indication of success other than as a theological discourse.

The process must provide the Golem with an Etheric body (which the Kabbalists would refer to as Nephesch). A Ruach would also have to be present within the Golem for it to function as the faculty of memory is attributed to the Ruach.

Almost 30 years ago, while sitting in a hot dusty Indian railway station outside of Pondicherry, I spoke to an old mystic[59] who was known to my teacher Vivandatta. The mystic told me a story of how some Tantric adepts created life out of earth and statues.

He said adepts were limited to what they could make. The energy that impregnated the form came from their bodies and vital energy. The process could be formed from the atmosphere, but when the form had finished its task had to be re-absorbed by the adept. A form created out of air could talk but a form created out of matter could not.

Rabbi Abraham Abulafia left us a legacy in Golem creation (which is a further attempt to explain the use of the 231 Gates) by adding flour to dust, then reciting the ritual of the 231 Gates. Next, he used an alchemical measuring process of mixing water and dust the obligatory Holy name of God were spoken.

Various houses are mentioned in this recipe but there is no indication as to which houses they refer, astrological or otherwise. They could relate to the old Arabic system of lunar astrology.

References to the Hebrew letters could refer to the elements, they do represent the elemental concept, which was a theme concentrated on by later Golem makers.

Many Talmudic scholars do not really consider that a Golem can be made and many consider them fairy tales. How they explain the historical documentation of the Golem of Prague[60&61] legend

---

This adds up to a total of 231 combinations of letters in successive formations.

[59] I studied Tantra there.

[60] This legend is not to be confused with that of Rabbi Elijah of Chelm who died in 1583.

[61] I refer the readers to three texts: *The Golem* by Gustav Meyrink. Victor Gollancz London, 1928. *The Golem, Legends of Prague* by Chayim Bloch, Vienna, Austria 1925. *The Golem* by Gershon Winkler, Judaica Press, New York 1980.

is a mystery. This Golem used to patrol certain areas of Prague and the Christian citizens were scared of it. Many cite this as myth, though there are many reports of it that exist, including letters from Prague officials who complained about the Golem. Fact or fiction, the Golem made a number of people very nervous!

Chapter Two

The Z2 DOCUMENTS

The Z2 papers are the most complex of all Golden Dawn documents, but the formula was familiar to adepts as they would have experienced the energy patterns in the neophyte grade. Of this, Mathers says:

> For this ritual betokeneth a certain person, substance or thing, which is taken from the dark world of matter, to be brought under the operation of the divine forces of the magic of the light.[62]

The Z2 formula brings through the light, or magnetising currents of energy, in a safe and focused way. This is needed when performing a variety of rituals but keeping a single flow of energy.

To quote from Mathers again (from the introduction to the Z2 documents) as to the breakdown or different levels of the Z2 rituals:

> Also herein are contained the commencements of all formulae of evocation, the development of which is further shown by the inner knowledge of the succeeding grades of the outer order. In the true knowledge of the application of the symbolism of the 'enterer' lies in the entrance of the knowledge of practical magic. Therefore are all the formula drawn from the ritual classed under five heads, according unto the letters of the name YEHESHUAH.

The Formulae of the Enterer is in two parts (General Exordium[63] and Particular Exordium) and is complex, for it works on many

---

[62] Introduction to the Z2 documents.
[63] See *Secret Teachings of the Golden Dawn* by Pat Zalewski (pages 139-151) Book I, for an explanation of this formula as applied to the Neophyte ritual.

levels. The two parts relate to the individual's outer and inner sphere. The breakdown of the five parts of the divine name are as follows:

YOD	(fire)	1. Evocation ritual (of spirits and elements etc.)
HEH	(water)	2. Talisman rituals plus the production of natural phenomena, as storms and earthquakes.[64]
SHIN	(spirit)	3. Spiritual development ritual.
		4. Transformation ritual.
		5. Invisibility ritual.
VAU	(air)	6. Divination ritual.
HEH	(earth)	7. Alchemy ritual.

Mathers took this formula of seven rituals from the first seven verses of Genesis. The Hebrew word 'BRAShITh', the first word of the Bible, was used by Mathers[65] to categorise the 'Formula of the Enterer' - The Particular Exordium.

Letter	Formula of the enterer test
Beth:	At the ending of the night
	At the limits of the light
	Thoth stood before the unborn ones of time.
Resh:	Then came the gods thereof,
	The aeons of the bornless beyond.
Aleph:	Then was the voice vibrated.
Shin:	Then was the name declared.
Tau:[66]	At the threshold of the entrance,
	betwixt the universe and infinite.
Yod:	In the Sign of the Enterer stood Thoth,
	As before him the aeons were proclaimed.

---

64   I have never seen a breakdown for causing storms etc. and can only presume that it relates to a talisman that can cause this effect.

65   Refer to *Notes on Genesis* by Alan Bennett (*Equinox II*). I came across some Whare Ra documents, copied from the Golden Dawn, that gave the key breakdown of the word 'BRAShITh' and applied it to the 'Formula of the Enterer'. I thought that Bennett was responsible for this work and found that the basis for it was a paper circulated among Golden Dawn members. The original Golden Dawn document (possibly by Mathers) consisted only of page 181 (in *The Equinox)* and Bennett did the rest.

66   This reversing of the Tau before the Yod was also in the Golden Dawn copy.

When the word BRAShITh is fully decoded:

Beth	This is the magical history
Resh	Of the dawning light
Aleph	Begun are the whirling motions
Shin	Formulated is the primal fire
Yod	Proclaimed is the reign of the gods of light
Tau	At the threshold of the infinite worlds

If this formula is applied practically to the seven sub-divisions of the Z2 and we have the following:

Verse One - Evocation.

"In the beginning God created et the heavens and et the earth.[67]"

The word 'et' (taken in its literal translation) stands for the Alpha and Omega the beginning and the end and stands for the letters of the Hebrew alphabet. This is shown in the book *Sepher Yetzirah.* The speaker of this verse is God and no-one else has the right to speak. Applied to ritual evocation[68], the force evoked cannot talk back and must perform its designated task. This is like the Golem, which could not speak.

Verse Two - Talisman.

"The earth was without form and empty, with darkness on the face of the depth, but God's spirit moved on the water's surface."

The original Hebrew words for form is Tohu and empty is Bohu. Tohu is the chaotic state before formation, while Bohu is something with chaos. These words[69] show the illusory concept of the face of the God's spirit as a reflective image. A talisman is an image of an angelic force or entity reflected upon an object, or is the object.

---

[67] This translation differs from, 'In the beginning God created the heavens and the earth.'

[68] Evocation must not be confused with invocation which is more in line with the principle of channeling or mediumship.

[69] See *The Bahir*, translated by A. Kaplan, for a discourse in the meaning of these two words.

Verse Three - Spiritual Development

"And God said 'Let there be Light' and there was Light."

The 'Light' is the pre-existent spirit about to make itself known(spiritual development). It is the acknowledgement of the Creator and a petition to receive its grace. This is shown in the letter Shin, the impregnated spirit.

Verse Four - Transformation

"God saw the Light that was good and he separated the Light from the darkness."

Transformation[70] occurs when the Light is transferred into something else, in this instance darkness. In Kabbalah, the light and dark are extremes of the same thing. They are analogous to the white and black pillars of the Tree of Life and mercy and severity. When using the ritual of transformation we are in a neutral state between the two extremes - the middle pillar.

Verse Five - Invisibility[71]

"God called the light 'day' and the darkness he called 'Night'. And there was evening, and there was morning - the first day."

The Zohar tells us[72] that a day was realised when night was introduced. This division is when the world is clothed in darkness-invisibility.

---

[70]   In Africa, late last century, Dr.R.Felkin witnessed a man changing into an animal when he attended a ceremony by a witch doctor. The events are recorded in a yet unpublished biography of Felkin by Connel Townsend. In the 1918 edition of England's *Cornhill Magazine* it relates the experience of a British officer serving in Nigeria who wounded and tracked a hyena and eventually found it had changed into human form. In England in the 1960's, a researcher investigating shape changing was invited to witness it by a Wiccan Priestess. The man was so shaken by his experiences that he gave up all future investigations into the paranormal.

[71]   See *Invisibility* by Steve Richards, Aquarian Press 1982. This is a fine little volume that gives some examples.

[72]   Vol 1. Folio 46a.

Verse Six. - Divination

"And God said: 'Let there be an expanse between the waters to separate water from water."

Water indicate illusion and that is what divination deals with. The practitioner must separate truth from illusion or water from water. Since water is timeless, the separation indicates a predictive truth or one that can be grasped and understood.

Verse Seven - Alchemy[73]

"So God made the expanse and separated the water under the expanse from the water above it. And it was so."

The higher and lower waters referred to relates to natural waters and those naturally distilled - the waters of the heaven and the waters of the earth. The distinction between the two is alchemical.

These seven rituals were the kernel of the Golden Dawn's occult teachings. The curriculum required the adepts to master one of the rituals in the hope that they would specialise in one area. Each area required many years training, and even a lifetime's work. Mathers tried to show, through his Z2 teachings, the way adepts could learn a system.

People may ask what is special about the 'Formulae of the Enterer' and comment that any ritual would work if faith and intent are strong. While this is true, some people forget that Mathers, like Crowley after him, tapped into an obscure power source and could use it for his own benefit. Jung called this drawing on the collective unconscious, but it is much more.

It is by studying modern physicists like Michael Talbot and David Bohm that we begin to understand what adepts like Mathers and Crowley were getting at. Bohm outlined his theory on a multidimensional reality in the book *Wholeness and Implicate*

[73] For a good example of practical alchemy in the Herbal Kingdom see *Practical handbook on Plant Alchemy,* by Manfred Junius. Inner Traditions International Ltd, 1985. A complete correspondence course on Alchemy in the vain as the now defunct Paracelsus Research Organisation can be obtained through 'Philosophers of Nature' P.O.Box 11218, Boulder, CO 80301, U.S.A.

Order[74]. He determined a link at sub-atomic level between our reality and its higher macrocosmic self.

Mathers' theory throws light onto this scientific concept as he breaks down Z2 into its seven component parts. These are interconnected through his YHShVh theory, or the biblical formula of Brashith. Once interconnected, Mathers used the fundamentals of the neophyte ceremony to quantify and expand them. The difference between this and other systems is the size of the system. It is the ability to draw on a higher power, even if that power is self created.

When Mathers put together the invocations of godforms and magical systems into one component, he had the ability to use all the magical subsystems from the past, whether they be Egyptian, Greek, Christian, Hebraic or Roman.

Using Michael Talbot's holographic theory, it is possible to shine lasers on an intangible mess, and produce a crystal clear image. Z2 rituals are like those lasers, with different levels of the entire picture shown to those who want them. Like lasers, rituals to have to be tuned to the same level of wholeness to present a clear picture.

I have only presented the barest of outlines of holographic theory and have no hesitation in recommending Talbot's books. His field is new and helps explain the universe from a perception which bring the mystical visionary and scientist closer.

INDEX FOR GENERAL REFERENCE TO THE ENTERER CEREMONY OF THE 0=0 GRADE[75]

A -   The ceremony itself. The place of the temple.

B -   The Hierophant.

C -   The officers.

D -   The candidate.

E -   The ceremony of opening.

---

[74]   His theories were expanded on from his initial work in the early 1950's through his friendship with Einstein and later Krishnamurti.

[75]   The next formula of the 'Enterer' breakdown and the formula for 'evocation' are taken from Golden Dawn Z2 papers by Mathers.

F - Hierophant states that he has received a dispensation from second order, and commands hegemon to prepare candidate. Candidate prepared. Speech of Hegemon.

G - Admission of candidate. First barring by Kerux. First baptism of the candidate with water and fire.

H - The Candidate is conducted to the foot of the altar. Hierophant asks "Wherefore hast thou come, etc." Candidate replies "I seek the hidden light, etc."

I - Candidate is asked whether he is willing to take the obligation. He assents; and is instructed now to kneel at the altar.

J - Administration of the obligation, and raising the neophyte from the kneeling position.

K - Candidate is placed in the North. Oration of the Hierophant, "The voice of my higher self, etc." Hierophant commands the mystic circumambulation in the path of darkness.

L - Procession. Candidate barred in South. Second baptism of water and fire. Speech of Hegemon. Allowing the candidate to proceed.

M - Hoodwink slipped up. Challenge of Hiereus. Speech of Hegemon. Speech of Hiereus. Candidate re-veiled and passed on.

N - Circumambulation. Barred in North. Third baptism. Speech of Hegemon allowing candidate to approach unto the gate of the East.

O - Hoodwink slipped up for the second time, Hierophant challenges. Hegemon answers for the candidate. Speech of Hierophant. Candidate passes on.

P - Candidate led to West of altar. Hierophant advances by the path of Samech. Officers form the triangle. Prayer of Hierophant.

Q - Candidate rises. Hierophant addresses him, "Long hast thou dwelt in darkness. Quit the night and seek the day."

Hoodwink finally removed, sceptres and swords joined. "We receive thee, etc." Then the mystic words.

R -   Hierophant indicates lamp of Kerux. He commands that the candidate be conducted to the East of the altar. He orders Hiereus to bestow signs, etc. Hiereus places candidate between pillars. Signs and words. He orders the fourth and final consecration to take place.

S -   Hegemon removes rope and invests candidate with his insignia. Hiereus then ordains the mystic circumambulation in the path of light.

T -   Hierophant lectures on the symbols. Proclamation by Kerux.

U -   Hierophant commands Hiereus to address candidate.

V -   Hierophant addresses Neophyte on subject of study.

W -   Blood produced. Speech of Kerux. Hiereus' final caution.

X -   The closing takes place.

When the above set of guidelines is then adopted directly to the principle of evocation, the following outline is a result:

Z2 FORMULA OF EVOCATION UNDER THE LETTER YOD

A -   The magic circle.

B -   The magician, wearing the great lamen of the hierophant; and his scarlet robe. A pentacle, whereon is engraved the sigil of the spirit to be invoked, has painted on the back of it the circle and cross as shown on the hierophant's lamen.

C -   The names and formulae to be employed.

D -   The symbol of the whole evocation.

E -   The construction of the circle and the placing of all the symbols, etc., employed, in the places properly allotted to them; so as to represent the interior of a G.D. Temple in the

0=0 Grade, and the purification and consecration of the actual piece of ground or place, selected for the performance of the evocation.

F - The invocation of the higher powers. Pentacle formed of three concentric bands, name and sigil therein, in proper colours, is to be bound thrice with a cord, and shrouded in black, thus bringing into action a blind force to be further directed or differentiated in the process of the ceremony. Announcement aloud of the object of the working; naming the spirit or spirits, which it is desired to evoke. This is pronounced standing in the centre of the circle and turning towards the quarter from which the spirit will come.

G - The name and sigil of the spirit, wrapped in a black cloth, or covering, is now placed within the circle, at the point corresponding to the West, representing the candidate. The consecration of baptism by water and fire of the sigil then takes place, and the proclamation in a loud and firm voice of the spirit (or spirits) to be evoked.

H - The veiled sigil is now to be placed at the foot of the altar. The magician then calls aloud the name of the spirit, summoning him to appear, stating for what purpose the spirit is evoked: what is desired in the operation; why the evocation is performed at this time, and finally solemnly affirming that the spirit shall be evoked by the ceremony.

I - Announcement aloud that all is prepared for the commencement of the actual evocation. If it be a good spirit the sigil is now to be placed within the white triangle on the altar, the magician places his left hand upon it, raises in his right hand the magical implement employed (usually the sword) erect; and commences the evocation of the spirit N. to visible appearance. The magician stands in the place of the Hierophant during the obligation, irrespective of the particular quarter of the Spirit. But, if the nature of that spirit be evil, then the sigil must be placed without and to the West of the white triangle and the magician shall be careful to keep the point of the magical sword upon the centre of the sigil.

J - Now let the magician imagine himself as clothed outwardly with the semblance of the form of the spirit to be evoked, and in this let him be careful not to identify himself with the spirit, which would be dangerous; but only to formulate a species of mask, worn for the time being. And if he knows not the symbolic form of the spirit then let him assume the form of an angel belonging unto the same class of operation, this form being assumed. Then let him pronounce aloud,, with a firm and solemn voice, a convenient and potent oration and exorcism of the spirit unto visible appearance. At the conclusion of this exorcism, taking the covered sigil in his left hand, let him smite it thrice with the flat blade of the magic sword. Then let him raise on high his arms to their utmost stretch, holding in his left hand the veiled sigil, and in his right the sword of art erect. At the same time stamping thrice upon the ground with his right foot.

K - The veiled and corded sigil is then to be placed in the Northern part of the hall at the edge of the circle, and the magician employs the oration of the Hierophant, from the throne of the East, modifying it slightly, as follows: "The voice of the exorcism said unto me, Let me shroud myself in darkness, peradventure thus may I manifest myself in Light, etc." The magician then proclaims aloud that the mystic circumambulation will take place.

L - The magician takes up the sigil in his left hand and circumambulates the magic circle once then passes to the South and halts. He stands (having placed the sigil on the ground) between it and the West, and repeats the oration of the Kerux. And again consecrates it with water and fire. Then takes it in his hand, facing westward saying, "Creature of ...., twice consecrate, thou mayest approach the gate of the West".

N - Magician moves to the West of the magical circle, holds the sigil in his left hand and the sword in his right, faces South West, and astrally masks himself with the form of the spirit, and for the first time partially opens the covering of the sigil, without however entirely removing it. He then smites it once with the flat blade of the sword, saying, in a loud, clear, and firm voice: "Thou canst not pass from concealment unto manifestation, save by the virtue of the name Elohim. Before all things are the chaos and darkness, and the gates of the land of night. I am He whose name is darkness. I am the great one of the path of the shades. I am the exorcist in the midst of the exorcism. Appear thou therefore without fear before me, so pass thou on." He then re-veils the sigil.

N - Take the sigil to the North, circumambulate first, halt, place sigil on the ground, stand between it and the East, repeat the oration of the kerux, again consecrate with fire and water. Then take it up, face North, and say "Creature of .... thrice consecrate, thou mayest approach the gate of the East".

O - Repeat section M in North East. Magician then passes to East, takes up sigil in left and sword in right hand. Assumes the mask of the spirit form, smites the sigil with the lotus wand or sword, and says, "Thou canst not pass from concealment unto manifestation save by virtue of the name YHVH. After the formless and the void and the darkness, then cometh the knowledge of the light. I am the light which riseth in the darkness. I am the exorcist in the midst of the exorcism. Appear thou therefore in visible form before me, for I am the wielder of the forces of the balance. Thou hast known me now, so pass thou on to the cubical altar of the universe."

P - He then recovers sigil and passes to altar, laying it thereon as before shown. He then passes to the East of the altar, holding the sigil and sword as already explained. Then doth he rehearse a most potent conjuration and invocation of the spirit unto visible appearance, using and reiterating all the divine, angelic, and magical names appropriate to this end neither omitting the signs, seals, sigils, lineal figures, signatures and the like from that conjuration.

Q - The magician now elevates the covered sigil towards heaven, removes the veil entirely, leaving it yet corded, crying with a loud voice, "Creature of .... long hast thou dwelt in darkness. Quit the night and seek the day". He then replaces it upon the altar, holds the magical sword erect above it, the pommel immediately above the centre thereof, and says, "By all the names, powers, and rites already rehearsed, I conjure thee thus into visible appearance." Then the mystic words.

R - Saith the magician, "As light hidden in the darkness can manifest therefrom, so shalt thou become manifest from concealment unto manifestation."

He then takes up the sigil, stands to East of altar, and faces West. He shall then rehearse a long conjuration to the powers and spirits immediately superior unto that one which he seeks to invoke, that they shall force him to manifest himself unto visible appearance.

He then places the sigil between the pillars, himself at the East facing West, then in the sign of the enterer doth he direct the whole current of his will upon the sigil. Thus he continueth until such time as he shall perceive his will power to be weakening, when he protects himself from the reflex of the current by the sign of silence, and drops his hands.

He now looks towards the quarter that the spirit is to appear in, and he should now see the first signs of his visible manifestation.

If he be not thus faintly visible, let the magician repeat the conjuration of the superiors of the spirit, from the place of the throne in the east. And this conjuration may be repeated thrice, each time ending with a new projection of will in the sign of the Enterer, etc. But if at the third time of repetition he appeareth not, then be it known that there is an error in the working.

So let the master of evocations replace the sigil upon the altar, holding the sword as usual: and thus doing, let him address a humble prayer unto the great gods of Heaven to correctly complete that evocation. He is then to take back the sigil to between the Pillars, and repeat the former processes, when assuredly that spirit will begin to manifest, but in a misty and ill-defined form. (But if, as is probable, the operator be naturally inclined unto evocation, then might that spirit perchance manifest earlier in the ceremony than this. Still, the ceremony is to be performed up to this point, whether he be there or not.)

Now as soon as the magician shall see the visible manifestation of that spirit's presence, he shall quit the station of the hierophant, and consecrate afresh with water and with fire, the sigil of the evoked spirit.

S - Now doth the master of evocations remove from the sigil the restricting cord, and holding the freed sigil in his left hand, he smites it with the flat blade of his sword, exclaiming, "By and in the names of ...... I do invoke upon thee the power of perfect manifestation unto visible appearance." He then circumambulates the circle thrice holding the sigil in his right hand.

T - The magician, standing in the place of the Hierophant, but turning towards the place of the spirit, and fixing his attention thereon now reads a potent invocation of the spirit unto visible appearance, having previously placed the sigil on the ground, within the circle, at the quarter where the spirit appears. This invocation should be some length; and should rehearse and reiterate the Divine and other names consonant with the working.

That spirit should now become fully and clearly visible, and should be able to speak with a direct voice, if consonant with his nature. The magician then proclaims aloud that the spirit N. hath been duly and properly evoked in accordance with the sacred rites.

U - The magician now addresses an invocation unto the lords of the plane of the spirit to compel him to perform that which the magician shall demand of him.

V - The magician carefully formulates his demands, questions, writes down any of the answers that may be advisable. The master of evocations now addresses a conjuration

unto the spirit evoked, binding him to hurt or injure naught
connected with him, or his assistants, or the place. And that
he deceive in nothing, and that he fail not to perform that
which he hath been commanded.

W -   He then dismisses that spirit by any suitable form, such as
those used in the higher grades of the outer. And if he will
not go, then shall the magician compel him by forces contrary
to his nature. But he must allow a few minutes for the spirit
to dematerialise the body in which he hath manifested, for
he will become less and less material by degrees. And note
well that the magician (or his companions if he have any)
shall never quit the circle during the process of evocation, or
afterwards, till the spirit hath quite vanished.

Seeing that in some cases, and with some constitutions,
there may be danger arising from the Astral conditions, and
currents established, and without the actual intention of the
spirit to harm, although if of a low nature, he would probably
endeavour to do so. Therefore, before the commencement
of the evocation, let the operator assure himself that
everything which may be necessary, be properly arranged
within the circle.

But if it be actually necessary to interrupt the process,
then let him stop at that point, veil and re-cord the sigil if it
have been unbound or uncovered, recite a license to depart
or a banishing formula and perform the lesser banishing rituals
of the pentagram and hexagram. Thus only may he in
comparative safety quit the circle.

Note: If the spirit is placed into a white triangle outside the
midheaven, he then will speak the truth of necessity.[76]

Before summoning a spirit to visible appearance that one should
have a good reason. I have performed many evocations and have
always had a good reason, and could not care if the spirit appeared.
In the late 1940's, a Whare Ra adept decided to evoke an entity
to visible appearance, and called on Jack Taylor and Percy

[76] This ends the Mathers paper.

Wilkinson[77] to assist. Jack was to see if the ritual was correct and Percy's job was to check the astrological configurations. Many saw the entity forming in the triangle at the crucial point in the ceremony. Unfortunately after the ceremony, the figure kept re-appearing at inconvenient times. The magus who had been in charge of the operation was told by Taylor that since the spirit was created from the etheric body, it had to re-absorbed before it drained his life force. A ceremony was performed by Taylor, the energy was reabsorbed and the magus had no more trouble.

The following ceremony is the full ritual for the evocation of the spirit Taphthartharath to visible appearance, described at the beginning of Chapter One. It is the only evocation ritual that has survived (that I know of) from the early Golden Dawn. It is a group ritual that has adhered to the outline of the 'Formula of the Enterer'. It was first published in Crowley's *Equinox* Volume One, Number three.[78] The version below is taken from Bennett's notebooks are different to the Crowley edition and I will add footnotes to explain why certain props, positions and conjurations are used.

---

[77] He reached the rank of 6=5 and later took over the leadership of the 'Order of the Table Round' (The Arthurian side Order to Whare Ra) after Taylor died.

[78] For the modified version see Yorke collection #225, New Folder 62.

THE RITUAL FOR THE EVOCATION UNTO
VISIBLE APPEARANCE OF THE GREAT SPIRIT
TAPHTHARTHARATH[79]

8	58	59	5	4	62	63	1
49	15	14	52	53	11	10	56
41	23	22	44	45	19	18	48
32	34	35	29	28	38	39	25
40	26	27	37	36	30	31	33
17	47	46	20	21	43	42	24
9	55	54	12	13	51	50	16
64	2	3	61	60	6	7	57

This is the sigil of Taphthartharath[80] has the Hebrew letters giving
a value of 400, 80, 400, 200, 400, 200, 400 which, when reduced by
Aiq Beker are 40, 8, 40,20,40,20,40.

You take the magic Square of Mercury and draw a line through
these numbers which gives you the above sigil.

Considerations

To be performed on the day and in the hour of Mercury: the
evocation itself commencing in the magical hour of Tafrac, under
the dominion of the great Angel of Mercury Raphael.

On Wednesday, May 13, 1896, this hour Tafrac[81] occurs
between 8 hours 32 minutes P.M and 9 hours 16 minutes, when
Mercury is in 17 degrees Gemini on the cusp of the Seventh House,
slightly to the South of due West.

---

[79]   I have decided to use the ritual of F.L.Gardner rather than Bennett's. There are
some differences in diagrams and the use of invoking for banishing pentagrams,
some of which are transposed in the Crowley copy.

[80]   This relates to section 'D' of the Yod formula.

[81]   Name of the eighth hour of daylight of which the Angel Raphael governs on
Wednesday.

Moon going to conjunctions with Mercury in 15[82] degrees Gemini. Mercury to conjunction with Neptune, Mercury 150 degrees Saturn.

The four elemental tablets shall be placed in the four quarters in the circle without. The tablet of union shall be placed on the altar in the circle within, upon this shall be placed the symbols of the Red Cross over the White triangle, as in the Neophyte Ceremony.[83]

The Form Of The Circle To Be Employed

Magical figures of Mercury are to be drawn in yellow-orange chalk upon the ground as shown. At the quarter where the spirit is to appear. A triangle within a circle is drawn[84]: at its points are to be placed three vessels burning on charcoal the incense of mercury.

---

[82]   The original paper had 14 degrees but with the use of the computer I have rectified this to 15 degrees.

[83] The rule is that when doing an evocation ceremony, the four Children of Horus are invoked along with the Kerubics just before the start of the ceremony by the Hierophant or the magus of art. Their function is important. They maintain balance of energy with the circle and triangle and outside. If the God-form evoked has too much fire or earth then the god-forms of the quarters rectify that. They also help stabilize the energy within the circle so that any evocation will be smooth and not leave any negative residue. They also keep the evoked form in the triangle. This allows others to be present (usually seated around the edge of the Portal) to watch the ceremony in safety.

[84]   The normal method was using chalk of an appropriate colour.

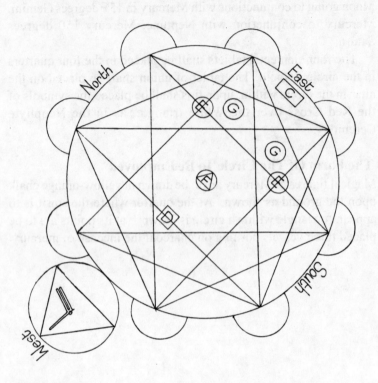

The Circle[85]

Magical Triangle For Evocation Of Taphthartharath

(The arms of the sigil in the Gardner version of the ritual (used here) do not point to the same letters as the Crowley version.)

---

[85] This circle is a combination of the Octagram, Octangle and Octagon (these three figures relating to Hod and Mercury). This comes from the Golden Dawn lecture 'Polygons and Polygrams'. The Octangle relates to the eight lettered name YHVH ADNI and can be reflected in three ways; reflected from every second point when it is called the octagon and from every third and fourth point when called the octagram. The octangle also represents the weak semi-quartile aspect of astrology and had to be reinforced by the octagram and octagon. The combinations relate to the strengthening aspect of both elements and planets. This may appear confusing, it suffices to say that when the three figures are transposed on top, all weak lines are omitted, with component parts strengthening each other to its maximum efficiency.

About the great circle[86] are disposed lamps burning olive oil impregnated with snake fat[87]. C is the chair of the chief operator. D is the altar, E and E are the pillars, G and G are handy and convenient tables whereon are set writing materials[88], the ingredients of the hell-broth[89], charcoal, incense, &, all as may be needed for this work. At F is placed a small brazen cauldron, heated over a lamp burning with spirit in which a snake has been preserved.

Operationis Personae[90]

V.H. Sor: S.S.D.D.[91]   Mighty Magus of Art.
V.H. Fra: I.A.[92]   Assistant Magus of Art.

The reinforcement of the intersecting lines are lines of power of the 'circle' with the key people or props at the junctions of the angular intersecting lines. This relates to section 'E' of the Yod formula (when the orange chalk marks are actually traced over in the opening). 'A' of the Yod formula involves the tracing of the circle in the astral (in a complex circle it is usually done over a light visible tracing in neutral chalk is done first so that the sword pattern traced afterwards is correct) some days before the actual orange chalk circle is drawn in the opening.

The original version of this circle was changed (by Florence Farr) so that the outer rim was a circle - Bennett made it an eight sided figure. I have to side with Bennett, from a Golden Dawn perspective Farr weakened the power of the circle by altering it. I do agree with her altering of the direction of the circle and triangle. The changes Florence Farr made to the Bennett ritual were good with the circle being the exception.

[86]   The directions given for the circle and triangle differ in the Gardner version of the rituals as compared to the Crowley publication.

[87]   This was used as an added incentive to Mercury, whose staff is the twin serpents of the caduceus. It also had the strength to raise the vibration of the auras of the officers so that through the senses the influence of the spirit of Mercury would be seen.

[88]   All of these are purified individually.

[89]   The ingredients for the hell-broth are mentioned in a letter from Bennett to F.L.Gardner:

    1. Gum ammoniacum 2 ozs.
    2. Coriander seed 2 ozs.
    3. One pint of olive oil.

Some milk was used as well. Possibly the ingredients listed here are incomplete. For the candles half a pound of spermaceli was utilized for the magus to read by.

[90]   All of this section comes under the heading of 'B' from the Yod Formula.

[91]   'Sapientia Sapienti Dona Data' is the motto of Florence Farr.

[92]   'Iehi Aour' is the motto for Alan Bennett.

V.H. Fra: A.A.[93]   Magus of the Fire.
V.H. Fra: D.P.A.L[94]   Magus of the Water.

The duties of the Magus of Art[95] will be to perform actual processes of invocations: to rule the assistants and command them all.

The Assistant Magus of Art shall act as Kerux in the circumambulations; he shall preside over the brewing of the hell-broth in the midst of the circle: he shall repeat such invocations as may be necessary at the command of the Magus of Art: and he shall beforehand prepare the place of working.

The Magus of Fire[96] shall preside over all magical lights, fires, candles, incense etc.: he shall perform the invoking and consecrating rituals at the command of the magus, and shall consecrate the temple by fire, and shall consecrate all fire used in due form.

The Magus of Water[97] shall preside over all the fluids used in the operation; over the water and the wine, the oil and the milk: he shall perform all banishing rituals at the opening of the ceremony: he shall purify the temple by water: he shall consecrate all watery things in due form.

Of The Robes And Insignia[98] [99]

The mighty Magus of Art shall wear a white robe,[100] yellow sash[101], red over-mantle[102], indigo nemys[103], upon her breast shall she shall bear a great tablet whereon is the magic seal of Mercury; and over

---

[93] 'Aequo Animo' was the motto of Charles Rosher.
[94] 'De Profundis ad Lucem' was the motto of F. L. Gardner.
[95] This is analogous with the position of Hierophant in the Neophyte Ceremony.
[96] This is the action of the Dadouchous in the Neophyte ceremony. What is not said here is that the magus of fire may have performed a separate ceremony to consecrate all items within the circle, such as writing implements and the like. This would have been more than a quick consecration and purification (done in conjunction with the magus of water) and would have involved reciting magical psalms and invocations, as given in the 'Key of Solomon the King'. I doubt this was done on the day of the ritual.
[97] These are the duties of the Stolistes in the Neophyte ceremony.
[98] This also comes under section 'B' of the Yod formula.
[99] The paper with the ritual written on it is section 'C' of the Yod Formula.
[100] This is basic Golden Dawn dress for Inner Order rituals such as this.
[101] This was the 5=6 symbol and was worn around the waist in the early days of

this the lamen bearing the signature of Taphthartharath, on its obverse the lamen of the Hierophant. She shall also wear a (air) dagger in the sash and a red rose cross on her heart: and she shall carry in her left hand the ankh of Thoth, and in her right hand the ibis wand.[104]

The Assistant Magus of Art shall wear a white robe, with the girdle of a snake skin[105]; a black[106] head-dress and lamen of the spirit[107], on its obverse the lamen of the hiereus. And he shall bear in right hand a sword; and in his left hand the magical candle:[108] and a black chain[109] around his neck.

The Magus of Fire shall wear a white robe and yellow sash; and the rose upon his breast; in his right hand a sword and in his left hand a red lamp (the symbol of hidden knowledge)[110].

The Magus of Water shall wear a white robe and a yellow sash and rose cross: he shall bear in his right hand a sword and in his left a cup of water.

---

the Order. It differed in function to the Grade sash.

[102]   This is the link to the Hierophant's red mantle in the Neophyte ceremony.

[103]   This is from the Path of Tau (Saturn). It shows the magus is an operator who works outside the four elements of Malkuth. All four element grade rituals are also considered to be Malkuth. When that is transcended, you are on the Path of Tau. It is a complex formula that jumps back and forth in Golden Dawn teachings.

[104]   This is an other word for the lotus wand. She would also be gripping the wand in the band of Mercury..

[105]   This attracts and prevents the energy of the spirit of Mercury getting negative as the snake skin is in empathy with it and it will not try to hurt itself.

[106]   The black signifies the darkness which conceals a threatening and avenging force ready to act if attacked. Black is a colour that absorbs negative energy like a sponge with water. The black restricts the growth of negativity by condensing it.

[107]   Same as that worn by the magus of the art.

[108]   The Golden Dawn, and its later off shoot, the Stella Matutina, used colored candles with the sigils carved on them in the complementary color. In this case it would be an orange candle with the sigil of the spirit in mauve. This would have been done in a separate ceremony. Possibly just after the candles were consecrated.

[109]   This is not symbolic of the black chain of mourning of the previous Golden Dawn rituals. Here it takes on an entirely different meaning. It is to remind the officer of his duties and to act if anything goes wrong.

[110]   In the Neophyte ceremony it is the Kerux's responsibility to carry the lamp but is now shifted to that of the Dadouchos.

OPENING

The chamber of art shall be duly prepared by the Assistant Magus of Art as aforementioned. He shall draw upon the ground the lineal figures; and shall trace over them with the magic sword: he shall place the furniture of the temple in order. The members shall be assembled and robed.

The Chief Magus rises, holding the ibis wand by its black end, and proclaims:

HEKAS, HEKAS, ESTE BEBELOI![111]

Fratres of the Order of the Rosy Cross, we are this day assembled together for the purpose of evoking unto visible appearance the spirit of Taphthartharath. That is to say, we envoke a force of terrible material power not yet enlightened by the Divine wisdom of Thoth and we propose to bring the blind force to that knowledge and thereby create between ourselves and the great thrice crowned one of occult wisdom, a lasting link to the glory of his name and the redemption of the blind force to wisdom and light.[112] *And before we can proceed further in the operation of so great danger, it is necessary that we should invoke Divine aid and assistance, without which would our work be indeed futile and of no avail. Wherefore being met thus together let us kneel down and pray:*

All kneel at four points.

From thy hands O Lord cometh all good! From thy hands flow down all grace and blessing: the characters of nature with thy fingers hast thou traced, but none can read them unless he hath been taught in thy school. Therefore even as servants look unto the hands of their masters, and handmaidens unto the hands of their mistresses, even so

---

[111] Roughly translated, this means that all those present who should not be here are to get out.

[112] This underlined section which was added in by Florence Farr was taken out by

our eyes look unto thee! For thou alone art our help, O Lord our God. Who should not extol thee, who should not praise thee, O Lord of the Universe! All is from thee, all belongeth Unto thee! Either thy love or thine Anger, all must again re-enter; for nothing canst thou lose; all must tend unto thy honour and majesty.

Thou art Lord alone and there is none beside thee! Thou dost what thou wilt with thy mighty arm, and none can escape from thee! Thou alone helpest in their necessity the humble, the meek-hearted and the poor, who submit themselves unto thee! Unto whom there is no like, whose dwelling is in Heaven, and in every virtuous and God-fearing heart.

O God the vast One - thou art in all things.

O nature, thou self from nothing: for what else shall I call thee!

In myself I am nothing, in thee I am self, and live in thy selfhood from nothing! Live thou in me, and being me unto that self which is thee! Amen!

All rise - a pause.

Magus of the Art:

Fratres of the Order of the Rosy Cross, let us purify and consecrate this place as the Hall of Dual Truth. magus of the water, I command thee to perform the Lesser Banishing Ritual of the Pentagram[113], to consecrate the water of purification, the wine, the oil, and the milk; and afterwards to purify the place of working with the consecrated water!

Magus of Water:

Mighty Magus of Art! All thy commands shall be fulfilled, and thy desires accomplished.

Crowley in the published version in the Equinox.

[113] The use of the banishing ritual here is in error. When doing an evocation ritual the area must be banished before the start so that the current brought in is not tainted with negative energy. In this ritual it is unacceptable to banish, especially

He passes to the East where he performs the Lesser Banishing Ritual of the Pentagram, and then to the North, where are collected in open vessels, the water, the wine, the oil, and the milk: and makes with his sword over them the banishing pentagram of water, saying:[114]

I exorcise ye impure, unclean and evil spirits that dwell in these creatures of water, oil, wine, and milk, in the name of EL, strong and mighty, and in the name of Gabriel, great angel of water, I command ye to depart and no longer pollute with your presence in the Hall of Twofold Truth!

Drawing over them the equilibrating pentagram of passives, and the invoking pentagram of water, he says:

In the name of HCOMA and by the names EMPH ARSL GAIOL I consecrate ye to the service of the magic of Light!

He places the wine upon the altar, the water he leaves at the North, the oil towards the South, the brazen vessel of milk on the tripod in the midst of the circle. The Magus of Art silently recites to herself the exhortation[115] of the Lords of the key of the Tablet of Union, afterwards saying silently:

I invoke ye, lords of the key of the Tablet of Union, to infuse into these elements of water and fire your mystic powers, and to cast into the midst of these opposing elements the Holy Powers of the great letter Shin: to gleam and shine in the midst of the balance, even in the cauldron of art wherein alike is fire and moisture.

After the consecration of the water, the Magus of the Water takes up the cup of water, and scatters water all around the edge of the circle saying:

---

when you have already invoked and linked with the current to bring it through into an already purified area.

[114]   This should have been done before the ceremony was started. Section 'E' of Yod does not tell them to do this at this point in the ceremony.

[115]   This is explained in the commentary on the portal ritual.

So first the priest who governeth the works of fire, must sprinkle with the lustral waters of the loud-resounding sea.

He then passes to the centre of the circle and scatters the water in the four quarters, saying:

I purify with water.

He resumes his place in the North.

Magus of the Art:

Magus of the Fire, I command you to consecrate this place by the Invoking ritual of the Hexagram, to consecrate the magic fire and lights; to illumine the lamps and place them about the circle in orderly disposition; and afterwards to consecrate this place with the Holy fire.

Magus of Fire:

Mighty Magus of the Art! all thy commands shall be obeyed and all thy desires accomplished.

He collects together at the South the incense, oil, charcoal, and magic candle, and performs Lesser Invoking Ritual of the Hexagram at the four quarters; then, extinguishing all lights, save one, he performs over these the banishing ritual of the pentagram of fire, saying:

I exorcise ye, evil and opposing spirits dwelling in this creature of fire, by the Holy and tremendous name of God the vast One, ELOHIM: and in the name of MICHAEL, great archangel of fire, that ye depart hence, no longer polluting with your presence the Hall of Twofold Truth.

He lights from that one flame the magical candle, and drawing over it the invoking pentagram of spirit active, he cries:

BITOM!

And then, drawing the invoking pentagram of fire, he says:

> *I, in the names of BITOM and by the names OIP TEA*
> *PEDOCE, I consecrate thee, O creature of fire, to the*
> *service of the works of the magic of Light!*

He lights from the magical candle the eight lamps, and the charcoal for the incense burners, after which he casts the incense on the coals in the censer and passes round the circle saying:

> *And, when all the phantoms are vanished, thou shalt see*
> *that Holy and formless fire, that fire which darts ands*
> *flashes through the hidden depths of the universe, hear*
> *thou the voice of fire.*

He passes to the centre of the circle and censes towards the four quarters saying:

> *I consecrate with fire.*

He resumes his place in the South. Chief Magus takes a fan, and fanning the air says:

> *I exorcise thee, creature of air, by these names, YHVH*
> *SHALOM that all evil and impure spirits now depart*
> *immediately.*

The Chief Magus makes banishing air pentagram then circumambulates saying:

> *Such a fire existeth extending through the rushing of*
> *the air, or even a fire formless whence cometh the image*
> *of a voice, or even a flashing light abounding, revolving*
> *whirling forth, crying aloud.*
> *Creature of air, in the names of EXARP, OROIBAH*
> *AOZIPI, I consecrate thee to the works of the magic of*
> *Light!*

Makes invoking pentagram of air. All face West. Assistant Magus then casts salt to all four quarters, all over the circle, and passes to West, and describes with his chain the banishing pentagram of earth, saying:

I exorcise thee, creature of earth, by and in the Divine names Adonai Ha Artez, Adonai Melekh Amen, and in the name of Aurial, great Archangel of earth, that every evil and impure spirit now depart immediately.

Circumambulates saying:

Stoop not down unto the darkly splendid world, wherein lieth continually a faithless depth, and Hades wrapt in gloom, delighting in intelligible images, precipitous, winding, a black ever-rolling abyss, ever espousing a body unluminous, formless and void.

Makes invoking pentagram of earth.

Creature of earth, in the names of EMOR DIAL HCTGA, I consecrate thee to the service of the magic of the Light!

Chief Magus:

We invoke ye, great Lords of the Watchtowers of the Universe! Guard ye our magic circle, and let no evil or impure spirit enter therein: strengthen and inspire us in this our operation of the magic Light. Let the mystic circumambulation take place in the path of life.

Assistant Magus of Art goes first, holding in his left the magic candle, and in his right the sword of art, with which latter he traces in the air the outer limits of the magic circle. All circumambulate thrice. He then, standing at the East and facing East, says:

Holy art thou, Lord of the Universe!
Holy art thou, whom Nature hath not formed!
Holy art thou, the Vast and the Mighty One!
Lord of Light and of the darkness![116]

---

[116]   This is an ancient adoration used by the Golden Dawn.

Chief Magus of Art:

Magus of the Fire, I command you to perform at the four quarters of the universe the invocation of the forces of Mercury by Solomon's Seal.[117]

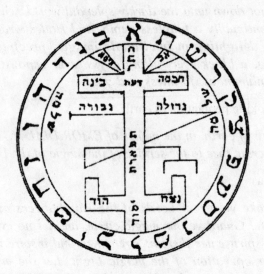

Solomon's Seal

Magus of Fire:

Mighty Magus of Art, all thy commands shall be obeyed, and all thy desires shall be accomplished!

He does it. The magus now advances to the centre of the circle, by the magical cauldron, wherein is the milk becoming heated, turns himself towards the fire of the spirit and recites:

---

[117]   Although the seal is unlisted in the descriptions of the ritual, it was a consecrated pentacle that was included in the *Key of Solomon the King* manuscripts. It was worn over the forehead. I am puzzled by this reference here as it implies it is worn by the magus of fire when it should be worn by the chief magus of the art. Mathers called this seal 'The Mystical figure of Solomon' - This is only given in the two MSS., Lansdowne 1202 and 1203. It was given by Levi in his *Dogme et Ritual de la Haute*, and by Tycho Brahe in his *Calendarium Naturale Magicum*. In each

'F'

INVOCATION TO THE HIGHER

Majesty of the Godhead, Wisdom crowned Thoth, Lord of the gates of the universe: Thee! Thee we invoke! Thou that manifesteth in thy symbolic form as ibis-headed one: thee, thee we invoke! Thou, who holdest in thy hand the magic wand of double power: thee we invoke! Thou who bearest in thy left hand the rose and cross of light and life: thee, thee we invoke! Thou whose head is of green, whose nemys is of night sky-blue; whose skin is of flaming orange, as though it burned in a furnace: thee, thee we invoke!

Behold, I am Yesterday, To-day, and the brother of the Morrow! For I am born again and again. Mine is the unseen force which created the Gods, and giveth life unto the dwellers in the watchtowers of the Universe.

I am the charioteer in the East, lord of the past and future, He who seeth by the Light that is within him.

I am the lord of resurrection, who cometh forth from the dusk, and whose birth is from the house of death.

O ye two divine hawks upon your pinnacles, who are keeping watch over the universe!

Ye who accompany the bier unto its resting place, and who pilots the ship of Ra, advancing onwards unto the heights of Heaven!

Lord of the shrine which standeth in the centre of the earth!

Behold He is in me and I in Him!

Mine is the radiance in which Ptah floateth over his firmament.

I travel upon high.

I tread upon the firmament of Nu.

---

instance it was published without the Hebrew words and letters, probably because these were so mangled by illiterate transcribers. After much labour and study of the figure, I believe the words in the body of the symbol to be intended for the ten Sephiroth arranged in the form of the Tree of Life, with the name of Solomon to right and to the left; while the surrounding characters are intended for the Twenty Two letters of the Hebrew alphabet. I have restored them.

*I raise a flame with a flashing lightning of mine eye,
ever rushing forward in the splendour daily glorified
Ra, giving life to every creature that treadeth upon the
earth.*

If I say come up upon the mountains,
The Celestial waters shall flow at my word:
For I am Ra incarnate,
Khephra created in flesh!
*I am the living image of my father Tmu, lord of the
City of the Sun!*
The god who commands is in my mouth:
The god of wisdom is in my heart:
My tongue is the sanctuary of truth:
And a God sitteth upon my lips!
My word is accomplished each day,
and the desire of my heart releases itself
like that of Ptah when he creates his works.
Since I am eternal, everything acts
according to my designs,
and everything obeys my words.

*Therefore do thou come forth unto Me from thine
abode in the silence, unutterable wisdom, all-light, all-
power. Thoth, Hermes, Mercury, Odin, by whatever name
I call thee, thou art still un-named and nameless for
eternity! Come thou forth, I say, and aid and guard me
in this work of art.*

*Thou, star of the East, that didst conduct the magi.
Thou art the same, all present in Heaven and Hell. Thou
that vibratest betwixt the Light and the darkness rising,
descending, changing forever, yet forever the same!*

The Sun is thy father!
Thy mother the moon!
The wind hath borne thee in its bosom:
*And earth hath never nourished the changeless
godhead of thy youth.*
*Come thou forth I say, come thou forth, and make all
spirits subject unto me!*
So that every spirit of the firmament,

> *And of the ether of the earth,*
> *And under the earth,*
> *On dry land,*
> *And in the water,*
> *Of whirling air,*
> *And of rushing fire,*
> *And every spell and scourge of God, may be obedient*
> *unto me!*

She binds a black cord thrice round the sigil of the spirit and veils it in black silk, saying:

> *Hear me, ye lords of truth in the Hall of Themis, hear ye my words, for I am made as ye! I now purpose with Divine aid, to call forth this day and hour of the spirit of Mercury, Taphthartharath, whose magical seal I now bind with this triple cord of bondage, and shroud in the black concealing darkness and in death! Even as I knot about this sigil the triple cord of bondage, so let the magic power of my will and words penetrate unto him, and bind him that he cannot move; but is presently forced by the mastery and majesty of the rites of power to manifest here before us without this circle of art, in the magical triangle which I have provided for his apparition.*
>
> *And even as I shroud from the light of day this signature of that spirit Taphthartharath, so do I render him in his place blind, deaf and dumb.*
>
> *That he may in no-wise move his place or call for aid upon his Gods; or hear another voice save mine or my companions', or see another path before him than the one unto this place.*

Sigil is placed outside the circle by Assistant Magus of Art

> *And the reason for this my working is, that I seek to obtain from the spirit Taphthartharath the knowledge of the realm of Kokab, and to this end I implore the divine assistance in the names of   ELOHIM TZABOATH, THOTH, METATRON, TAPHAEL, MICHAEL, BENI-ELOHIM, TIRIEL!*

'G'

Chief resumes her seat. The three others pass to the West and point their swords in menace at the veiled and corded sigil. The Assistant Magus then lights the sigil onto the edge of the circle, and says:

> *Who gives permission to admit to the Hall of Dual Truth this creature of sigils?*

Magus of Art:

> *I, S.S.D.D., Soror of the Order of the Golden Dawn, Theorica Adepta Minora of the Order of the Rose of Ruby and the Cross of Gold!*

I.A.:

> *Creature of sigils, impure and unconsecrate! Thou canst not enter our magic circle!*

D.P.A.L.:

> *Creature of sigils I purify thee with water.*

A.E.A.:

> *Creature of sigils I consecrate thee by fire.*

Magus of the Art, in a loud voice cries seven times[118] the name of the spirit, vibrating strongly and then says:

'H'

> *Assistant Magus of Art, I command thee to place the sigil at the foot of the altar.*

I.A.:

> *Mighty Magus of Art, all your commands shall be obeyed and your desires shall be fulfilled.*

He does so. The Magus of Art, standing on the throne of the East, then proclaims:

---

[118]   This represents the numbers of Hebrew letters in the name of the spirit.

THE INVOCATION

O thou mighty and powerful spirit Taphthartharath, I bind and conjure thee very potently, that thou do appear in visible form before us in the magical triangle without this circle of art. I demand that Thou shall speedily come hither from thy dark abodes and retreats, in the sphere of Kokab, and thou do presently appear before us in pleasing form, not seeking to terrify us with vain apparitions, for we are armed with words of double power, and therefore without fear! and I moreover demand, binding and conjuring thee by the mighty name of ELOHIM TZABOATH, that thou teach us how we may acquire the power to know all things that appertain unto the knowledge of THOTH who ruleth the occult wisdom and Power. And I am about to invoke thee in the magical Hour of TAFRAC, and with the hour we desire to form a link through thee. Show us how best to control thee and those spirits of KOKAB which are beneath thee, and on this day, for that in this day and hour the great angel KOKAB, RAPHAEL, reigneth-beneath whose dominion art thou-and I shall swear to thee, here in the Hall of the Twofold Manifestation of Truth, that, as liveth and ruleth for ever more the Lord of the Universe; that even as I and my companions are of the Order of the Rose of Ruby and the Cross of Gold; that even as in us is the knowledge of the rites of power ineffable:

THOU SHALT this day become manifest unto visible appearance before us, in the magical triangle without this circle of art:

'I'

It should now have arrived at the magical hour Trafrac, commencing at 8h. 32'P.M. If not, then the adepti seat themselves and await that time. When it is fulfilled, the Assistant Magus places the sigil on the altar in the right quarter: The magus advances to the East of the altar, lays her left hand upon it, her right holding the sword with its point upon the centre of the sigil. The Associate Magus holds the magical candle for her to be read by: and the magus of fire holds the Book of Invocations, turning the pages that she may read continually.

She recites:

> *Hear ye, ye Lords of Truth, hear ye invoked powers of the sphere of KOKAB, that all is now ready for the commencement of this evocation!*

'J'

THE POTENT EXORCISM

To be said assuming the mask or form[119] of the spirit Taphthartharath.

(TAU)
O thou mighty spirit of Mercury, Taphthartharath!
I bind, command and very potently do conjure thee:

(PEH)
By the Majesty of the terrible name ELOHIM TZBOATH, the Gods of the armies of the BENI-ELOHIM, by and in the name of MIKAL, great Archangel of God, that ruleth the Sphere of KOKAB, by and in the name of TIRIEL, the mighty Intelligence of KOKAB; By and in the name of the Sephirah HOD, and in the name of thy sphere KOKAB! that thou come forth here now, in this present day and hour, and appear in visible form before us: in the great magical triangle without this circle of art.

(TAU)
I bind and conjure thee anew: By the magical figures which are traced upon the ground: By the magic seal of Mercury I bear on my breast: By the eight magic

---

[119]   An astral Shell of the God-form must be built up around the individual.

*lamps that flame around me: By thy seal and sigil which
I bear upon my heart: That thou come forth, here now,
in this present day and hour, and appear in visible and
material form before us, in the great magic triangle
without this circle of art.*

(RESH)

*I bind and conjure thee anew: By the wisdom of Thoth
the mighty God: By the light of the magic fire: By the
unutterable glory of the godhead within me: By all
powerful names and rites: that thou come forth, here,
now in this present day and hour, and appear in visible
and material form before us, in the great magical triangle
without this circle of art.*

(TAU)

But if thou art disobedient and unwilling to come:
    Then I will curse[120] thee by the mighty names of God!
    And I will cast ye down from thy power and place!
    And I will torment thee with new and terrible names!
    And I will blot out thy place from the Universe;
    *And thou shalt never rise again! So come thou forth
quickly, thou Mighty spirit Taphthartharath, come thou
forth quickly from thy abodes and retreats! Come unto
us, and appear before us in visible and material form
within the great magical triangle without this circle of
art, courteously answering all our demands, and see thou
that thou deceive us in nowise-lest.*

    *Take up the veiled sigil and strike it thrice with the
blade of the magic sword, then hold it in the left*

---

[120] To use a curse in a ritual is taking a step backwards, and goes against everything the adept has learnt. The curse appears in the 'Key of Solomon the King' manuscript and no doubt it was used in this ritual because of this. It is ill advised to curse the spirit in evocation when you may want to include its power in a talisman ritual. Spirits do not forgive and to use a curse shows a lack of control of the ritual. Curses have a habit of bouncing back on people who use them, even more so when cursing a powerful spirit such as Taphthartharath.

aloft in the air, at the same time stamping thrice with right foot.[121]

'K'

Assistant Magus now takes the sigil and places it in the North: S.S.D.D. returns to her seat, takes lotus wand (or ibis sceptre) and says:

The voice of the exorcist says unto me, let me shroud myself in darkness, from the darkness come I forth ere my birth, from silence of primal sleep. And the Voice of Ages answered unto my soul: 'Creature of Mercury, who art called Taphthartharath! The Light shineth in thy darkness, but thy darkness comprehendeth it not!'

Let the mystic circumambulation take place in the path of darkness, with the magic light of occult science to guide our way!

'L'

I.A. takes up sigil in left hand and candle in right. Starting at North they circumambulate once.

S.S.D.D. rises and passes round the temple before them, halting at the gate of the West. Sigil barred by I.A., purified and consecrated:

S.S.D.D., as Hiereus, assuming the mask of the spirit, strikes the sigil (now partly barred) once with the magic sword and says:

Thou canst not pass from concealment unto manifestation save by the virtue of the name ELOHIM! Before all things

---

[121] The stamping of the foot gets rid of negative tendencies and cuts the cords that bind the spirit. The middle of the Sword relates to the sephira of Geburah (this is the sword of the Hiereus) and this is the power that forces the spirit's hand. An analogy of this is when someone is apprehended by the law and looks for a method of escape. The arresting officer simply pulls back his coat to reveal his pistol. The inference is clear without direct force.

*are the chaos and the darkness, and the gates of the
land of night. I am he whose name is darkness; I am the
great one of the paths of the shades! I am the exorcist in
the midst of the exorcism: appear thou therefore without
fear before me, for I am he in whom fear is not!*

Thou hast known me so pass thou on!

'N'

Magus of Art passes around throne of East, Assistant Magus reveils
the sigil and carries it round once more. They halt, bare, purify and
consecrate sigil as before: they approach the gate of the East. Sigil
unveiled: S.S.D.D. smiting sigil once with lotus wand.

'O'

*Thou canst not pass from concealment unto manifestation
save by virtue of the name YHVH. After the formless and
the void and the darkness cometh the knowledge of the
light. I am that light which riseth in the darkness: I am
the exorcist in the midst of the exorcism: appear thou
therefore in visible form before me, for I am the wielder
of the forces of balance.*

*Thou hast known me now, so pass thou on unto the
cubical altar of the universe!*

'P'

Sigil re-veiled, and conducted to altar, placed on West of triangle;
S.S.D.D. passes to altar holding sigil and sword as before. On her
right hand is A.E.A. with the magic candle: on her left is D.P.A.L.
with the ritual. Behind her to the East of the magical cauldron is
I.A. casting unto the milk at each appropriate moment the right
ingredient. Afterwards, as S.S.D.D. names each magical name,
I.A. draws in the perfected hell-broth the sigils, etc., appropriate
thereunto: at which time S.S.D.D. recites the:

STRONGER AND MORE POTENT CONJURATION

Come forth! Come forth! Come forth unto us! spirit of
KOKAB TAPHTHARATHARATH, I conjure thee! Come!
Accept of us these magical sacrifices, prepared to give
thee body and form. Herein are blended the magical
elements of thy body, the symbols of thy mighty being.
For the sweet scent of mace is that which shall purify
thee finally from the bondage of evil. And the heat of the
magical fire is my will which volatilises the gross matter
of thy Chaos, enabling thee to manifest thyself in
pleasing form before us. And the flesh of the serpent is
symbol of thy body, which we destroy by water and fire,
that it may be renewed before us. And the blood of the
Serpent is the symbol of the magic of the word Messiah[122]
whereby we triumph over Nahash. And the all-blending
milk is the magical water of thy purification.

And the fire which flames over all is the utter (assistant
lights hell-broth) *power of our scared rites!*

Come forth! Come forth! Come forth unto us! Spirit
of Mercury. O Taphthartharath. I bind and conjure thee
by him that sitteth forever on the Throne of thy Planet,
the knower, the master, the all-dominating by wisdom,
Thoth the great king, lord of the upper and lower crowns!
I bind and conjure thee by the great name IAHDONHI!
Whose power is set flaming above thy palaces, and ruleth
over thee in the midst of thy gloomy habitations.

And by the powers of the mighty letter Beth: which is
the house of our God, and the crown of our
understanding and knowledge.

---

[122] When using Gematria, both the words Serpent and Messiah have a numerical
value of 358 (these numbers reduce up to 16) and relate to the 16th
Path, associated to the Key of the Hierophant. Crowley (in his *Equinox* Volume)
puts it this way:' ...the dogma is that the head of the serpent (n) is "bruised," being
replaced by "M" , the letter of sacrifice, and God, the letter alike of virginity (YOD
=Scorpio) and of original deity (YOD= the foundation or type of all letters).Thus
the word may be read: "The sacrifice of the virgin born Divine One triumphant
(CHETH, the Chariot) through the spirit," while NChSh reads "Death entering
(realm of spirit)."...

*And by the great magic word StiBeTTChePhMeFShiSS[123]
which calleth thee from thy place as thou fleest before
the presence of the spirit of Light and the Crown! And by
the name ZABOATH! which symbolises thy passage from
Mercury to Gemini unto us in Malkuth:*

*Come   forth,   Come   forth,   Come   forth!
TAPHTHARATHARATH!*

*In the name of IAHDONHI: I invoke thee: appear!
appear! TAPHTHARATHARATH!*

*In the name ELOHIM TZABOATH: I invoke thee:
appear! appear! TAPHTHARATHARATH!*

*In the name of MIKHAEL! I invoke thee: appear!
appear! TAPHTHARATHARATH!*

*In the name of RAPHAEL: I invoke thee: appear!
appear! TAPHTHARATHARATH!*

*In the name of TIRIEL: I invoke thee: appear! appear!
TAPHTHARATHARATH!*

*In the name of ASBOGA[124]: I invoke thee: appear!
appear! TAPHTHARATHARATH!*

*In the name of DIN[125] and DONI: I invoke thee:
appear! appear! TAPHTHARATHARATH!*

*In the name of TAPHTHARATHARATH: I invoke thee:
appear! appear!*

*O thou mighty Angel who art lord of the 14th degree
of Gemini, wherein now Mercury takes refuge, send thou
unto me that powerful but blind force in the form of
TAPHTHARATHARATH . I conjure thee by the names of
Nghanenel, he who rejoiceth.*

*Come   forth   unto   us   therefore,   O
TAPHTHARATHARATH, TAPHTHARATHARATH, and
appear thou in visible and material form before us in the*

---

[123] This word is made from the Coptic letters of the paths, and initial letters of
the sephiroth, of the left hand side of the Tree of Life.

[124]   This name is sometimes called eight extended. It is based on a numerical
compilation.

[125]   This relates to the number 64 which is the total number of squares in the
kamea of Mercury.

*great magical triangle without this circle of art! And if
any other magus of art, or any other school than ours,
is now invoking thee by potent spells; or if thou art bound
by thy vow, or thy duties, or the terrible bonds of the
magic of Hell; then I let shine upon thee the glory of the
symbol of the rose and cross; and I tell thee by that symbol
that thou art free of all vows, of all bonds, for what time
thou comest hither to obey my will!*

*Or if any other master or masters of the magic of
light of the Order of the Rose of the Ruby and the Cross
of Gold is now binding and invoking thee by the supreme,
absolute and fearful power of this our art; then I
command and conjure thee by every name and rite
already rehearsed that thou send unto us an ambassador
to declare unto us the reason for thy disobedience.*

*But if thou art yet disobedient and unwilling to come,
then I curse thee by the mighty names of God, and I
will cast thee forth from thy power and place. And I
will torment thee by horrible and terrible rites. And I
will blot out thy place from the Universe and thou shalt
NEVER rise again!*[126]

*So come thou forth!, thou spirit of Mercury!
TAPHTHARATHARATH! come thou forth quickly, I
advise and command thee.*

*Come thou forth from thy abodes and retreats. Come
thou forth unto us, and appear before us in this magical
triangle without this circle of art: in fair and human form,
courteously answering in an audible voice all our
demands. As it is written:*

"Kiss the Son lest He be angry!
If His anger be kindled, yea, but a little-
Blessed are they that put their trust in him!"

The Mighty Magus of Art lifts up the sigil towards Heaven, removes
the black veil, and cries:

---

[126] This paragraph with its threats and cursing should be omitted.

Creature of KOKAB, long hast thou dwelt in darkness!
Quit the night and seek the day!

Sigil is replaced to West of the triangle; Magus holds Sword and erect (point upwards) over its centre, and lays her left hand upon it, saying:

By all the names and powers and rights already
rehearsed, I conjure thee thus unto visible apparition:

KHABS AM PEKHET
KNOX OM PAX
LIGHT IN EXTENSION

Saith the Magus of Art:

'R'

As the Light becomes hidden in darkness can manifest
therefrom. SO SHALT THOU become manifest from
concealment unto manifestation!

The Magus of Art takes up the sigil, stands at the East of the altar, facing West, and says:

CONJURATION OF THE INTELLIGENCE TIRIEL

TIRIEL, Angel, of God, in the name of IAHDONHI, O conjure thee send unto us this spirit TAPHTHARATHARATH. Do thou force him to manifest before us without this circle of art.

TIRIEL, in the name of ELOHIM TZABOATH, send to us in form material this spirit TAPHTHARATHARATH.

TIRIEL, in the name of BENI ELOHIM, send to us in form material this spirit TAPHTHARATHARATH.

TIRIEL, in the name of MIKAEL, send to us in form material this spirit TAPHTHARATHARATH.

TIRIEL, in the name of RAPHAEL, send to us in visible form this spirit TAPHTHARATHARATH.

TIRIEL, in the name of HOD, send to us in visible

form this spirit TAPHTHARATHARATH.

O TIRIEL, O TIRIEL: in all the mighty signs and seals and symbols here gathered together, I conjure thee in the name of the highest to force this spirit TAPHTHARATHARATH unto visible manifestation before us, in the great triangle without this circle of art.

The magus now places the sigil between the Mystic Pillars, and attacks it as the Enterer, directing upon it her whole will: following this projection by the sign of silence. If he does not yet appear, then repeat the invocation to Tiriel from the throne of the East. This process may be repeated thrice. But if not even then the spirit come, then an error hath been committed, in which case replace the sigil on altar, holding sword as usual and say:

THE PRAYER UNTO
THE GREAT GOD OF HEAVEN

O ye great Lords of the Hall of the Twofold Manifestation of Truth, who preside over the weighing of the souls in the place of judgement before AESHOORI[127], give me your hands for I am made of ye! Give me your hands, give me your magic powers, that I may have given unto me the force and the power and the might irresistible, which shall compel this disobedient and malignant spirit, TAPHTHARATHARATH, to appear before me, that I may accomplish this evocation of arts according to all my wants and all my desires. In myself I am nothing: in ye I am all Self, and exist in the selfhood of the mighty to eternity! O Thoth, who makest victorious the word of AESHOORI against his adversaries, make thou my word, who and OSIRIS, triumphant and victorious over this spirit: TAPHTHAR ATHARATH! Amen.

---

[127] This is the Coptic title for Osiris.

Return to the place of the Hierophant, and repeat, charging. He now will certainly appear. But as soon as he appears, again let the sigil be purified and censed by the Magus of Art. The removing from the middle of the sigil the cord of bondage, and holding that sigil in her left hand, she will smite it with the flat blade of her magic sword, saying:

'S'

By and in the names of IAHDONAHI, ELOHIM TZABOATH, MIKAEL, RAPHAEL AND URIEL: I invoke upon thee the power of perfect manifestation unto visible appearance!

I.A. now takes the sigil in his right hand and circumambulates thrice. He places sigil on the ground at the place of spirit.

'T'

S.S.D.D., from the place of the Hierophant, now recites: (I.A. with sword guarding the place of spirit, D.P.A.L. holding the book; and A.E. holding the magical candle for her to read by)

AN EXTREMELY POWERFUL CONJURATION

Behold! Thou great powerful prince and spirit TAPHTHARATHARATH, we have conjured thee hither in this day and hour, to demand of thee certain matters relative to the secret magical knowledge which may be conveyed to us from thy great master Thoth through thee. But, before we can proceed further, it is necessary that thou do assume a shape more distinctly material and visible. Therefore, in order that thou mayest appear more fully visible, and in order that thou mayest know that we are possessed of the means, rites, powers and privileges of binding and compelling thee unto obedience, do we rehearse before thee yet again the mighty words; The names, the sigils, and the powers of the conjurations of fearful efficacy: and learn that if thou wert under any bond or spell, or in distant lands or elsewhere employed, yet nothing should enable thee to resist the power of our terrible conjuration; for it thou art disobedient and unwilling to come, we shall curse and imprecate thee most horribly by the fearful names of God the vast one; and we shall tear from thee thy rank and thy power, and we shall cast thee down unto the fearful abode of the chained ones and shells, and thou shalt never rise again!

Wherefore, make haste, O thou mighty spirit TAPHARATHARATH, and appear very visibly before us, in the magical triangle, without this circle of art. I bind and conjure thee unto very visible appearance in the divine and terrible name IAHDONAI! by the name IAHDONAI! and in the name IAHDONAI! I command thee to assume before us a very visible and material Form. And by the mighty name of God the vast one, ELOHIM TZABOATH! And in the name ELOHIM TZABOATH! And by the name ELOHIM TZABOATH! I bind and conjure thee that thou should stand forth very visibly before us. I bind and conjure thee unto more visible appearance, O thou spirit, TAPHTHARATHARATH! By the name of MIKAEL! And in the name of MIKAEL! By and in the name of MIKAEL!

I bind and conjure thee that thou stand forth very visibly, endowed with an audible voice, speaking truth in the language wherein I have called thee forth.

Let IAHDONAI, ELOHIM TZABOATH, MIKAEL, RAPHAEL, BENI-ELOHIM, TIRIEL, ASBOGA, DIN, DONI, HOD, KOKAB and every name and spell and scourge of God the vast One bind thee to obey my words and will.

Behold the standards, symbols and seals and ensigns of our God: obey and fear them, O thou mighty and potent spirit TAPHTHARATHARATH!

Behold our robes, ornaments, insignia and weapons: and say, are not these things thou fearest?

Behold the magic fire, the mystic lamps, the blinding radiance of the flashing tablets![128]

Behold the magical liquids of the material basis; it is these that have given thee form!

Hear thou the magic spells and names and chants which bind thee!

TAPHTHARATHARATH!

TAPHTHARATHARATH!

TAPHTHARATHARATH!

TAPHTHARATHARATH!

TAPHTHARATHARATH!

TAPHTHARATHARATH!

Arise! Move! Appear!

Zodacar Eca od Zodamerhnu odo kikale Imayah piape piamoe; od VAOAN![129]

And at this time a spirit be duly and rightly materialised, then pass to the request of the Mighty Magus of Art; but if not, then doth the magus of art assume the God-form of Thoth, and say:

Thou comest not! Then will I work and work again. I will destroy thee and uproot thee out of Heaven and earth and Hell. thy place shall become empty; and the horror of horrors shall abide in thy heart, and I will overwhelm thee with fear and trembling, for "SOUL mastering terror" is my name.[130]

at this point he manifests, then pass on to the final Request of the

---

[128]   A flashing tablet is any symbol in colour with its complementary. In this instance the reference is to the five Enochian Tablets.

[129]   This is a combination of Enochian and English (Imayah = I may) and a rough translation is 'Move therefore and appear, open the mysteries so I may balance righteousness and truth.'

[130]   You can control an entity when you bring him into your dimension, but beyond that, threats are meaningless. An adept has no power to deal with an entity in its own level. The adept summons and deals with part of the entity that comes into our dimension, not the whole being. Threats and curses only bore it. If it comes, it does not do so because it is frightened. The object of the exercise here is to bring the portal of the ritual to where one can tap into the ray or level where the emanations of the spirit are apparent.

Mighty Magus of Art; if not, continue holding the arms in the Sign of Apophis[131].

> *Brother Assistant Magus! Thou wilt write me the name of this evil serpent, this spirit TAPHTHARATHARATH, on a piece of pure vellum[132], and thou shalt place thereon also His seal and character; That I may curse, condemn and utterly destroy Him for his disobedience and mockery of the divine and terrible names of God the vast one.*

Assistant Magus does this.

> *Hear ye my curse, O lords of the twofold manifestation of Truth. I have evoked the spirit TAPHTHARATHARATH in due form by the formula of THOTH. But he obeys me not, he makes no strong manifestation. Wherefore bear ye witness and give ye power unto my utter condemnation of the mocker of your mysteries.*
> *I curse and blast thee, O thou spirit*
>   *TAPHTHARATHARATH. I curse thy life and blast thy being. I consign thee unto the lowest hell of Abaddon.*
>   *By the whole power of the Order of the Rose of Ruby and the Cross of Gold-for that thou hast failed at their behest, and hast mocked by thy disobedience at their God-born knowledge-by that Order which riseth even unto the white throne of God himself do I curse thy life and blast thy being; and consign thee unto the lowermost Hell of Abaddon!*

> *In the names IAHDONHI, ELOHIM TZABOATH, MIKAEL, RAPHAEL, BENI-ELOHIM and TIRIEL: I curse thy Life!   And blast thy being! Down! Sink down to the depths of horror.*

---

[131] The V position of the hands when placed in the Zodiac circle shows them touching 0 degrees Virgo and 0 degrees Taurus. This is the transmutation of the forces of the earth Signs into growth through the influence of the Moon and Mercury. It is the manifestation of Mercury through the earth so the entity's form can be perceived.

[132] This is a type of parchment prepared from either lambskin, kidskin or calfskin.

*By every name, symbol, sign and rite that has this day
been practised in this magic circle; by every power, of
the Gods, of the mighty Order to which we all belong!
I curse thy Life!   And blast thy being!
all, fall down to torment unspeakable!
If thou dost not appear then will I complete the fearful
sentence of this curse. God will not help thee. thou hast
mocked His name.*

Taking the slip of vellum and thrusting it into the magical fire.

*I bid thee, O sacred fire of art, by the names and Powers
which gave birth unto the spirit of the Primal fire: I
bind and conjure thee by every name of God, the vast
One, that hath rule, authority and domination over thee;
that thou do spiritually burn, blast, destroy and
condemn this spirit TAPHTHARATHARATH, whose
name and seal are written herein, causing him to endure
the most horrible tortures as of an eternal and
consuming fire, so long as He shall not come at my
behest!*

*The earth shall suffocate him, for mine are its powers,
and fire shall torment him, for mine is its magic. And
air shall not fan him, nor water shall cool him. But
torment unspeakable, horror undying, terror
unaltering, pain unendurable; the words of my curse
shall be on Him for ever; God shall not hear Him, nor
help Him ever, and the curse shall be on Him for ever
and ever!*

So soon as he shall appear, extinguish that fire with consecrated
water, and cry:

*O thou mighty spirit TAPHTHARATHARATH, for as much
as thou art come, albeit tardily, I do revoke my magic
curse, and free thee from all its bonds save only from
those that bind thee here!*

He having appeared, the Assistant Magus of Art holds aloft his
Sword, saying:

*Hear Ye, great lord of the Hall of Dual Truth; Hear ye,
immortal powers of the magic of Light, that this spirit
TAPHTHARATHARATH hath been duly and properly
invoked in accordance with scared rites of the power
ineffable.*

'U'

The Mighty Magus of Art now says:

*O ye great lords of the glory and light of the radiant orb
of Kokab; ye in whom are vested the knowledge of the
mighty powers, the knowledge of all the hidden arts and
sciences of the magic and of the mystery! Ye! Ye! I invoke
and conjure!   Cause ye this mighty Serpent
TAPHTHARATHARATH to perform all our demands:
manifest ye through him the majesty of your presences,
the divinity of your knowledge, that we may all be led
yet one step nearer unto the consummation of the mighty
work, one step nearer unto the great white throne of the
God-head; and that, in so doing, His being may become
more glorified and enlightened, more capable of
receiving the influx of that divine spirit which dwells in
the heart of man and God!*

S.S.D.D. now formulates the desires as follows:

*O thou great potent spirit TAPHTHARATHARATH, I
do command and very potently conjure thee by the
majesty of Thoth, the great God, lord of Amenta, king
and lord eternal of the magic of Light:*
*That thou teach us continually the mysteries of the
art of magic, declaring unto us now in what best manner
may each of us progress towards the accomplishment of
the great Work. Teach us the mysteries of all hidden arts
and Sciences which are under the dominion of Mercury,
and finally swear thou by the great magic sigil that I
hold in my hand, that thou wilt in future always speedily
appear before us; coming whensoever we enable thee*

*by the offerings and sacrifices of thy nature! To the end
that thou mayest be a perpetual link of communication
between the great god Thoth under his three forms and
ourselves.*

'V'

THE FINAL ADMONITION

*O thou mighty and Potent Prince of spirits
TAPHTHARATHARATH : for as much as thou hast obeyed
us in all demands, I now finally bind and conjure thee:*
    *That thou hereafter harm me not, or these my
companions, or this place or ought pertaining unto all
of us[133]: that thou faithfully perform all these things even
as thou hast sworn by the great and all-powerful names
of God the vast one; and that thou dost deceive us in
nothing, and for as much as thou hast been obedient
unto our call, andhast sworn to obey our commands:*
    *Therefore do thou feel and receive these grateful
odours of the fine perfumes of our art, which are
agreeable unto thee.*

Magus of Fire burns much incense.

'W'

*And now I say unto thee, in the name of IHSVH, depart
in peace unto thy habitations and abodes in the invisible.
I give unto thee the blessing of God in the name of
IAHDONHI: may the influx of the divine light inspire
thee and lead thee unto the ways of peace!*
    Shalom! Shalom! Shalom!

Reverse circumambulation and closing rituals by banishing ritual of
hexagram (Mercury) and pentagram (air and then earth).

---

[133] This may refer to the R.R. et A.C. but it is unclear, and I feel that one must
protect the power of the group or Order - being specific would be a lot better.

Chapter Three

STRUCTURES

The Adeptus Minor examining evocation has to study the classification of spiritual entities, both good and evil. This can be considered in two ways. The first is through the sephiroth system of the Kabbalah, and the second is through the seven stage pulsation system that equates with our subtle bodies and chakras.

The Kabbalistic system has been explained clearly in other volumes, so it is important to deal with the system of subtle bodies. I will relate them, by analogy, to the seven subtle bodies of man.

The first level is the divine, spiritual or soul body. This brings together all necessary spiritual information from God. It establishes our life principles. It has knowledge of all past lives and is constantly adjusting to the experiences of our present incarnation.

The second level is the causal body[134]. This links the personality with the planet. It is the umbilical cord with our surroundings. It deals with our reactions to collective energies or what Jung refers to as the collective unconscious (and includes the influence of astrological configurations).

The third level is the higher mental body[135]. This upper level of the mental body processes ideas and basic information on a collective or abstract scale.

The fourth level is the lower mental body. Though this is but a lower part of the third level, it personalises ideas and concepts into aspects that can be easily understood.

The fifth level is the astral emotional body[136].

---

[134]   See 'Causal Body' by A.E. Powell.
[135]   See 'Mental Body' by A.E. Powell.
[136]   See 'Astral Body' by A.E. Powell.

"The astral body is the total accumulation of the personality. It acts as a screen to filter karmic patterns, diseases, and information from past lives into one's consciousness. Some of these patterns extend from genetic levels in the physical body. The emotional body provides a sense of emotional stability and psychological security... "[137]

There is a separation of the emotional body in Westerners and in the East, the astral and emotional bodies are united.

The sixth level is the etheric Body:

"The etheric body has one objective. This is to vitalise and energise the physical body and integrate into it the energy body of the Earth and of the solar system. It is a web of energy streams, of lines of force and light...Along these lines of energy the cosmic forces flow, as the blood flows through the veins and arteries..."[138]

The seventh level is the physical body and the field of matter and is the sum expression of the other bodies.

THE STRUCTURE OF THE SEVEN RAYS

Golden Dawn co-founder, Wynn Westcott, in his Flying Roll lecture No.17, spoke about the seven rays:

"Science teaches, and has rediscovered a great truth, that however valuable the seven colours of the prism may be, there are rays invisible and not so demonstrated here by space. Beyond the red end of the spectrum begins the violet, and these have a great chemical or Yetsiratic[139] force.."

Westcott wrote this lecture in 1893, only five years after Madame Blavatsky published her first concept of the seven rays in her massive work, *Secret Doctrine*, which is used as a bible for her Theosophical Society. Westcott and Mathers were familiar with

---

[137]   *Gem Elixirs and Vibrational Healing*, Vol 1. by Gurudas.
[138]   *Esoteric Healing* by Alice Bailey.
[139]   One of the Four Worlds of the Kabbalists and called the World of Formation. It relates to the Mental or Intellectual World.

the Theosophical Society, and Mathers had met Madame Blavatsky. The seven rays theory inspired the Golden Dawn when it came to construct its Vault.

Another description of the rays comes from the book *Gem Elixirs and Vibrational Healing, Vol. 2*, by Gurudas:

"The seven rays are a function of physics integrating with the chakras and their extensions into the universe. The rays are the functions of physics that create and correlate holographic physical existence with the concepts of the physics of consciousness...The rays are a constant progressing element. They are a force that comes down from the soul level itself to become self-actualising...It is only that the ancients attributed the sevenfold colour spectrum to the seven rays as a point of visual aid[140], because there is also a degree of synchronicity and forbearance in behavioural patterns both spiritual and psychological with the forces of light stimulated within the self. They perceptually have been assigned colours as a visual aid in learning their content and meaning as energy."

The Golden Dawn believed the rays come through the planets yet touched everything. But the planets are only a sheath for the seven rays and planetary influence is not the dominating factor. The planets are a suitable vehicle for the energy to manifest on a certain level. Mathers tells us that all creatures must come through one of these rays as a doorway to manifestation. Whoever controls this doorway has mastery over the entity who enters it.

There has been nothing published on the Golden Dawn theory of the seven rays, yet in the New Zealand temple, Whare Ra, they were taken seriously. When I was admitted into the 5=6 level of the R.R.et A.C. I found that my mentor, Jack Taylor, frequently studied the seven rays through the works of Alice Bailey.

Mrs. Felkin, the head of Whare Ra, gave a number of lectures on the Vault and the influence of the seven rays in esoteric study. This information is closely allied with Alice Bailey's work, though two of the lectures were dated 1918 and 1921, some years before Bailey published her findings. The names of the rays are identical

---

[140] This relates to rays having no color associated to them, but are given here as a point of reference only.

with those given by Bailey.[141]

The Golden Dawn believed that within seven rays' structure there are a further seven rays. The adept draws from these sub-rays to correctly integrate with the main ray. This is closely allied to the concept of the seven Heavens within each Heaven of ancient Hebrew *Hecaloth* Literature[142]. Each ray affects the physical body of the Adept and the Kabbalistic Soul[143] (though there is still a dominant ray for all levels). Rays affect the various entities and they must conform or utilise the energy of a particular ray if they are to function in our solar system. They are governed by certain laws, the seven ray theory being just one.

When associating entities to various rays, there will be overlaps, especially when entities from one group have the same function as an entity from another. The first point to consider is the grouping of the entity, as this is the predominating ray. In every ray there are seven sub-rays and so the similar entities from different groups would share the same sub-ray.

Rather than change the ray number to coincide with colour and planetary arrangement of the Golden Dawn, I have left them in the order given by Alice Bailey to avoid confusion and make comparisons easier. This was the order of the rays taught at Whare Ra temple before Bailey's publications.

The formula for ray interpretation as given below will differ from that advocated by Alice Bailey. It takes into consideration the Adepts' make-up, the type of entity they can expect (categorised according to the seven rays that control it). Each of these rays coincide with the seven subtle levels.

---

[141]   Mrs. Felkin stated that her teachers taught much of the same material as Alice Bailey's and that some messages were received by both.

[142]   The colors and planetary associations given by Alice Bailey differ from that of the Golden Dawn.

[143]   For a full discourse on the Kabbalistic Soul and its analogy to Eastern Subtle Anatomy see *The Kabbalah and the Golden Dawn* by P.J. Zalewski. (Thoth Publications).

FIRST RAY

Purpose: Spiritual development
Chakra: Crown [144]
Colour: Red[145]

This ray shows the Creator/Destroyer concept, depending how the power of this ray is manipulated. If uncontrolled it shows the power of wilful destruction and thoughtless action. It comes from the activation of deeper levels of consciousness so a clearer spiritual purpose emerges.

To integrate with this ray, adepts have to utilise the crown chakra. If this centre is out of alignment and the adept tries to control a powerful force (through evocation), it places a strain on the intuitive faculties. This is like being cast adrift with no reference point and a loss of equilibrium. The individual would find a sense of loss and an inability to cling to reality. Logic is thrown out the window, showing a distorted viewpoint. Israel Regardie told of an individual who committed suicide after using the Golden Dawn's Enochian system of magic. Regardie believed the individual was unbalanced and the strain of working the complex Enochian system was the last straw.

Paul Foster Case, the head of Builders of the Adytum, who was once a Golden Dawn chief, blamed the Enochian system for the death of a friend who also killed himself and the order refuses to admit anyone who practices the system because it is 'too dangerous'. But it is more likely that the chief's friend died because his Crown centre was over stimulated and he could not tell the difference from reality and illusion. I have often seen this and have noted that in all cases the Crown chakra was extremely overactive. Entities of destruction and hate are those who dwell in the negative side of this ray; specially those evoked to cause havoc. This is the ray that is infamous among magicians who bring forth a creature for acts of destruction. It is the ray of the active approach, which if

---

[144]   The Golden Dawn did not consider the Seven Chakra centers, but its later off-shoots, such as the Stella Matutina did. Through the science of Radionics, the Chakra centers have been analyzed carefully and there has been much written about them.

[145]   The color of the rays and the chakras are not necessarily the same.

ill used, can bring about death and pestilence.

Entities on the positive side of this ray are those who provide protection and assistance to the adept. It involves calling an entity of great power. Power enough to be able to perform the tasks set of it. It also needs a great deal of power to control. The brow chakra must be in correct alignment (with the other chakras), for perception and intuition plays an important part of this ray. Handled correctly, this part of the ray can be an unstoppable force.

SECOND RAY

Purpose: Love, wisdom and creativity
Chakra: Brow.
Colour: Orange

This is the ray of the teacher/healer and one of magnetic attraction for the truth. It forms a balanced structure and brings people together. It initiates, directs and creates. This is the ray of the peacemaker or diplomat and planned unification for spiritual purpose. The Kabbalistic Sephiroth of Chesed, meaning mercy, is linked to this ray.

The brow chakra governs the second ray and if this is out of alignment the adept will find it difficult to banish the entity evoked. Possession is a consequence of dealing with entities under the second ray.

Hermetic orders such as the Golden Dawn, have in their records accounts where possession has occurred and it taken more than a Banishing Ritual of the Pentagram[146] to dislodge the entity (as some of the published texts would have us believe). I have mentioned in the previous chapter about the plight of Euan Campbell and his obsession after using the Abra-Melin system. The following quote is from a copy of the letter he sent to the *Occult Review* in 1929 as example of process of possession:

"The New Moon of May 1st brought a recurrence of the trouble, this time very much more powerful, and necessitated an almost intolerable effort of will to cast it off. Also it was about this time that I first saw the entity which was rapidly obsessing me. It was

---

[146]   As given in Regardie's *Golden Dawn* vol. 1, page 106.

not altogether unlovely to look at. The eyes were closed and it was bearded with long flowing hair. It seemed a blind force slowly waking to activity...Not one of these incidents happened when I was asleep. Always I found myself awake with terror upon me and struggling violently to cast off the spell. I have had nightmares before, but no nightmare that I ever had could hold my mind in its grip for minutes at a time as this thing did, or send me plunging through a ten foot high window to the ground below..."

Campbell was a shrewd individual, and not one to be frightened by anything occult orientated. He was a competent adept, yet even he had to call on the help of Mrs. Felkin to help him get rid of the entity. This was only accomplished over a long time and some difficulty.

Campbell had done everything correctly, but his internal mechanism was not prepared for what happened during evocation. According to Jack Taylor, Campbell had a widely unbalanced brow chakra[147] and Taylor helped him in trying balance this up through the use of colour healing techniques.

The ray produces entities that are subtle in their approach. They are often so subtle that few are aware of their presence, but as they get stronger and will try to possess the adept[148]. When directed, they will take possession of the person or thing they are directed at during evocation. They must be banished quickly once they have finished their task. Entities under this ray act independently and the wording you use with them during ritual must be precise.

The negative side of this ray produces over confidence, the entities under this influence will self generate, if given the chance and can become impossible to control.

On the positive side, they offer and give self assurance to the adept and have a habit of getting to the heart of the matter quickly. They love exposure and revealing truth. They are present in group religions and push individuals to extremes in these areas unless carefully watched.

---

[147] Taylor could see the chakras and found Campbell's 'spinning erratically'.
[148] In Campbell's case, he told a friend it was three months after the actual working that he noticed something was wrong.

THIRD RAY

Purpose: Active intelligence.
Chakra: Throat.
Colour: Yellow

This ray shows the hidden part of the intellect at its best, especially through the faculty of memory. This is the ray of creativity and the ray of illusion. Its powerful influence shows new developments but does not reveal what areas would suit its influence.

The solar influence is the primary influence in our solar system. The third ray relates to the Kabbalistic influence of Tiphareth, meaning beauty, seated at the centre of the Tree of Life.

The physical centre attributed to this ray is the throat chakra. It relates to memory and drawing from past experiences enabling sense to be made from abstract concepts. This is the centre of social interaction. It is the experimental area where those who have a vision try and apply it to reality.

The entities that the third ray governs are the elementals[149]. The elementals are more of a blind force than any other group or entity. Within the Golden Dawn framework there are four basic types of elemental. The Gnomes are the elementals of Earth and they are governed by their King Ghob. The undines are the water elementals (they are also called nymphs) and their ruler is called Nixsa. The elementals of air are called sylphs, (they are also called fairies) their ruler is Paralda. The salamanders are the fire elementals and their ruler is Djinn.

When the ray is positive, the elementals work on creating material items. When the ray is negative the elementals can disrupt others. Elementals have limited power and are too varied to concentrate on detail. Any elemental sent by the adept to harass others, will have a limited attention span.

One of the favourite tasks of Golden Dawn adepti was to send elementals to locate books or manuscripts. Jack Taylor once

---

[149]   Most would place the elementals under Malkuth, but in dealing with the seven rays, things are mixed and complex. Malkuth is not mentioned, though it does relate to earth. The rays do come from an outside influence and hence the earth is omitted as an influence in favour of the Sun - the next primary source of life governing us.

referred me to a then out of print book called *The Cannon*, by William Stirling to research. This book was part of a library collection of Whare Ra that had been dispersed when the temple closed. Jack thought it was part of the National Library of New Zealand's collection and I would have to look for it there. That night, I met the chief of Whare Ra temple (who had not spoken to Taylor for 20 years) who told me that he had a book that may interest me. He placed a battered 80 year old copy of *The Cannon* in front of me.

Years later, Taylor told me that he had asked the elementals to assist me in obtaining this book, though he admitted that he had not seen such a prompt service. He had nearly fallen over backwards when I showed him the book the next day.

FOURTH RAY

Purpose: Harmony through conflict, The healer.
Chakra: Heart.
Colour: Green.

This ray brings out the deep inner awareness needed to tune into one's surroundings - through nature and spiritually. Deep changes within the self must have some outlet and this is the mainstay of this ray. It is something hard to start and difficult to stop. This ray sparks a number of choices and the conflict comes from in trying to make a decision. The fourth ray relates to the Kabbalistic Sephiroth of Binah, or understanding. The planetary association of Saturn to this ray does not refer to the mundane astrological interpretation, but a psychic meaning as given by psychics such as Edgar Cayce and Arthur Ford. These writers show Saturn as a planet of sudden changes of circumstance where the soul is left alone for self evaluation.

The degree that this Chakra can be awakened or opened will depend on how forms or energies are seen. The ray initiates a perception of the spirit in material terms, so structure is important on a spiritual and sociological level. If this centre is not aligned correctly it can make a person retreat from reality and lose touch with the world around them.

When Jack Taylor was Hierophant at Whare Ra, he was approached by a member to enter the 5=6 grade. Taylor declined because he saw that the individual's brow chakra was overactive. Eventually another Hierophant put the person through to the 5=6 level. As soon as the new 5=6 started inner order work he had a mental breakdown, and spent six years in a mental institution.

When our Thoth-Hermes Temple was established in Wellington, the same 5=6 approached me to discuss esoteric subjects. I noticed a large black spot (psychically) in his aura. On contacting Taylor about this person, he confirmed that there was something wrong with the man and gave me his background.

Entities under this ray enhance the confidence and control of the adept. Notoriety and glamour are also an area where these entities work. They inflate the ego, but they also bring results. After their work is finished and they depart, they can leave one slightly on a 'downer', which can lead to depression. Also they can cause havoc to business decisions if sent to plague someone. In one case, someone I knew sent entities under this ray to break up a partnership that had been causing him problems. Within a few months, the partnership broke up with the two individuals going in different directions. When the person who sent the entities thought they had done enough, he discharged them from their task and the two partners suddenly started talking and resumed their business relationship.

FIFTH RAY

Purpose: Science or knowledge.
Chakra: Solar plexus.
Colour: Blue

This ray shows the ordered world of the scholar and scientist. It is the ray of the planner and analyser. If uncontrolled, it leads to a pre-occupation with trivia. The action undertaken with this ray is swift. Structure and form is important, for the individual must have the capacity to channel the energy into the correct format. The efforts of this ray are channelled to the masses with scientific break throughs. The Kabbalistic association to this ray is the Sephiroth of Hod, meaning splendour or glory.

The part of the body attributed to this ray is the solar plexus centre which analyses the situation based on the present, ignoring past and future. The individual who experiences life through this sense, lives for the moment, and shows the impulsive side of their nature. The psychic influence of this centre is telepathy, on an individual and group level. It creates attunement of the senses.

Entities under this ray bestow gifts of logic, commerce, safe journeys and communications. One incident relating to use of entities under the fifth ray happened during a particular stressful time at my work. The office was in chaos, and I had to find a submission that had been 'filed' and was lost. The situation was critical and related to an expensive project.

After searching for hours and getting nowhere, I decided to start early the next morning. I cleaned out my tray and left for home. Later that night, I called an entity under this ray to help locate the file. The next day found the missing file sitting in my tray. After questioning everyone in the office, no one knew how it had got there.

On the negative side of things one can call forth these entities to cause havoc and disruption to any logical sequence. Jack Taylor told me of an incident that happened in the 1920's, when an Adept at Whare Ra had to appear in court and was doubtful of the outcome. He invoked an entity a week before the court date, and to the surprise of everyone, the Judge found that the preparation work of the prosecution was so bad, that he dismissed the case to teach them a lesson.

SIXTH RAY

Purpose: Ray of devotion.
Chakra: Sacral.
Colour: Indigo

This ray shows the manifestation of faith on a huge scale. In its first impulse, this ray shows the impetus that gets people into forms or structures. It is not the form itself, but the impetus behind it. In its first impulse, the ray can bring awareness of something other than the physical. In its intermediate stage it creates a balance between the day-to-day life and the spiritual. Taken to extremes, this ray creates an individual who will do anything for his beliefs. This is not the fanaticism of previous rays but one who is still in touch with the spiritual essence, for this governs everything he or she does. It is the laying down of oneself or giving one's all for a belief, to win at any cost, it is the ray of inspiration.

The Kabbalistic association here is the Sephiroth of Netzach, meaning victory.

The sacral centre governs this ray and it is a force of such magnetism that people are attracted to and can be mesmerised by it. The magnetic personality type has this centre working overtime. The control here can be either an affinity or a strong obsessive attraction. Many individuals in the media possess a strong centre, as do some politicians. Normally this centre will work by swaying members of the opposite sex. It does not have to be overtly sexual, but a type of energy that always generates people around you.

Entities who come under this ray can try and induce sexual favours from another. On a wider level, they can attract attention to a cause, whether it be individual or group motivated. I once asked Jack Taylor about entities under this ray and their appearance in religious and political groups, and he gave me the following example:

"Just after the World War Two, I spoke with a former member of the Nazi Party whom was very clairvoyant in his own right. He told that when he attended some of the mass rallies both before and during the War, he found a strong abundance of entities ever present, more so than anything he had previously witnessed. During a speech of Hitler's, he found himself quite close to him and found that choirs of various entities attended his speeches and whipped up things to high pitch fervour of adulation. After a while he found the whole process sickening but the power generated at rallies like that were real and perverse."

This is the ray where the entities have a wide frame of reference and are hard to control. Mass hysteria is an example of the negative side of this ray. On the positive side of things, this ray provides support but is limited to the point where it can be controlled.

SEVENTH RAY

Purpose: Ceremonial magic.
Chakra: Base.
Colour: Violet.

This ray shows the result of the manipulation of forces or form, from one dimension to another. It is the ray of the magician, alchemist, healer and teacher of the ancient mystery traditions. The ray's theme is unification through diverse and natural methods. It is also the ray of fulfilment, through the study of mystery[150]. The Kabbalistic association here is to the Sephiroth of Yesod, meaning foundation, for it is the place where all are united before entry to a new era.

The integration point of this ray is the base chakra. This centre is the foundation or springboard that opens up other centres. It is where the stored energy is released and brings about the Kundalini experience. This is the area of perception, and the experience one has here depends on the individual's personal development. Distortions and visionary work are controlled by this chakra.

The entities under this ray are varied. There are those which some call the incubus and sucubus. Another choir of entities that could be applied here are those that draw from the sexual centres of both men and women. Rarely are creatures under this ray summoned as they usually appear involuntarily and when least expected.

They are vampirific and attach themselves like shells to the subtle bodies and can cause diseases. Sometimes an Adept will send an entity to plague another with sickness and these are the entities of this ray. Sometimes these entities are mindless and are like jellyfish who drift with the tide and attach themselves to anything. Other times they are malicious and seek to destroy things. The biblical plagues of Egypt relate to entities under this ray.

---

[150] This is the ray which is coming into prominence on Earth at the moment.

LEVELS OF INTEGRATION

There are gaps in the Golden Dawn papers on angelic classification. Using the Kabbalistic system we can put them in four worlds and have ten stages for each level (a full Kabbalistic tree in each world). There are some of Mathers' teachings in this area that in my opinion are inaccurate. An example of this is the placement of the elementals and applying them to Malkuth.

The angelic hierarchies have different subtle layers similar to humanity. Some of these levels can equate with the soul plane (the first level of existence), our innermost kernel of spiritual projection.

To partly defend Mathers, he could have provided the Golden Dawn with deep levels of spiritual chains but it appears he decided to leave it up to the adepts to work out these out for themselves. I do not go along with this type of thinking because it gets away from the collective thinking process the Golden Dawn encourages. There are times to go things alone and periods to work with the group. The classification of angelic entities is definitely a group area for experiment.

Dion Fortune realised this and in her book *The Cosmic Doctrine*[151] you will find a strong leaning towards the different level theory rather than a Kabbalistic one. If you compare the *The Cosmic Doctrine* with Alice Bailey's book *A Treatise on Cosmic Fire*[152] the teachings appear to have come but from a single source, whose roots are entrenched in the Theosophical teachings of Madame Blavatsky.

When Dion Fortune showed the *The Cosmic Doctrine* to Moina Mathers, she was told that it was incompatible with Golden Dawn teachings. Possibly this was because Dion Fortune was only 2=9[153] in the Golden Dawn ranking system at the time, and 'it was not done' for an Outer Order student to present a chief with a full set of spiritual teachings.

Since an example of evocation has been given on the Spirit Taphthartharath I would suggest to the reader to look at *The Cosmic*

---

[151] Said to have been received from her teachers in the winter of 1923\24.

[152] First printed in 1925.

[153] Regardie told me in 1983 that Dion Fortune did not get beyond the 2=9 in the A.O. order under Moina Mathers, but later worked up to the 5=6 in Stella Matutina.

Doctrine, and in particular the chapter on the *Evolution of a Planetary Being*. This chapter is a miniature Genesis on the development of planetary hierarchies of spirit. The concepts as laid down in *The Cosmic Doctrine* are universal and do not interfere with Golden Dawn teachings.

Whether this teaching came from Fortune is another matter entirely.[154] It is a difficult book to read but with perseverance it will be invaluable for the study of angelic beings, and helps adepts know what they are up against.

To help explain who does what in the angelic world, three books on the subject are obligatory. The first is *Dictionary of Angels* by Gustav Davidson and the second is the *Dictionary of Demons* by Fred Gettings. The third book is Mathers *The Book of Sacred Magic of Abra-Melin the Mage*, which lists many of the names of spirits (mentioned in the other two texts) but for the first time places them in some form of overall hierarchy. The four princes of the elements or directions (Oriens, Paimon, Ariton, Amaimon) learnt in the Golden Dawn papers, take on completely new meanings when placed on the Abra-Melin genealogy.

Before the Abra-Melin book was published, its angelic structure was circulated among the Golden Dawn's elite.

The four princes and superior spirits[155]:-

LUCIFER, LEVIATAN, SATAN, BELIAL.

The eight sub-princes be:-

ASTAROT, MAGOT, ASMODEE, BELZEBUD, ORIENS, PAIMON, ARITON, AMAIMON.

The spirits common unto these four sub-princes, namely:-

ORIENS	PAIMON	ARITON	AMIAMON
Hosen	Saraph	Proxosos	Habhi
Acuar	Tirana	Alluph	Nercamay
Nilen	Morel	Traci	Enaia
Mulach	Malutens	Iparkas	Nuditon

---

[154] See *Magical Life of Dion Fortune* by Alan Richardson, pages 144-145.

[155] You will note that these names are not all classified as negative or Qlippothic, for the Hebrew belief is that all angels serve God whether for good or evil.

Melna	Melhaer	Ruach	Apolhun
Schabuach	Mermo	Melamud	Poter
Sched	Ekdulon	Mantiens	Obedama
Sachiel	Moschel	Pereuch	Deccal
Asperim	Katini	Torfora	Badad
Coelen	Chuschi	Tasma	Pachid
Parek	Rachiar	Nogar	Adon
Trapis	Nagid	Ethanim	Patid
Pareht	Emphastison	Paraseh	Gerevil
Elmis	Asmiel	Irminom	Asturel
Nuthon	Lmoiol	Imink	Plirok
Tagnon	Parmatus	Iaresin	Gorilon
Lirion	Plegit	Ogilen	Tarados
Losimon	Ragaras	Igilon	Gosegas
Astrega	Parusur	Igis	Aherom
Igarak	Geloma	Kilik	Remoron
Ekalike	Isekel	Elzegan	Ipakol
Haril	Kadolon	Iogion	Zaragil
Irroron	Ilagas	Balalos	Oroia
Lagasuf	Alagas	Alpas	Soterion
Romages	Promakos	Metafel	Darascon
Kelen	Erenutes	Najin	Tulot
Platien	Atloton	Afarorp	Morilen
Ramaratz	Nogen	Molin	

ASTAROT and ASDMODEE share the following spirits:

Amaniel	Orinel	Timira	Dramas
Amalin	Kirik	Bubana	Buk
Raner	Semlin	Ambolin	Abutes
Exteron	Laboux	Circaron	Ethan
Taret	Badlet	Buriul	Oman
Carasch	Dimurgos	Roggiol	Loriol
Isigi	Tioron	Darokin	Horanar
Abahin	Goleg	Guagamon	Laginx
Etaliz	Agel	Lemel	Udaman
Bialot	Gagalos	Ragalim	Finaxos
Akanef	Omages	Agrax	Sagares
Afray	Ugales	Hermiala	Haligax

Gugonix	Opilm	Daguler	Pachel
Nimalon			

AMAIMON and ARITON share the following spirits:

Hauges	Agibol	Rigolen	Grasemin
Elafon	Trisaga	Gagalin	Cleraca
Elaton	Pafesla		

ASMODEE and MAGOT share the following spirits:

Toun	Magog	Diopos	Disolel
Biriel	Sifon	Kele	Magiros
Sartabakim	Lundo	Sobe	Inokos
Mabakiel	Apot	Opun	

ASTAROT has the following spirits:

Aman	Camal	Toxai	Kataron
Rax	Gonigin	Schelagon	Ginar
Isiamon	Bahal	Darek	Ischigas
Golen	Gromenis	Rigios	Nimerix
Herg	Arigolin	Okiri	Fagani
Hipolos	Ileson	Camonix	Bafamal
Alan	Apormenos	Ombalat	Quartas
Ugirpen	Araex	Lepaca	Kolofe

MAGOT and KORE share the following spirits:

Nacheran	Katolin	Luesaf	Masuab
Urigo	Faturab	Fersebus	Baruel
Ubarin	Butarab	Ischiron	Odax
Roler	Arotor	Hemis	Arpiron
Sorriolenen	Megalak	Anagotos	Sikastin
Petunof	Mantan	Mekelboc	Tigafon
Tagora	Debam	Tiraim	Irix
Madail	Abagiron	Pandoli	Nenisem
Cobel	Sobel	Laboneton	Arioth
Marag	Kamusil	Kaitar	Scharak
Maisadul	Agilas	Kolam	Kiligil

Corodon	Hepogon	Daglas	Hagion
Egakireh	Paramor	Olisermon	Rimog
Horminos	Hagog	Mimosa	Amchison
Ilarax	Makalos	Locater	Colvam
Batternis			

The spirits under ASMODEE are :

Onei	Ormion	Preches	Maggid
Sclavak	Mebbesser	Bacaron	Holba
Hifarion	Gilarion	Eniuri	Abadir
Sbarionat	Utifa	Omet	

The spirits under BELZEBUD are :

Alcanor	Amatia	Bilifares	Lamarion
Diralisen	Licanen	Dimirag	Elponen
Ergamen	Gotifan	Nimorup	Carelena
Lamalon	Igurim	Akium	Dorak
Tachan	Ikonok	Kemel	Bilico
Tromes	Balfori	Arolen	Lirochi
Nominon	Iamai	Arogor	Holastri
Racamuli	Samalo	Plison	Raederaf
Borol	Sorosma	Corilon	Gramon
Magalast	Zagalo	Pellipis	Natalis
Namiros	Adirael	Kabada	Kipokis
Orgosil	Arcon	Ambolon	Lamalon
Bilifor			

The following spirits are under ORIEN:

Sarisel	Gasarons	Sorosma	Turitel
Balaken	Gagison	Mafalac	Agab

The following spirits are under PAIMON:

Aglafos	Agafali	Dison	Achniel
Sudoron	Kabersa	Ebaron	Zalanes
Ugola	Came	Roffles	Menolik
Tacaros	Astolit	Rukum	

The following spirits are under ARITON:

Anader	Ekorok	Sibolas	Saris
Sekabin	Caromos	Rosaron	Sapason
Notiser	Flaxon	Harombrub	Megalosin
Miliom	Ilemlis	Galak	Androcos
Maranton	Caron	Reginon	Elerion
Sermeot	Irmenos		

The following spirits are under AMAIMON:

Romeroc	Ramison	Scrilis	Buriol
Taralim	Burasen	Akesoli	Erekia
Illirkim	Labisi	Akoros	Mames
Glesi	Vision	Effrigis	Apelki
Dalep	Dresop	Hergotis	Nilima

Chapter Four

THE ASTROLOGICAL CONNECTION[156]

The Taoist philosopher Lao Tzu once said, "Without stirring abroad one can know the whole world; Without looking out the window one can see the way of heaven..." Although Lao Tzu was not referring to astrology, his saying is appropriate to this art. From ancient times to today, mankind has observed the stars and their effects. Those few who studied this philosophy in its relationship to the world and its mysteries, found their perceptions increasing. They developed an awareness of microcosmic and macrocosmic energy fields and forces. Astrology became an internalised symbolism of wisdom. A deeper understanding and insight of the laws of life lead the seekers to refine their comprehension into spiritual dimensions.[157]

Although occultists may not make astrology a career, they must use this tool as an aid in magical work. Astrology is used to chart times for operations (electional astrology). Astrological charts (sidereal calculations) are used to locate directions of planets upon whose powers are drawn during a working. The purpose of such timing is to ensure the working is being performed during a moment where the cosmic energies are best aligned.

An astrological understanding enables the occultist to link up all energies, correspondences, and essential natures towards a wholeness. There is an awareness of the weaknesses and strengths which the occultist can balance or counter-check, so that all runs smoothly in the working. I am not just referring to external

---

[156] Though included in the evocation section of the book, this chapter applies to all features of the Z2.

[157] *Astrology, Karma and Transformation* Stephen Arroyo.

influences, as internal energies must also be handled and directed. Evocation or any magical working is generally for internal transformation. The right timing of an operation in accordance with internal and the cosmic energies prevailing at the time, can ensure the ritual's success. This is harmony between astrological, seasonal, biological, tattvic, etc., in accordance with the energy being evoked so the desired forces can be attracted or impregnated into an object, or directed to a desired purpose.

Outlined below are various points to observe when using astrology in your work.

Planetary Cycles

These cycles are periods of time broken up into divisions with each section associated to a planet which is the strongest at any given time. The commonly used divisions are the days of the week and the hours within each day and night.

Each day of the week has an associated planet:

Monday	-	Moon
Tuesday	-	Mars
Wednesday	-	Mercury
Thursday	-	Jupiter
Friday	-	Venus
Saturday	-	Saturn
Sunday	-	Sun

Day and night are two cycles. The planetary hours of a day commence at sunrise at your geographical location, of any day. From that time to sunset, the day is divided into 12 divisions. Each of those divisions is a planetary hour. The night divisions are calculated in the same way, from sunset to sunrise, and the 12 divisions therein. Sunrise and sunset never occur at the same time each day in a six month period, the planetary hours adjust in length throughout each six month period. They are not the ordinary 60 minute hour.

The order of cycle that the planets rotate throughout the days and nights is an esoteric one and is as follows: Sun, Venus, Mercury,

Table I
Planetary Hours

Ruling Hour	Sun	Mon	Tue	Weds	Thurs	Fri	Sat
1	Sun	Moon	Mars	Mercury	Jupiter	Venus	Saturn
2	Venus	Saturn	Sun	Moon	Mars	Mercury	Jupiter
3	Mercury	Jupiter	Venus	Saturn	Sun	Moon	Mars
4	Moon	Mars	Mercury	Jupiter	Venus	Saturn	Sun
5	Saturn	Sun	Moon	Mars	Mercury	Jupiter	Venus
6	Jupiter	Venus	Saturn	Sun	Moon	Mars	Mercury
7	Mars	Mercury	Jupiter	Venus	Saturn	Sun	Moon
8	Sun	Moon	Mars	Mercury	Jupiter	Venus	Saturn
9	Venus	Saturn	Sun	Mercury	Jupiter	Venus	Jupiter
10	Mercury	Jupiter	Venus	Moon	Mars	Mercury	Mars
11	Moon	Mars	Mercury	Saturn	Sun	Moon	Sun
12	Saturn	Sun	Moon	Jupiter	Venus	Saturn	Venus

Table II

**Planets, Archangels, Angels, Metals that Govern
the Planets and Days of the Week**

Planet	Sun	Moon	Mars	Mercury	Jupiter	Venus	Saturn
Archangel	Raphael	Gabriel	Khamael	Michael	Tzadiqel	Haniel	Tzaphqiel
Angel	Michael	Gabriel	Zamael	Raphael	Sachiel	Anael	Cassiel
Metal	Gold	Silver	Iron	Mercury	Tin	Copper	Lead
Zodiac	Leo	Cancer	Aries	Gemini	Sagittarius	Taurus	Aquarius
Months			Scorpio	Virgo	Pisces	Libra	Capricorn

Moon, Saturn, Jupiter, Mars. The planets associated to the first hour from sunrise and the first hour from sunset is the planet of the particular day. For example, if a Wednesday, Mercury starts the day. The second hour will be the Moon, then Saturn, Jupiter, Mars, Sun, Venus, then Mercury and so on. The same method occurs for the night hours, if a Wednesday commencing with Mercury.

The outer planets, Uranus, Neptune and Pluto have been omitted. These operate on a transformative, larger, mass scale rather than a personalised scale of the other planets. When doing workings for these planets use their co-rulership planets. For example Moon for Neptune, Mercury for Uranus and Mars for Pluto.

The next associations are the archangels and angels of the planets as given in the table below. These are the names called for assistance during ritual, therefore you would use the names associated to the planetary vibration of your working.

Table III

Magical Names of the Hours

Day Hour	Angel	Night Hour	Angel
1	Thamur	1	Rana
2	Ourer	2	Netos
3	Thaine'	3	Tafrac
4	Neron	4	Sassue
5	Yayon	5	Agla
6	Abai	6	Caerra
7	Nathalon	7	Salam
8	Beron	8	Yayn
9	Barol	9	Yanor
10	Thanu	10	Nasnia
11	Athor	11	Salla
12	Mathon	12	Sadedali

The occultist will time the working on the day and hour most in tune with the nature of the working. For example, if the working was of a Jupiter energy, the Jupiter hour on a Thursday would be the chosen time.

This can be taken further by taking the planetary/zodiac month (which is important) and the planetary year, (which is less important). This year is calculated from the year of your birth, the first year being under the governance of the Sun and following years continued in the order as given above.

Planetary hours will not affect everyone in the same way. If you have badly afflicted planets in your own natal horoscope (the chart at the time of your birth) then those are the planetary hours you may find difficult.

A planetary hour more effectively starts 15 minutes after the calculated time.

Astrology

The method of astrological calculation used by the occultist for an evocation is sidereal astrology. Sidereal astrology calculates the true position of the planets, and the zodiac belt at the allotted time the chart is drawn up and is calculated for the geographical latitude and longitude. During evocation you only need rotate your chart that is calculated for your working until its East Point (Antivertex) faces your geographical East. This will show you in which direction to face for any planet to draw its power or make adoration.

When you calculate your chart, include all planets, Lunar Nodes, the Vertex and Antivertex. Calculate also three other charts for the same moment. One chart should include the Fixed Stars; the second the asteroids; the third some of the Arabic Parts, such as Parts of fortune, fate, spirit, life, religion, occultism, alchemy, death, etc. The importance of the affects of these charts is in the order as given. All these charts are compared to your planetary chart for aspect analysis, as any strong 'contacts' may prove influential to your working which you may have to balance. The aspect of most importance is the direct conjunction.

The type of Sidereal charts calculated are Electional Charts. Electional astrology[158] is where an astrological chart is drawn up

---

[158] *Electional Astrology* by Vivien E. Robson, Samuel Weiser, Inc., Reprint 1972.

to elect a time for your working. This method increases the possible success of your work by your operating at the elected time, which is supposed to be when the prevailing celestial energies are potentially auspicious. It is always advisable to have charts for more than one time for your proposed activity, so that the charts can be compared for the most auspicious time.

It is rare to have all planets in a chart fortified for an ideal election, but occultists must do their best with what is available even if a week, month, six month, year or more wait is necessary. Waiting too long is ridiculous, so I suggest that you find a time where it is most harmonious and balance what is discordant. But don't go ahead through impatience when a two month wait would make all the difference.

Electional astrology is quite an in depth subject on its own, and cannot be entered into here in detail. Following are some general principles to observe in an Election:

1.   Choose the significators ruling the evocation and fortify them. For example, the Moon is important in all elections; the zodiac signs placed on the ascendant and mid-heaven and the placing of their planetary rulers; the planet(s) most in affinity with the object of evocation to be fortified. The planets should be in their exaltation or rulership, not in their detriment or fall or badly aspected.

2.   The Electional chart is compared with your own horoscope of the time you were born - your Natal Chart (Sidereal calculation). This will show you whether it is safe to continue. If there are strong malefic aspects you must calculate another more auspicious time.

3.   Observe all other astrological points. For example, Retrograde planets which show delay or difficulty; Sun placed in the ascendant may undo all benefit unless Leo or Aries is rising; the Moon in the ascendant is said to be unfavourable for almost everything unless strong by its sign and very well aspected; Cauda Draconis should not be in the ascendant or conjunct the Sun or Moon; the Fortuna must be fortified; and always take into account the Eclipse cycles and their affect at the time of operation.

4.   Quadruplicities: Cardinal signs on the ascendant are for speedy conclusions. Fixed signs are for slowness or permanence, and Mutable signs are for change, transition or diffusion.

5.   The predominance of elements in the chart must also be observed. For example, if you are evoking a Fire energy, you do not have a predominance of important points or planets in water signs.

6.   The Moon in Evocation: Special attention must be paid to the Moon's cycles and their prevailing energies together with the Moon's position in the Electional chart and its aspects to your natal chart. For example, whether the Moon is waxing or waning, whether it is 'Combust', and in good aspect or position; avoid the degree of fall (three degrees Scorpio), and 12 degrees on either side of the Nodes; avoid cadent positions or via combusta; she is weakened if she is slow in motion or in Capricorn, Aries or Libra, or void of course; her worst possible zodiac position would be between 15 degrees Libra to 15 degrees Scorpio.

7.   Planetary exaltation and fall degrees: Sun is exalted at 19 degrees Aries, Moon at 3 degrees Taurus, Caput Draconis at 3 degrees Gemini and Cauda Draconis at 3 degrees Sagittarius, Jupiter at 15 degrees Cancer, Saturn at 21 degrees Libra, Mercury at 15 degrees Virgo, Uranus at 19 degrees Scorpio, Pluto at 14 degrees Leo, Mars at 28 degrees Capricorn, Neptune at 19 degrees Aquarius, and Venus at 27 degrees Pisces. The Fall degree of each of the above is the exact opposite degree and zodiac sign.

Lunar Mansions

Lunar Mansions are a type of Lunar zodiac that divides the 360 degree zodiac belt up into 28 divisions. These divisions are directly related to the fixed stars and constellations rather than to the actual zodiac signs. Each division is 12 degrees 51 minutes 25.7 seconds. The first Mansion commences at the exact degree of the constellations that is at 0 degrees right ascension (the equinoctial point from which calculations are taken from). This starting degree changes with the precession of the equinoxes. For example, at a rough guess this starting point for the first Lunar Mansion in 1990 would be about 5 degrees Pisces 18 minutes 5 seconds. Therefore, the first Lunar Mansion would run from 5 degrees Pisces 18 minutes to 18 degrees Pisces 9 minutes 20.7 seconds.

Each Lunar Mansion has a specific meaning and influence to the energy of the working you will be performing therefore timing your work also, if possible, in an appropriate Lunar Mansion would be beneficial. This is of more importance for evocation

Magical Influence of Arabic Lunar Mansions

1. Purpose: For general good fortune and happiness.
    Image: In a square table on a silver ring the image of woman, well clothed, sitting on a chair, her right hand being lifted to her head.
    Aromatic: Musk, Camphor, Calamus Aromaticus.
    Ruling Spirit: Anixiel

2. Purpose: For revenge, separation, enmity and ill-will.
    Image: A soldier sitting on a horse, and holding a serpent in his right hand.
    Aromatic: Red Myrrh, Storax.
    Ruling Spirit: Azariel

3. Purpose: For Royal and official favour and good entertainment.
    Image: The head of a man sealed in Silver.
    Aromatic: Red Sanders.
    Ruling Spirit: Gabriel

4. Purpose: To procure love between two people.
    Image: Two images embracing one another and sealed in white wax.
    Aromatic: Lignum Aloes, Amber.
    Ruling Spirit: Dirachiel

5. Purpose: To obtain every good thing.
    Image: A man well clothed, holding up his hands in prayer and sealed in silver.
    Aromatic: None listed other than 'good odours'.
    Ruling Spirit: Scheliel

6. Purpose: For victory in war.
   Image: An eagle with the face of a man sealed in tin.
   Aromatic: Brimstone
   Ruling Spirit: Amnediel

7. Purpose: To cause infirmities.
   Image: A mutilated man, covering his eyes with his
                 hands. Sealed in Lead.
   Aromatic: Pine resin
   Ruling Spirit: Barbiel

8. Purpose: To facilitate child-bearing and to cure illness.
   Image: The head of a lion, sealed in Gold.
   Aromatic: Amber
   Ruling Spirit: Ardefiel

9. Purpose: For fear reverence and worship.
   Image: A man riding on a lion, his left hand holding its
                 ear, and on his right a bracelet of gold. Sealed
                 in Gold.
   Aromatic: Sweet odours and Saffron.
   Ruling Spirit: Neciel

10. Purpose: For the separation of lovers.
    Image: A dragon fighting with a man. Sealed in Black
                 lead.
    Aromatic: Lion's hair, Asafoetida.
    Ruling Spirit: Jazerial

11. Purpose: For the agreement of married people.
    Image: A man and woman, in white, embracing one
                 another. Sealed in red wax.
    Aromatic: Lignum Aloes, Amber.
    Ruling Spirit: Jazeriel

12. Purpose: For separation and divorce.
    Image: A dog biting its tail. Sealed in red Copper.
    Aromatic: Hair of a black dog and cat.
    Ruling Spirit: Ergediel

13. Purpose: For friendship and good will.
    Image: A man sitting and writing letters.
    Aromatic: Frankincense, Nutmeg.
    Ruling Spirit: Atliel

14. Purpose: For gaining merchandise.
    Image: A man sitting on a chair, holding a balance in
                    his hand. Sealed in Silver.
    Aromatic: Pleasant spices.
    Ruling Spirit: Azeruel

15. Purpose: Against thieves and robbers.
    Image: An ape. Sealed in Iron.
    Aromatic: Hair of an ape.
    Ruling Spirit: Adriel

16. Purpose: Against fevers and venomous creatures.
    Image: A snake with its tail above its head.
    Aromatic: Hartshorn.
    Ruling Spirit: Egibiel

17. Purpose: For aiding childbirth.
    Image: A woman holding her hands before her face.
                    Sealed in copper.
    Aromatic: Liquid storax.
    Ruling Spirit: Amutiel

18. Purpose: Hunting
    Image: A centaur, sealed in tin.
    Aromatic: Head of a wolf.
    Ruling Spirit: Kyriel

19. Purpose: Destruction of someone.
    Image: Man with a double face, in brass.
    Aromatic: Brimstone and jet, plus hair of victim.
    Ruling Spirit: Bethnael

20. Purpose: Security of runaways.
    Image: Man with wings on his feet sealed in iron.
    Aromatic: Argent vive.
    Ruling Spirit: Geliel

21. Purpose: Destruction and wasting.
    Image: Cat with dog's head, sealed in iron.
    Aromatic: Hair from a dog's head.
    Ruling Spirit: Requiel

22. Purpose: Increasing cattle or livestock.
    Image: Woman and infant branded in hide of animal
                    one wanted to increase.
    Aromatic: Hair of animal in question.
    Ruling Spirit: Abrinael.

23. Purpose: Preservation of trees and harvest.
    Image: Man planting. Made from wood of fig tree.
    Aromatic: Flowers of fig tree.
    Ruling Spirit: Aziel

24. Purpose: Love and favour.
    Image: Woman washing and combing her hair. Sealed
                    in white wax and mastic.
    Aromatic: Good odours.
    Ruling Spirit: Tagriel

25. Purpose: To destroy waters of fountains, baths and pits.
    Image: Winged man holding a damaged vessel, made
                    of clay.
    Aromatic: Asafoetida, Storax.
    Ruling Spirit: Atheniel

26. Purpose: Catching fish.
    Image: Image of a fish in copper.
    Aromatic: Skin of a fish.
    Ruling Spirit: Amnixiel

27. Purpose: Destruction of a person.
    Image: Black man in hair dress casting a lance with
                    his right hand. Sealed in Iron.
    Aromatic: Storax.
    Ruling Spirit: Geniel.

28. Purpose: Reconciliation with Royalty.
    Image: Crowned King sealed in white wax and mastic.
    Aromatic: Lignum Aloes.
    Ruling Spirit: Enediel

General influences and brief meanings of the Constellations: [159,160]

The following information on the constellations can be utilised depending on which part of the globe we live, and which constellations pass over us. A plastic planet sphere, will tell you what constellations pass overhead and at what times. This, when combined with Natal astrology, will give impetus to the ritual. The meanings of each constellation (both ancient and modern) are taken from the mythology behind them. These myths were formulated by studying the individual meanings of the fixed stars and their clusters (mainly from the Arabic) and the observation of Ptolemy[161]. It was Ptolemy, and those like him, who equated stars and star clusters, giving each the meanings of the planets in our solar system. The magnitude of each star governed the importance of the influence. The early myths associated with each constellations took all that into consideration. By applying that principle, the twelve constellations of the zodiac and the hidden meanings of their influence become more apparent, (though much of this is lost in some aspects of modern astrology).[162] Included in the following list one will find the names of some constellations that were named for a while then underwent numerous changes, with some passing into abeyance. I have included some these as well, with the presently accepted variations of the constellations. Also I have omitted some of the Chinese and Arabic[163] names, but their meanings have been taken into consideration when formulating the meanings of each constellation listed below. Due to overlaps of the figures on the constellations, this has been a difficult task.

The way to draw upon the influences of these constellations is simple. When writing a ritual, include the constellation in your

---

[159] See *Allen's Book on Star Names* for an exhaustive study of the myths associated to the Stars and Constellations.

[160] For those of you who wish to find out where the original names of the constellations came from see *The 12th Planet* by Zecharia Sitchin.

[161] See his *Tetrabiblos* for more detailed information.

[162] See *The 12th Planet* by Zecharia Sitchin. The author relies on cuneiform tablets to propose an interesting theory on how man first knew the origins of the zodiac.

[163] I have used the collective meanings of the old Arabic fixed stars in some of the newer constellations where the origin of the name was in doubt.

petition or invocation and face the direction it will be in. A symbol of the constellation can be traced with one of the magical implements.

1. Andromeda: Enduring love after hardship.
2. Antinous: Love and sacrifice.
3. Antila Pneumatica: Spiritual insight and prosperity.
4. Apus: Flight and travel.
5. Aquarius: Spiritual change.
6. Aquila: Spiritual protection and transformation due to sacrifice and estrangement from loved ones.
7. Ara: Unification for victory.
8. Argo Navis: Travel and adventure, usually over water and not without danger, in following one's spiritual desires.
9. Aries: Victory due to travel, warlike emphasis on goals.
10 Auriga: Mobility, travel, nourishment and concealment of faults.
11. Bootes: Excessive zeal, prosperity and a strong link to a spiritual path.
12. Caelum: Artistic inclinations, desire to construct and build along with enscribing.
13. Camelopardalis: Travel, patience and endurance, especially for a loved one.
14. Cancer: Protection from hardship, strong leaning to spiritual pursuits.
15. Canes Venataci: Hunting, searching.
16. Canis Major: Protection and devotion.
17. Canis Minor: Problems with water, bad luck to travel over water.
18. Capricornicus: Transformation and change: adjusting to one's surroundings, survival.
19: Cassiopea: Pride, conceit, revenge, power ill used.
20. Centauris: Good for hunting, teaching the sciences (including medicine) and prophecy.
21. Cepheus: Quick voyage, good government, swift justice, positive for the innocent and negative for the guilty, strong spiritual pursuits, fame.
22. Cerberus: Guarded by things around us that we can only control through appeasement. It is the protector against evil.

23. Cetus: Emotional disturbances, making one face their own fears.
24. Chamaeleon: An adaptable nature and a born survivor. Travel and constant change.
25. Circimus: Violent, revengeful and greedy.
26. Columba Noae: Strength of spirit, peace and good news for messages.
27. Coma Berenices: An agreement or pact made but not kept, but consolation afterwards through the intervention of a mediator.
28. Corona Australis: Problems given by those in a position of authority.
29. Corona Borealis: Good fortune on the heels of bad. A quick marriage.
30. Corvus: A greedy and untrustworthy individual who is incapable of any position of responsibility.
31. Crater: Delayed nourishment. Wasted ability.
32. Crux: Staying power, responsibilities and slow to change.
33. Custos Messium: Prosperity and growth.
34. Cygnus: Deceit in matters of love.
35. Delphinus: Persuasive messages, Spiritual reward for services rendered. Marriage proposal from unlikely source.
36. Dorado: Decorative with little practical use.
37. Draco: Obstacles placed in the way of success.
38. Equuleus: Youth, friendship and pleasure.
39. Equuleus Pictoris: Imagination and artistic ability.
40. Eridanus: Revenge, travel.
41. Felis: Cautiousness, watchfulness, unpredictability.
42. Fornax Chemica: Enthusiasm, practicality.
43. Rederichi Honores: Fame, peace, high office, with warlike ability if needed.
44. Gemini: Fraternal love and extremes - all or nothing as an approach, good for sport and travel and any form of communication. There is also a loss of a partner.
45. Globus Aerostaticus: Changeable nature, travel and also danger.
46. Grus: Devotion, watchfulness, habit forming.
47. Hercules: Strength of character with dangerous inclinations

towards passion and violence - especially if challenged.

48. Horologium Oscillatorium: Punctuality, planning, patience.

49. Hydra: Scapegoat for the troubles of others, travel.

50. Hydrus: Treacherous and cunning in concealment.

51. Indus: Unfathomable nature, keen insight into spiritual matters.

52. Lacerta[164]: Intellect, power and justice.

53. Leo: Strength, but eventually vanquished by a more powerful opponent.

54. Leo Minor: Noble and fearless, acts on behalf of others.

55. Lepus: Quickness of mind, madness, timidity, uncertainty.

56. Libra: Facing the consequences of one's actions.

57. Lupus: Nothing is sacred in the search of knowledge and religion.

58. Lynx: Predator and life long hunter.

59. Lyra: Love and harmony through communications.

60. Machina Electrica: Advancement of science, idealistic concepts.

61. Microscopium: Meticulous, scientific.

62. Monocres: Fertility, life long partnership, purity of thought and action.

63. Mons Maenalus: Success through hard work and effort.

64. Mons Mensae: Difficulties and obstacles overcome with peasce as a reward.

65. Musca Australis: Working for the good of those around us.

66. Musca Borealis: Adaptability, seeking help from the world of Spirits.

67. Noctua: Wisdom and watchfulness.

68. Norma et Regula: Good for sciences and shows and affinity for the occult.

69. Nubecula Major: Imagination and high ideals used for the good of all.

70. Nubecula Minor: High ideals not shared with others due to isolation.

71. Octans Hadleianus: Science and an ability to heal through psychic perceptions.

---

[164] The figure was changed a number of times by Bode and Royer. Helevius's drawing is nothing like the function of the constellation which is more in line with the design of Bode and Royer.

72. Officina Typographica: Communications and the preservations of knowledge, science and literature.

73. Ophiuchus Serpentarius: Triumph over illness or accidents.

74. Orion: Self confidence that defies logic and pays for it. Problems with wounds or poisoning.

75. Pavo: Vanity, beauty, travel and longevity.

76. Pegasus: Successful journey but at a price. Ambition beyond one's ability.

77. Perseus: Adventure and love, violence eventually leads to ones undoing.

78. Phoenix: Immortality through the cyclic nature of change.

79. Pisces: Pursuit, help and support from those around us.

80. Piscis Australis: Transformation, protection and change through hardship.

81. Piscis Volans: Swiftness and unexpected flight with imagination.

82. Psalterium Georgianum: Joviality and good natured.

83. Pyxis Nautica: Travel, calculating, ambitious and forethought into any task undertaken so that danger is minimised.

84. Quadrans Muralis: Scientific concepts applied but limited to a small area.

85. Reticulum Rhomboidalis[165]: Restriction and self centeredness and tenacity.

86. Robur Carolinum: Sanctuary from danger, due to science.

88. Sagitta: Help through an aggressive act.

89. Sagittarius: Fatal accidents, strength.

90. Scorpio: Passing through the gate, self destruction, both good and bad times equally.

91. Sculptor: New creations, artistic ability, imagination.

92. Scutum: Power, honour and bravery.

93. Serpens: Danger by poison, longevity and immortality by observing the actions of others.

94. Sextans Uraniae: Science and destruction by Fire.

95. Tarandus: Travel and obscurity.

---

[165] This is the Star system that many claim the bulk of UFO craft come from and are the main abduction culprits. The old description certainly fits what has been published about them. See 'Behold a Pale Horse' by William Cooper for additional information and also the 'Watchers' by Raymond Fowler.

96.   Taurus: Infatuation and stubbornness, travel by sea, taking what we want from life by stealth.
97.   Taurus Poniatovii: Fame, high office, changeability.
98.   Telescopium: Intellect, interest in science and occult matters.
99.   Telescopium Herschelii: Science and spiritual interests.
100.   Triangulum: Honour, love.
101.   Triangulum Minor: Help through a lover.
102.   Traingulum Australe: Limited help from a friend or lover.
103.   Tucana: gentleness, unselfishness.
104.   Ursa Major: Deception through lust, wrongful vengeance.
105.   Ursa Minor: propriety, travel, strength, labour.
106.   Via laceta: Comfort, help, sympathy.
107.   Virgo: Grief, death, renewal.
108.   Vulpecula et Answer: Hunting, cunning, travel.

Magical Image of the Decans

This was taken by the Golden Dawn from earlier documents. Examples of this nature are given in Agrippa (Book 2) which is not so dissimilar from this work. Though not part of the Shem-Hamphoresch paper, it was often attached to it and given out at the 4=7 level. This was used in practical terms to elect a horoscope for a particular working as follows. The Image of the Decan in which the Ascendant stood, related to the Magus, and the Mid-heaven point gave the magical image of the power about to be utilised, for example the Evoked entity. By studying the imagery of these two points of the horoscope one could then determine if the timing was favourable to perform the ritual. For those of you who wish to study this method further I suggest the book *Zodiac Within Each Sign* by Sakoian and Acker which is the best I have seen on the meanings of the Decanates and also the Duads. Fuller meanings can be applied to the Decanates and more sense can be made of the magical images.

A magical image[166] was a type of talisman in which the energy of the constellations could be tapped and utilised, and, its story was generally incorporated into the ritual. The following descriptions

---

[166]   The formation of the Court cards of the Tarot has much in common with the imagery of the Decans.

of the Decanates were probably written by an early occult author, due to the old fashioned spelling and phraseology. This was adopted into the Golden Dawn by either Mathers or Westcott.

ARIES

1st Decan. Mars. Therein ascendeth a man tall, dark, powerful and restless, clothed in a white tunic and scarlet mantle, having keen flame-coloured eyes. And in his hand a sharp sword. It is a Decan of boldness, fierceness, resolution and shamelessness.

2nd Decan. Sun. Therein ascendeth a woman clothed in green robes, with one leg uncovered from the knee to the ankle. This is the Decan of pride, nobility, wealth and rule.

3rd Decan. Venus. Therein ascendeth a restless man, clothed in scarlet robes, having golden bracelets on his hands and arms. It is the Decan of subtlety, beauty, etc.

TAURUS

1st Decan. Mercury. Therein ascendeth a woman with long beautiful hair, clothed in flame coloured robes. It is a Decan of ploughing, sowing, building and earthy wisdom.

2nd Decan. Luna. Therein ascendeth a man (like the previous figure of the first Decan of Aries) but having feet cloven like an ox-hoof. It is a Decan of power, nobility and rule over the people.

3rd. Decan. Saturn. Therein ascendeth a man of swarthy complexion and large white teeth projecting from his mouth, a body like that of an elephant, but with long legs. And there arise with him a horse, stag and calf. It is a Decan of misery, slavery, necessity, madness and baseness.

GEMINI

1st Decan. Jupiter. Therein ascendeth a beautiful woman, and with her two horses. It is a Decan of writing, calculations, giving and receiving money, and of wisdom in unprofitable things.

2nd Decan. Mars. Therein ariseth an eagle headed man, wearing a steel helmet surmounted by a crown, and having a bow and arrows in his hand. It is a Decan of pressure, burden, pressure, labour, subtlety and dishonesty.

3rd Decan. Sun. Therein ariseth a man clothed in a coat of mail with two arrows and a quiver. It is a Decan of disdain, mirth and jollity and of many unprofitable words.

CANCER

1st Decan. Venus. Therein ascendeth a man having a distorted face, and hands, and his body is like that of a horse having white feet with a garland of leaves around his body. It is a Decan of dominion, science, love, mirth, subtlety and magistracy.

2nd Decan. Mercury. Therein ascendeth a woman beautiful of countenance, wearing on her head a green myrtle wreath, holding in her hands a lyre, and she singeth of love and gladness. A Decan of pleasure, mirth, abundance and plenty.

3rd Decan. Luna. Therein ascendeth a swift-footed person holding a viper in his hand, and having dogs running before him. It is a Decan of running, hunting, pursuing, acquiring goods by war and of contention among men.

LEO

1st Decan. Saturn. Therein ascendeth a man in sordid raiment, and with him ascendeth a noble man on horseback accompanied by bears and dogs. A Decan of boldness, liberality, victory, cruelty, lust and violence.

2nd Decan. Jupiter. Therein ascendeth a man covered with a white myrtle wreath and holding a bow in his hand. It is a Decan of love, pleasure, society and avoiding quarrels and carefulness in parting with goods.

3rd. Decan. Mars. Therein ascendeth a dark and swarthy man, hairy, holding in one hand a drawn sword and in the other a shield. It is a decan of quarrelling, ignorance, pretended knowledge, wrangling, victory over the low and base, and of drawing swords.

VIRGO

1st Decan. Sol. Therein ariseth a Virgin clothed in linen, holding an apple or a pomegranate in her hand. A Decan of sowing, ploughing, planting herbs, colonisation of storing money and food.

2nd Decan. Venus. Therein ariseth a man, tall, fair and large, and with him a woman holding her hand in a black oil jar. It is a Decan of gain, covetness, taking of goods and rising by care and treasuring up.

3rd. Decan. Mercury. Therein ascendeth an old man leaning on a staff and wrapped in a mantle. It is a Decan of old age, slothfulness and depopulation.

LIBRA

1st Decan. Luna. Therein ariseth a dark man, having in his right hand a spear and a laurel branch and in his left hand a book. It is a Decan of justice, aid, truth, and helping the poor.

2nd Decan. Saturn. Therein ariseth a man dark and of unpleasant face. It is a 'face' of ill deeds, yet of singing and mirth and gluttony, sodomy and following evil pleasures.

3rd Decan. Jupiter. Therein ariseth a man riding an ass with a wolf going before him. A Decan of quietness, ease, plenty, good life and dance.

SCORPIO

1st Decan. Mars. Therein ascendeth a man holding in his right hand a lance and in his left hand a human head. A Decan of strife, sadness, treachery, deceit, destruction and ill will.

2nd Decan. Sol. Therein ascendeth a man riding on a camel and holding a Scorpion in his hand. A Decan of affronts, detection, strife, stirring up of quarrels, science and detection.

3rd Decan. Venus. Therein ascendeth a horse and a wolf. A Decan of war, drunkenness, fornication, wealth, pride and of rage and violence against women.

SAGITTARIUS

1st Decan. Mercury. Therein ascendeth a man with three bodies, one red, one white and one black. It is a Decan of boldness, freedom welfare, liberality and of fields and gardens.

2nd Decan. Sol. Therein ascendeth a man leading cows, and having before him and ape and a bear. It is a Decan of fear, lamentation, grief, anxiety and disturbance.

3rd Decan. Saturn. Therein ascendth a man holding another by the hair and slaying. It is a Decan of ill will, levity, envy, obstinacy and swiftness in all things evil, and of deceitful acts.

CAPRICORN

1st Decan. Jupiter. Therein ascendeth a man holding in his right hand an arrow or javelin, and in his left a lapwing. It is a Decan of wandering travel, labour and joy, alternate gain and loss, weakness and necessity.

2nd Decan. Mars. Therein ascendeth a man with an ape running before him. It is a Decan of ever seeking of what cannot be known or cannot be attained.

3rd Decan. Sol. Therein ascendeth a man holding a book which he opens and shuts. It is a Decan of covetousness, suspicion, careful ordering of matters, but with discontent.

AQUARIUS

1st Decan. Venus. Therein ascendeth a man with bowed head and a bag in his hand. It is a Decan of poverty, anxiety, grieving after gain, and never resting from labour, loss and violence.

2nd Decan. Mercury. Therein ariseth a man arrayed like a King. looking with pride and conceit on all around him. It is a Decan of beauty, dominance, conceit, good manners and self esteem yet notwithstanding modest.

3rd Decan. Luna. Therein ascendth a man with a small head clothed like a woman and having and old man with him. It is a Decan of abundance and compliments, detections and affronts.

PISCES

1st Decan. Saturn. Therein ariseth a man with two bodies but joining their heads together. It is a Decan of many thoughts, anxiety, of journeying from place to place, of misery, of seeking riches and food.

2nd Decan. Jupiter. Therein ascendeth a grave man pointing to the sky. It is a Decan of self praise, and of seeking after great and high aims.

3rd Decan. Mars. Therein standeth a man of grace and thoughtful countenance, carrying a bird in his hand and before him a woman and a ass. It is a Decan of pleasure, fornication, of quietness and of peacemaking.

The Golden Dawn lecture on the Shem-Hamphoresch has not been included in this section[167], for although it is analogous to the Quinaries of the zodiac, its real function is through the process of both Invocation and Evocation. How this can be applied will be included in a later chapter.

Herbs, Incense, Oils, Consecration Water:

When preparing for evocation, incenses, anointing oils and consecration waters must be prepared, and if dried or fresh herbs are being used these must be located and harvested. As your evocation ceremony is timed according to attunement to surrounding energies, so must any operation preparing the tools of evocation, such as talismans, incenses, and oils.[168]

Herbs, from which incenses, oils and waters are prepared, also have their own astrological associations. The practitioner will only choose a herb that is of the same astrological association as the evocation to be performed.

In the Golden Dawn, the adept is taught that nothing must be left unprepared for a full ritual, especially evocation. The Adept must prepare the sprinkling waters of purification, incense and anointing oil. Some of the ingredients for the recipes may have to be bought, so that adept is shown how to re-energise the products. This must be done as a purchased product does not leave surety of being made or harvested and dried during the most favourable times, either by moon cycles or astrological influences. Such re-energising is performed when influences are favourable. It is better if Adepts have access to the fresh plants and can alchemically prepare the product themselves. The sprinkling waters are used for consecration of the working area. Water is generally consecrated

---

[167] See *Kabbalah of the Golden Dawn* (Thoth Publications) by Pat Zalewski for the full papers and associated seals.

[168] The book *Herbs in Magic and Alchemy* by C. L. Zalewski, Prism Press, provides an easy to follow guide and reference for this work.

through ritual and in some instances through the use of ash of a certain incense or herb together with sea salt.

When preparing consecration of water for an evocation ritual an incense that relates specifically to the ray or planetary influence should be selected.

The anointing oil is used to anoint the candles and the adept. The oil tunes the adept to the planetary energy, through aroma. Its function is to work through the various subtle bodies and chakra centres. The degree of potency of the oil and of the type used will effect the subtle centres that the adept uses to see and control the evocation. This process would require a book in itself, though I would recommend *Flower Essences and Vibrational Healing* by Gurudas.

Incenses attract the spirit being evoked and provide an atmosphere from which the spirit can form a material base. If the individual's subtle bodies and centres can be attuned to this incense (usually by meditation on it before the ceremony) the alignment of the subtle bodies will be receptive to the incense. In other words, the energy emitted from the adept can be injected or linked to the incense without any loss of energy. When an entity is called through evocation by controlling the incense the adept also controls the evoked spirit's form. Incense cannot be confined to one space, but the will of the operator, through his own energy, restricts the evoked spirit to the triangle of the art.

It will be up to the individual to research and make their own selection of herbs for oils and incense. One can only work on personal experience and this takes time. It is easy to buy a book, put your finger on a column and presto, come up with an instant result. Since the methods of categorising oils, herbs under certain planetary influences vary greatly from text to text in their methodology, it would be better for the individual to make up their own list and stick to it. I do not suggest looking at hundreds of herbs, but simply a small selection that you consider will work.

Chapter Five

METHODS OF OPERATION

Ritual of the Pentagram[169]
by MacGregor Mathers

The pentagram is a powerful symbol representing the operation of the eternal spirit and the four elements under the divine presidency of the letters of the name Yeheshuah. The elements themselves in the symbol of the cross[170] are governed by YHVH. But the letter Shin, representing the Ruach Elohim, the divine spirit, being added thereto, the name becometh Yeheshuah or Yehovashah - the latter when the letter Shin is placed between the ruling earth and the other three letters of Tetragrammaton.[171]

From each re-entering angle of the pentagram, therefore, issueth a ray, representing a radiation from the divine. Therefore it is called the Flaming Pentagram or Star of Great Light, in affirmation of the forces of the divine light to be found therein.

Traced as a symbol of good, it should be placed with the single

---

[169]   I was tempted to rewrite this paper because Mathers does waffle. However I decided to add some footnotes to clarify what Mathers is getting at. This paper on the pentagram (taken from Felkin's master copy, copied 19th September, 1914) differs slightly from what Regardie published, and I have included some omissions he made, plus the occasional sentence I have written for the sake of clarity.

[170]   The symbol of the elements only makes a cross when one refers to the line traced on the 5 lower Sephiroth of Tree of Life, and not from the Zodiac signs which form a square.

[171]   Regardie said he had found no reference to where the Golden Dawn had got the pentagram ritual. The associations of the letters of YHShVH to the 'correct' points of the pentagram have been around for many centuries. The early Masonic rituals had them, and later Rosicrucian organisations also used this symbol. Eliphas Levi instructed his students in it (published in Lucifer magazine 1894-95, some 20 years after his death). The French occultist Papus (Dr. Gerard Encausse) used this version of the pentagram with the Hebrew letters as part of the badge for his Rosicrucian organization.

point upward, representing the rule of the divine spirit. For if thou shouldst write it with the two points upward, it is an evil symbol, affirming the empire of matter over that of the divine spirit which should govern it. See that thou does it not.[172]

Yet, if there may arise an absolute necessity for working or conversing with a spirit of an evil nature, and that to retain him before thee without tormenting him. Thou hast to employ the symbol of the pentagram reversed (For, know thou well, thou canst have no right to injure or hurt evil spirits to gratify curiosity or caprice) in such a case, thou shalt hold the blade of thy magical sword upon the single lowest point of the pentagram, until such time as thou shalt license him to depart. Also, revile not evil spirits, but remember the Archangel Michael of whom St. Jude speaketh, when contending with Satan does not bring a railing accusation against him but said 'The Lord rebuke thee.'

Now, if thou wilt draw the pentagram to have by thee as a symbol, thou shalt make it of the colours already taught, upon a black background. These shall be the sign of the pentagram; the wheel, the lion, the eagle, the ox, and the man, and each hath an angle assigned unto it for a dominion. Each angle of the 10 representeth the name of a Sephiroth. Hence ariseth the 'Supreme Ritual of the Pentagram', according to the angle from which the pentagram is traced. The circle or wheel answereth to the all pervading spirit: The laborious ox is the symbol of earth; the lion is

---

[172] I do not agree with the concept of the inverted pentagram being evil, it simply depends on the system one works from. I could think of a few instances where the upright pentagram could be used as a symbol of evil.

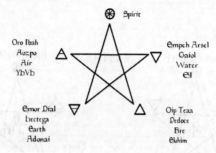

the vehemence of fire; the eagle is the water flying aloft as with wings when she is vaporised by the force of heat: the man is the air, subtle and thoughtful, penetrating hidden things.[173]

At all times complete the circle of the place before commencing an invocation.[174] The currents leading from fire to air and from earth to water are those of spirit, the meditation of the active and passive elements. These two spirit pentagrams should precede and close invocations[175] as the equilibration of the elements, and as establishing the harmony of their influence. In closing, these currents are reversed.

They are the invoking and banishing pentagrams of the spirit; the sigil of the wheel spirit should be traced in their centre[176].

---

[173]   People have asked me why certain elements and signs are placed on certain points of the pentagram. The above diagram answers that question. The signs are reduced to elements and all the associations are made.

[174]   This circle is the area cleared (usually by the Banishing Ritual of the Pentagram), sometimes this is also referred to as the Portal. At Whare Ra Temple they put white tape on the floor so that the area cleared was defined. This area would vary, according to the ritual.

[175]   This is slightly confusing in its wording. I was taught when invoking an element or sign one first used the banishing pentagram of earth to clear the area, then the active or passive, the invoked element, then the closing active or passive followed by a banishing earth pentagram. According to Jack Taylor, the final banishing pentagram of earth clears the air of any trapped energy left behind.

[176]   Because the pentagram represents our Universe, the center position of power is analogous to the Sun, source of all life and light.

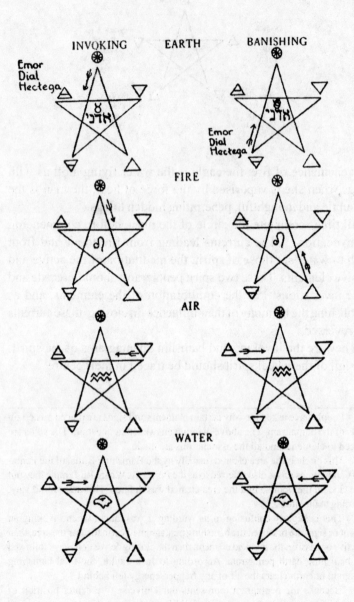

In the invoking pentagram[177] of earth the current descendeth from the spirit to the earth. In the banishing pentagram, the current is reversed. The sigil of the ox should be traced in the centre[178]

These two pentagrams are in general used for invocation or banishing, and their use is given to the Neophyte of the First Order of the Golden Dawn under the title of the 'Lesser Ritual of the Pentagram'. This 'Lesser Ritual of the Pentagram' should be only used in general and unimportant invocations.[179] Its use is permitted to the Outer Order, so that Neophytes may have protection against opposing forces, and also that they may form some idea of how to attract and to come into communication with spiritual and invisible things. The banishing pentagram of earth will also serve thee for protection if thou trace it in the air between thee and any opposing astral force.[180]

In all cases of tracing a pentagram, the angle should be carefully closed at the finishing point.

The invoking pentagram of air commenceth from water, and that of water commenceth from the angle of air. Those of fire and earth begin from the angle of spirit. The Kerubic sign of the element is to be traced in the centre. The banishing signs are the reversing

---

[177]   Unfortunately an aspect of the pentagram Ritual is the one most forgotten, especially in modern day Golden Dawn temples, is the use of the coloured pentagram. When invoking an element the whole pentagram is done in the colour of the element Invoked. When the Active and passive pentagrams are utilized they are done in white, representing the Power of Kether. When invoking or banishing a sign the pentagram is usually done in the color of the sign. The colour of the element or sign is usually done in the complementary color or the element or sign. I suggest to those who wish to learn this method properly that they make a color diagram of each pentagram (element and sign) on a black background, then visualize it until it becomes second nature to them.

[178]   This point is also confusing. When banishing any negativity the elemental symbol of earth is used. In the case of psychic attack that the earth element alone will not contain, then the symbol of the ox is used. There are two distinct levels here, a higher and lower form, each used when the occasion arises. The earth symbol will generally suffice for any normal banishing.

[179]   This may have been Mathers' intention when he first wrote this paper but in the Golden Dawn, the banishing pentagram of earth was often used in cases of exorcisms. I have seen some related papers on the subject by Brodie Innes where this point is made clear.

[180]   Taylor maintained that the pentagram of earth was for the etheric level and the pentagram of the ox was for the astral level. I have found this a good rule to use.

of the current. But before all things, complete the circle of the place wherein thou workest, seeing that it is the key of the rest. Unless you want to limit or confine that force, make not a circle around each pentagram, unless for the purposes of tracing the pentagram truly. In concentrating the force upon a symbol or talisman, thou shalt make the circle with the pentagram upon it so that as to gather the force together thereon.

RULE: *Invoke towards, and banish from, the point to which the element is attributed.*[181]

Air hath a watery symbol (Aquarius), because it is the container of rain and moisture. Fire hath the form of a lion - serpent (Leo). Water hath the alchemic eagle of distillation (eagle's head). Earth hath the laborious symbol of the ox. spirit is produced if the One is operating in all things.[182]

The elements vibrate between the cardinal points for they have not an unchangeable abode therein, though they are allotted to the four quarters in the invocations of the ceremonies of the First Order. This attribution is derived from the nature of the winds. For the easterly wind is of the nature of air more especially. The South wind bringeth into action the nature of fire. West winds bring with them the moisture and rain. North winds are cold and dry like earth. The South-West wind is violent and explosive - the mingling of the contrary elements of fire and water. And also the North-East Wind

---

The earth element can also be used in the astral, depending on the ability of the operator. In training anyone in this ritual, I would suggest this method of separating one level from the other, which at the 5=6 grade one should be able to do.

[181]   The reason for this will be obvious when the zodiac signs are used. By invoking you take from, in this instance the signs, and banishing you send the energy back to the sign in question.

[182]   Again Mathers has muddied the waters. The question most would ask is why not simply use the elemental symbols? I mentioned earlier the distinction between the different levels of the pentagram's use and the use of the elements and signs. By using the Kerubic emblems 'all one's eggs are in one basket'. What Mathers has given here is the highest form of the pentagram (taken from the Supreme Ritual) that goes further than the elemental or astrological sign. In existing temples all this is explained even though it is not written down. Whare Ra word of mouth teachings were very explicit. What we have now is three levels of the use of the pentagram. This highest level will be discussed when using the names from the Enochian Tablets.

is cold and deadly. The North-West and South-West winds are more harmonious uniting the influence of the two active and passive elements.[183]

The above association of the pentagram as placed on the zodiac circle works on the position of the fixed signs.

The invoking pentagram of air commenceth from water, and that of water commenceth from the angle of air. Those of fire and earth begin from the angle of spirit. The Kerubic sign of the element is to be traced in the centre. The banishing signs are the reverse direction.

Yet their natural position in the zodiac is fire in the East, earth in the South, air in the West, water in the North.[184] Therefore they vibrate:

West and East, fire between East and South, water between North and West, earth between South and North. spirit also vibrateth between height and depth. So that, if thou invokest, it is better to look towards the positions of the Winds, since the earth, ever whirling on her poles, is more subject to their influence. But if thou wilt go in the spirit vision unto their abode it is better for thee to take their position in the zodiac.[185]

Air and water have much in common, and because one is the container of the other, therefore have their symbols been at all times transferred, and the eagle assigned to air and Aquarius to water. Nevertheless, it is better that they should be attributed as before stated and for the foregoing reason it is that the invoking sign of the one and the banishing sign of the other counterchange in the pentagram.

---

[183]   The use of the old rabbinical term for the winds is confusing, but they are analogous with the Kerubics or Cherubs as Psalms 18: show: 'And he rode upon a Cherub, and did fly: he did fly upon the wings of the Wind.'

[184]   Mathers is referring to the position of the Cardinal signs, and their relationship to the elements.

[185]   To understand what Mathers is getting at here is like trying to translate 'double Dutch'. He maintains the use of general directions, forming the Microcosm of the Cardinal points in the Universe. If Mathers did not make an error in this paper, then I guess that these relate to the elemental forms of the pentagram only, mainly for work on the Etheric plane, considering the pentagrams are based on the Fixed signs (and different directions in space). For Astral work he suggests we face the true directions when invoking. I would be happy if this paragraph were omitted from the pentagram paper for on the surface it looks as if Mathers gets the position

When thou dealest with the pentagram of spirit thou shalt give the saluting sign of the 5=6 Grade, and for the earth the sign of Zelator, and for the air that of Theoricus, and for water that of Practicus, and for fire, that of Philosophus.[186]

If thou wilt use a pentagram to invoke or banish the zodiacal forces, thou shalt use the pentagram of the element unto which the sign is referred, and trace in its centre the usual sigil of the sign thus:

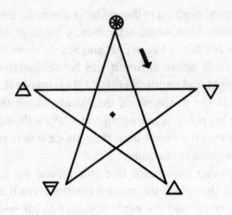

---

of the pentagram on the Zodiac mixed up with the Cardinal and air between Fixed signs. This is not the first time he does this - he does it in the Enochian Chess papers as well.

[186]   The instructions in this paragraph are often ignored in some temples and I feel this is a bad error, for it prevents the student from getting the full benefit of the pentagram's power. The pentagram used with the Grade signs gives the person performing them access to the power of the Order to reinforce his or her performance.

[187]   I came across an interesting version of the pentagram used in alchemical workings. This version used the alchemical symbols of Sulphur (fire) and Salt (water) with the Mercury symbol (Shin - spirit). Jack Taylor passed this on to me and was unaware of its origin.

And whenever thou shalt trace a sigil of any nature, thou must commence at the left hand of the sigil and pass to the right following the course of the Sun.[187] Whenever thou invokest the forces of the zodiacal signs, as distinct from the elements, thou shalt erect an astrological scheme of the heavens for the time of the working so that thou mayest know toward what quarter or direction thou should face in the working. For the same sign may be in the East at one time of the day and the West in another.[188]

Whenever thou shalt prepare to commence any magical work or operation, it will be advisable for thee to clear and consecrate the place, by performing the 'Lesser Banishing Ritual of the Pentagram'. In certain cases, especially when working by or with the forces of the planets, it may be wise also to use the Lesser Banishing Ritual of the Hexagram.

ADDENDUM

In order that a force and a current and a colour and a sound may be united in the same symbol, unto each angel of the pentagram certain Hebrew divine names and names from the angelic tablets are allotted. These are to be pronounced with the invoking and banishing pentagrams as thou mayest see in the foregoing diagrams entitled 'The attributions of the angles of the pentagram being the Key to the Ritual'. Herein, during ordinary invocation without the use of the tablets of the elements, thou shalt pronounce the divine name AL with the pentagram of water, and Elohim with fire, etc. But if thou art working with the elemental or enochian tablets, thou shalt use the divine names in the angelic language drawn therefrom.

For the earth, Emor Dial Hectga, etc., and from spirit, the four words: Exarp in the East, Hcoma in the West: Nanta in the North: and Bitom in the South.[189]

---

[188]   With the advent of computers, this can be done quickly. Sadly the true directional facing of a constellation is neglected by a number of modern day temples.
[189]   Here we have the clear definition of the Three layers of the pentagram. The elements (for the Etheric Level), signs (for the Astral\Emotional levels) and the Enochian Tablets (for the Mental level) the highest level. These equate with the lowest subtle bodies of man (excluding the physical) and we must gradually attune ourselves to each of these levels so that they are easily recognizable and accessed.

In the pronunciation of all these names, thou shalt take a deep breath and vibrate them as much as possible inwardly with the outgoing breath, not necessarily loudly, but with the vibration thus: A-a-a-el-ll. Or Em-or-r-Di-a-ll Hec—te-e-g-ah. If thou wilt, thou mayest also trace the letters or sigils of these names.

To invoke the forces of the four elements at once, at the four quarters, commence at the East and there trace the equilibrating pentagram of the actives and the ivoking pentagram of air and pronounce the proper names. Thence shalt thou carry round the point of thy wand to the South and thereon trace the equilibrating pentagram of the actives and the invoking pentagram of fire and pronounce the proper names. Pass to the West, trace the equilibrating pentagram for passives and invoking pentagram for water and pronounce the proper names; thence to the North, trace the equilibrating pentagram of the passives and the invoking pentagram of earth, pronounce the proper names, and then complete the circle of the place.

In the same manner shalt thou banish, unless thou desirest to retain certain of the forces for a time. All invocations shall be opened and closed with the 'Kabbalistic Sign of the Cross'. In certain cases other names, as those angels and spirits, may be pronounced towards their proper quarters and their names and sigils traced in the air.

If thou workest with but one element, thou shalt make (if it be an active element such as fire or air) the equilibrating pentagrams for actives only and the element's own invoking pentagram of the one element at the four quarters and not those of the other elements. And if it be a passive element, earth or water, thou shalt make the equilibrating pentagram of passives and the invoking pentagram of the one element at the four quarters. In closing and banishing, follow the same law. Also, see that thou pronouncest the proper names with the proper pentagrams and that thou dost complete the 'Circle of the Place' wherein thou workest. The pentagram is also called the symbol of the Microcosm or lesser world, and the hexagram is the symbol of the Macrocosm or greater world. Never make banishing symbols whether pentagrams or hexagrams in the Tomb of C.R.C., only declare the elemental spirits to be set free in the name of YEHESHUA.

RITUAL OF THE HEXAGRAM[190]
by
MacGregor Mathers

The hexagram is a powerful symbol representing the operation of the seven planets under the presidency of the Sephiroth, and of the letters of the seven-lettered name, ARARITA. ARARITA is a 'divine name of Seven Letters' formed of the Hebrew initials of the sentence: 'One is his beginning. One his individuality. His permutation is one.'[191]

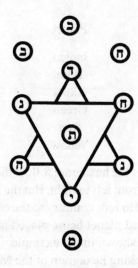

---

[190]   Although I have included the Mathers lecture here, I have used the diagrams of the unicusal hexagram which is much easier. This was first used as a magical hexagram (to the best of my knowledge) by Giordano Bruno. It was also part of the Golden Dawn paper 'Polygons and Polygrams'. I came across a note that some Golden Dawn members did experiment with it instead of the standard hexagram, but it was never deemed official. Since I have elected to use the unicusal hexagram the following paper is an abridged form of the one issued by Mathers. The 'four forms' aspect of this paper being omitted and certain references to the various triangles which have no relationship to the unicusal hexagram. Using the unicusal hexagram the 'Lesser Ritual of the Hexagram' becomes null and void because the 'four forms' are not used.

It is called the 'Signet' or 'Symbol of the Macrocosm', just as the pentagram is called the 'Signet Star' or symbol of the Microcosm. As in the case of the pentagram, each re-entering angle of the hexagram, issueth a Ray representing a radiation from the divine. Therefore it is called the Flaming Hexagram, or the Six-rayed Signet Star. Usually, it is traced with the single point uppermost. It is not an evil symbol with the two points upward, and this is a point of difference from the pentagram.

Now if thou dost draw the hexagram to have by thee as a symbol thou shalt make it in the colours already taught and upon a black background. These are the planetary powers allotted unto the angles of the hexagram.[192]

Invoked Direction	Planet	Sephiroth
To Saturn	Indigo	Black
To Luna	Blue	Puce
To Jupiter	Violet	Blue
To Venus	Green	Green
To Mars	Red	Red
To Mercury	Yellow	Orange

All invoking forms of the hexagram follow the course of the Sun in their current, that is from left to right. But the banishing hexagrams are traced from right to left, contrary to the course of the Sun. The symbol of the invoked planet being placed in the top triangle just above the centre, as shown in the example.

When using the invoking hexagram of the Moon, it should not be used in her decrease, or if there is anything negative astrologically taking place.[193]

---

[191]   'AChD RASh AChDUThU RASh YChUDu ThMURHZU AChD'

[192]   There are two colours allotted to the hexagram. One is for the planets and the other is when one is working through the Sephiroth. The planets are the paths of the King Scale and the Sephiroth are the Queen Scale. When using both these energies in ritual the predominant framework (whether Sephiroth or planet) decides the colour selected. If the ritual is written in such a way that more than one invoking hexagram is used, I suggest that the difference between the energy of the Sephiroth (angels etc.) and planet be acute. So there is no problem in identifying what energy you are bringing through.

[193]   Mathers went into some elaboration on the timing of the use of the Lunar hexagram, especially with Sun -Moon conjunctions and I have simplified things with this last sentence.

In all rituals of the hexagram as in those of the pentagram, thou shalt complete the circle of the place. Thou shalt not trace any external circle round each hexagram itself unless thou wishest to confine the force to one place, as in charging a symbol or talisman.

From the attribution of the planets, one to each angel of the hexagram, shalt thou see the reason of the sympathy existing between each superior planet and one certain inferior planet. That is, that to which it is exactly opposite in the hexagram:

BANISHING - UNSYMPATHETIC

Superior Planets	Inferior Planets
Saturn	Venus
Jupiter	Mercury
Mars	Luna

In the midst of all this is the fire of the Sun.

INVOKING - SYMPATHETIC

Superior Planets	Inferior Planets
Saturn	Luna
Jupiter	Mercury
Mars	Venus

In the 'Supreme Ritual of the Hexagram' the signs of the 5=6 Grade are to be given, but not those in the grades of the First Order, notwithstanding these latter are made us of in the 'Supreme Ritual of the Pentagram'. And because the hexagram is the Signet Star of the Macrocosm or Greater world, therefore is to be employed in all invocations of the forces of the Sephiroth: though the Signet Star of the pentagram represents their operations in the Luna world, in the elements and in Man.

If thou wilt deal with the forces of the supernal triad of the Sephiroth, thou shalt make use of the following:

Sephiroth	Planet
Kether	Saturn[194]

---

[194] Since the discovery of Pluto, Neptune is associated to Kether, Uranus for Chokmah and Pluto for Daath. I utilised an 11 pointed star for the invocation of the slower moving planets with success. Tracing it is complicated, but gradually you

Chokmah	Saturn
Binah	Saturn
Chesed	Jupiter
Geburah	Mars
Tiphareth	Sun
Netzach	Venus
Hod	Mercury
Yesod	Luna
Malkuth	Luna

Know also that the Sephiroth are not to be invoked on every slight occasion, but only with due care and solemnity. Above all, the forces of Kether and Chokmah demand the greatest purity and solemnity of heart and mind in him who would penetrate their mysteries. For such high knowledge is only to be obtained by him whose genius can stand in the presence of the Holy Ones. See that thou usest the divine names with all reverence and humility for cursed is he that taketh the name of the vast One in vain. All hexagrams are to be traced proportionately.

ADDENDUM

Now in the 'Supreme Ritual of the Hexagram', when thou shalt wish to attract in addition to the forces of the planet, those of a sign of the zodiac wherein he then is, thou shalt trace in the centre of the invoking hexagram of the planet, the symbol of that sign of the zodiac beneath his own; and if this not be sufficient, thou shalt also trace the invoking pentagram of the sign as it is directed in the 'Ritual of the Pentagram'.[195]

---

get used to it and it is not that difficult at all. In the Golden Dawn (according to Regardie) many of the members thought there should have been magic squares and sigils for the slower moving planets. Apparently Mathers promised his members to work on them but as far as I am aware they were never completed before 1900. I have written up kameas and sigils for these slower moving planets for our Thoth Hermes temple.

[195]   This is a 'short cut' where only one hexagram need be done for both planet and sign. I am not happy with it, nor the suggestion of the dual use be considered though this is up to the individual.

In the tracing of the hexagram of any planet thou shalt pronounce therewith in a vibratory manner as before taught, both the divine name of the Sephirah which ruleth the planet and the seven-lettered name ARARITA, and also the particular letter of the that name which is referred to that particular planet. Now if thou shalt wish to invoke the forces of one particular planet, thou shalt find in that quarter of the Heavens he will situate at the time of working...and shalt trace his invoking hexagram and pronounce the proper names, and invoke what angels and forces of that nature may be required, and trace their sigils in the air.

When thou hast finished thy invocation thou shalt in most cases license them to depart and perform the 'Banishing Ritual of the Planet' which shall be converse of the invoking one. But in cases of charging a tablet, or symbol or talisman, thou shalt not perform the banishing symbols upon it, which would have the effect of entirely de-charging it and reducing it to the condition it was when it was first made - that is to say dead and lifeless.[196]

If thou wishest to bring the rays of all or several planets into action at the same time, thou shalt discover their quarter in the Heavens for the time of the working... and invoke their forces as before laid down... And conclude with the ...'Banishing Ritual of the Hexagram'. And ever remember to complete the circle of the place wherein thou workest, following the course of the Sun.

---

[196]   I do not agree with this statement entirely. If an object is constructed on the correct time then it will be charged with the ionization of the moment. Any ritual afterwards of course adds to its power but in this instance the banishing over it, accidentally or otherwise, would not diminish its power at construction (as Mathers said), but this should be almost sufficient in its purpose for the project.

Invoking   Banishing

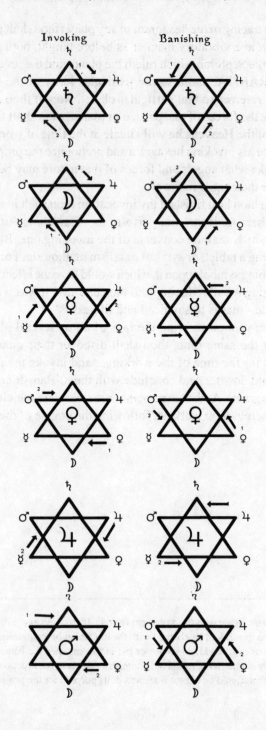

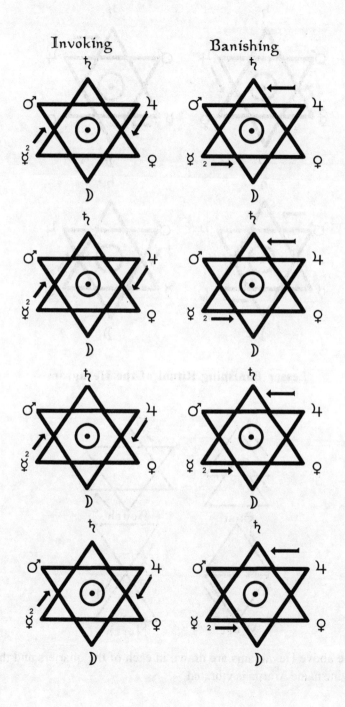

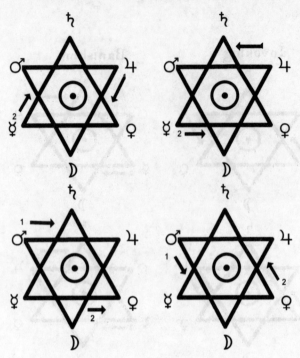

Lesser Banishing Ritual of the Hexagram

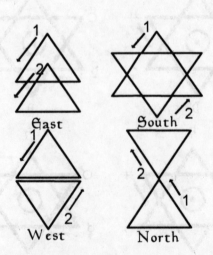

The above Hexagrams are drawn in each of the quarters and the divine name Ararita is vibrated.

LOTUS WAND[197]
by MacGregor Mathers.

This is for general use in magical working. It is to be carried by the Z.A.M. at all meetings of the Second Order at which he has the right to attend.

1. It is to be made by himself, unassisted.
2. Consecrated by himself.
3. Used by himself alone.
4. Untouched by any other person.
5. Untouched by any other person.

It will be thus free from external influences other than his own, on the human plane.

The wand has the upper end white, the lower black. Between them there are twelve colours referring to the zodiac signs, in the positive or masculine scale of colour (paths of the King Scale P.Z). At the upper end of the white is fixed a lotus flower in three whorls

[197] The symbol of the Lotus, as held by the gods on the Egyptian frescoes, symbolized life, death and rebirth. On one level it resembles the River Nile with its two branches. To the Egyptians this was the river of life and death. On a higher level it represents the Sun, the source of light and power to our Solar system. The Golden Dawn adage to the twelve signs shows a definite link to the Solar system in Microcosm.

of 26 petals: the outer eight, the middle eight, and the innermost 10. The calyx has four lobes or sepals of orange colour. The flower centre is orange or gold. The lotus wand should be 24-40 inches long[198] and of wood, about half an inch thick. The several bands of white, 12 colours and black may be painted or enamelled, or formed of coloured papers pasted on. The length of colours should be such that the white is a little the longest, then the black.[199] The colours must be clear, brilliant and correct.

These are as follows:

White

Aries	Red
Taurus	Reddish Orange
Gemini	Orange
Cancer	Amber
Leo	Lemonish Yellow
Virgo	Yellowish Green
Libra	Emerald
Scorpio	Greenish Blue
Sagittarius	Bright Blue
Capricornicus	Indigo
Aquarius	Violet
Pisces	Crimson

Black

The lotus flower may be made of sheet metal or card board, in three whorls of eight, eight and 10 petals, white internally and tips curved a little, olive outside with five markings as shown in the diagram. The centre is orange, or a brass bolt to keep all together will do. On the white portion of the wand, the owner's motto may be inscribed.

---

[198]   The cut wands that were handed out to the Z.A.M's at Whare Ra were exactly 24 inches long. This length is ideal because you can banish or invoke over an altar without trying to hit the ceiling.

[199]   The Whare Ra wands had each zodiac division one and three quarter inches in length.

Symbolism and Use of the Lotus Wand

As a general rule, use the white end in invocation and the black
end to banish. The white end may be used to banish by tracing a
banishing symbol an evil an opposing force which has resisted other
efforts. By this is meant, that whatever band you are holding the
wand, whether white for spiritual things or black for mundane
matters, by the blue, Sagittarius, or by the Red for Fiery triplicity,
you are, when invoking, to direct the white end of the extremity to
the quarter desired. When banishing, to point the black end to that
quarter.

The wand is never to be inverted, so that when the very material
forces are concerned, the black end may be the most suitable for
invocation, but with the greatest caution.

In working on the plane of the zodiac, hold the wand by the
portion you refer to between the thumb and the two fingers.

If a planetary working be required, hold the wand by the portion
representing the day or night house[200] of the planet, or else by the
sign in which the planet is at the time. [201]

Planet	Day - House	Night - House
Saturn	Capricorn	Aquarius
Jupiter	Sagittarius	Pisces
Mars	Aries	Scorpio
Venus	Libra	Taurus
Mercury	Gemini	Virgo
Sun	Leo	
Moon	Cancer	

Should the action be with the elements, one of the signs of the
triplicity of that element should be held according to the nature of

---

[200]   The day and night house uses the rulership of the old Zodiac as their
reference points.

[201]   The breadth of coverage of the lotus wand which covers greater areas than
the elemental fire wand. Part of the Invocation process not mentioned in the text
is the use of the wand for Circumambulation and Exorcism, which it is used with
the magical sword. Its power works through all the subtle bodies and is only
limited by the Will of the operator.

the elements intended to be invoked. Thus bearing in mind that the Kerubic emblem is the most powerful action of the element in the triplicity.

Sign	Northern Hemisphere	Southern Hemisphere [202]
Leo	Violent heat of Summer	Deep Winter
Aries	Beginning warmth of Spring	Waning heat in Autumn
Sagittarius	Waning of heat in Autumn	Growing warmth of Summer

Hold the wand by the white portion for all divine and spiritual matters or for the Sephirotic influences, and for the process of rising in the Planes.

Hold the wand by the black part only for material and mundane matters.[203]

The ten upper and inner petals refer to the purity of the ten Sephiroth. The middle eight refer to the counter-charged natural and spiritual forces of air and fire. The lowest and outer eight refer to the powers of earth and water. The centre and amber portion refers to the spiritual Sun, while the outer calyx of four orange sepals shows the actions of the Sun upon the life of the things by differentiation.

The lotus flower is not to be touched in working, but in Sephirotic and spiritual things, the flower is to be inclined towards the forehead; and to rise in the planes, the orange coloured centre is to be fully directed to the forehead.

---

[202]   I have included the Southern Hemisphere associations for those who have had to re-adjust many of the principles of the meaning of the signs from an elemental viewpoint.

[203]   And for banishing or getting rid of any negative force.

Addendum[204]

The Monk Trithemius was one of the first magicians to make the point that when evoking and invoking a force one should rise to the level of that force and be dominant to it. This is the purpose of the lotus wand. The action of rising through the planes gives added control. By knowledge of the seven subtle bodies of man the Z.A.M can learn to know which level to rise and understand the amount of control and power needed. The lotus wand is more powerful than the elemental wand, and while some of their areas may overlap, the lotus wand can be used as a separate elemental weapon. But the elemental wand must be used with the other three implements.

At Whare Ra Temple, Jack Taylor taught that before any evocation or invocation with the wand, the adept would use the wand as a vehicle to get to the desired level. One would then feel and identify this level so that when it was invoked or evoked it was easily identifiable. Taylor used to hold classes for adepts to do this by recognising the energy of the planetary, zodiacal and Sephirotic forces. It was a process where the subtle bodies of the adept would become empathic to the force then Taylor would explain how to dominate it[205].

---

[204] This Addendum is based on the notes from a discussion I gave on the subject of temple weapons, at Thoth-Hermes Temple in Wellington in 1985.

[205] This caused a huge number of problems for those Wardens or teachers who did not bother with it. More than one turned up on Taylor's doorstep to complain that he was poaching their students. However Mrs. Felkin gave him free rein in this area by never rebuking him or mentioning the subject.

Consecration of the Lotus Wand[206]

1. a. Private room
   b. White triangle
   c. Red cross of six squares
   d. Incense and rose
   e. Lamp, or a vessel of fire
   f. water in a vase
   g. Salt on a platter
   h. Astrological figure for the consecration
   i. Ritual of Pentagram
   j. New wand
   k. White linen or silk wrapper
   l. Table for an altar
   m. black altar cover
2. Find position of East
3. Prepare an invocation of the forces of the sign of the zodiac
4. Place altar in middle of room, cover and drape with black cloth.
5. Place upon the cross and triangle of the Neophyte ceremony, water at the base of the triangle, incense and rose in East, above cross, lamp in South.
6. Light lamp
7. Stand at West, holding wand, facing East.
8. Hold wand by black portion.
9. Say:

Hekas, Hekas, este Bebeloi

10. Perform Lesser Banishing Ritual of Pentagram.
11. Place wand on altar.
12. Light incense from lamp.
13. Sprinkle salt into water.
14. Purify room first with water, then with fire, as in Neophyte ritual. Repeating two passages from the 31st path: water:

---

[206]   This is taken from an early undated Golden Dawn paper.

So therefore first the Priest who governeth the works of fire, must sprinkle with the lustral waters of the loud resounding sea.

15. fire:

    And when all the Phantoms have vanished thou shalt see the Holy and formless fire, that fire that darts and flashes through the hidden depths of the Universe, hear thou the voice of fire!

16. Take up wand again, by the white portion, circumambulate the room three times and at West, facing East, repeat the adoration:

    Holy art thou, Lord of the Universe!
    Holy art thou whom nature hath not formed!
    Holy art thou! The vast and the mighty one!
    Lord of the Light and of the darkness!

17. Perform Supreme invoking Ritual of the Pentagram at four quarters of the room, tracing proper pentagram at each quarter.

18. Stand in the Eastern quarter; face East; hold the wand by the white portion; give the sign of the Adeptus Minor. Look upward, hold the wand on high and say:

    Oh Harpocrates, Lord of Silence, who art enthroned upon the lotus. Twenty-six are the petals of the lotus flower of the wand. Oh Lord of Creation! They are the numbers of thy name. In the name of YHVH let the divine light descend.

19. Facing, consecutively, the quarter where each sign is, repeat in each of the 12 directions the invocation which follows, using the appropriate divine angelic names for each sign. Begin with Aries, Hold wand at the appropriate coloured part, and in left hand the element from off the altar which is referred to the sign and say:

The heaven is above and the earth is beneath. And betwixt the light and the darkness the colours vibrate. I supplicate the powers and forces governing the nature, place and authority of the sign......, By the Majesty of the divine name......, with which in earth life and language, I ascribe to the Hebrew letter ...., to which is allotted the symbolic tribe.... and over which is the Angel...., to bestow this present day and hour, and confirm their mystic and potent influence upon the (Colour).....band of this lotus wand, which I hereby dedicate to purity and to occult work, and may its grasp strengthen me in the work of the character of (sign).... and his attributes.

As this is recited, trace in the air with the lotus end, the invoking pentagram of the sign required, and hold the corresponding element from the altar in the left hand, while facing each of the 12 zodiac directions.

20. Lay the wand on the altar, lotus end towards the East.
21. Stand at the West of the altar, face east, raise hands, and say:

Oh Isis! Great Goddess of the Forces of Nature, let thine influence descend and consecrate this wand which I dedicate to Thee for the performance of the works of the Magic of the Light.

22. Wrap the wand in silk or linen.
24. Purify the room with water and fire, as at first.
25. Perform reverse circumambulation.
26. Standing at the West of the altar, face East, and recite:

In the name of YEHESHUAH, I now set free the spirits that may have been imprisoned by this ceremony.

27. Perform Lesser Banishing Ritual of the Pentagram.

THE MAGICAL SWORD [207]

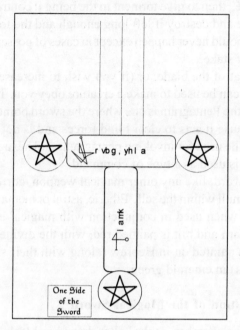

The sword should be of medium height and weight and there should be five pentagrams on it, one for each Sephiroth[208]. The tops or points of the pentagrams should face the direction of the hand that holds it. The sword of the Z.A.M. is similar to the sword held by the Imperator in the Neophyte ritual, with its base in Malkuth and its point and power of influence from Geburah. It is distinct from the air dagger, for like the lotus wand, the sword can be used as a separate weapon and has more power to deal with powerful forces.

It can clear a negative influence away from a purified area of working by using the astral form of the point to draw a circle of protection. During a ritual the sword is never pointed downward unless it is for a specific purpose. A downward pointing sword is a sign of capitulation by the Adept, by the very forces he is trying to command. The point of the sword is rarely used unless an entity disobeys your command. A sword is only pointed briefly, to warn

---

[207] This is taken from a Thoth-Hermes temple document and is a re-written version of the Golden Dawn paper on the subject.

[208] This was the Whare Ra teaching.

the force. Its main function is to threaten and if that makes no difference, then to give torment to the being it controls. The point can injure and destroy if left long enough and the focus is strong, but this should never happen except in cases of possession or when a life is at stake.

The flat of the blade, or (if you wish to increase your power) the edge, can be used to make a creature obey you. The Banishing Ritual of the Pentagram is one where the sword point can be safely used because it acts to clear blind forces and is not specific. The point can be used for invoking pentagrams and hexagrams for here the point is used as a type of command.

The sword, like any other magical weapon, corresponds to an inside stimuli within the self. Etheric, astral or mental it will get the job done when used in conjunction with magical expertise. The sword guard and hilt is painted red, with the divine names (from Geburah) painted on in Hebrew (along with their sigils from the rose cross) in emerald green.

Consecration of the Magical Sword[209]

Prepare the chamber, central altar draped in black, red cross and white triangle, rose and incense, cup and water, lamp, plate and alt. White robe, sash, rose cross, lotus wand, new sword, red cloak and lamen[210]. An invocation to Mars and Geburah (love and strength to be especially emphasised), An astrological figure to show the position of Mars at the time of the working.

1. Place sword on altar, hilt to East, near incense, point to West, near water.
2. Take up lotus wand, by black part.
3. Stand at West of altar, facing east.
4. Say:

    Hekas Hekas Este Bebeloi

5. Take cup and purify with water, sprinkling to all four quarters.
6. Say:

---

209   Taken from an early undated Golden Dawn paper.
210   This was the Lamen of the Praemonstrator with the Sigil of Mars, traced from the rose cross on the back.

And first the Priest who governeth the works of fire must sprinkle with the lustral waters of the loud resounding sea.

7. Put down cup on altar.
8. Take up incense and wave it as you pass round the four quarters.
9. Say:

And when after all the phantoms have vanished thou shalt see the Holy and formless fire, that fire which darts and flashes through the hidden depth of the Universe, hear thou the voice of fire.

10. Put down incense and take up lotus wand by the white band.
11. Circumambulate three times with Sol then return to West, facing East, say ADORATION:

Holy art Thou Lord of the Universe!
Holy art Thou whom nature hath not Formed!
Holy Art Thou the Vast and the Mighty One!
Lord of the Light and of the Darkness!

12. Perform Lesser Invoking Ritual of the Hexagram of Mars, holding wand by white band. Do LVX formulae.
13. Return to West of altar.

14. Turn to face the direction in which you have found Mars so that the altar is between your self and Mars (for convenience).
15. Describe in the air the invoking pentagram for the sign that Mars is in.
16. Describe invoking hexagram of Mars, saying: Elohim Gibor. Then still holding wand by white band.
17. Recite your invocation to the power of Geburah and the Forces of Mars, tracing the sigil of each as you read it:

Oh Mighty Power who governeth Geburah, thou strong and terrible divine Elohim Gibor. I beseech thee to bestow upon this magic sword and might to slay the evil and weakness I may encounter. In the fiery sphere of Madim, strength and fidelity. May the great Archangel Kamael bestow

*upon me, courage wherewith to use it aright, and may
the powerful angels of the order of the Seraphim scorch
with their flames and feebleness of purpose which would
hinder my search for the true Light.*

18. Then trace in the air, slowly, above the sword, and as if standing
    upon it, the invoking hexagram of Mars. Do this with the lotus
    end, still holding the white band (the wand at this point is vertical
    above the sword).
19. Next trace over the sword the letters of the names in the
    invocation and their several sigils.
20. Put wand down.
21. Take up the cup and purify new sword. Put down cup.
22. Take up incense and wave it over the new sword. Put down
    incense.
23. Take up new sword and with it perform lesser invoking Ritual
    of the Hexagram and also trace invoking hexagram of Mars,
    repeating the name ARARITA and ELOHIM GIBOR.
24. Lay down sword.
25. Purify chamber as before with cup.
26. Purify with incense as before.
27. Reverse circumambulation three times and say.

*In the name of YEHESHUAH, I now set free any spirits
that may have been imprisoned by this ceremony.*

28. Perform, with the sword, the Lesser Banishing Ritual of the
    Hexagram.
29. Perform, with sword, Lesser Banishing Ritual of the
    Pentagram.
30. Finish with Kabbalistic cross.
31. Wrap up sword and make sure no one else may touch it.

THE ROSE CROSS
by MacGregor Mathers.

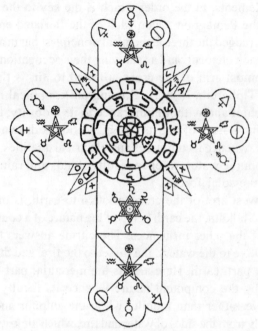

The rose cross[211] is a synthesis of the masculine, positive or rainbow scale of colour attributions, which is also called the 'Scale of the King'.[212] The four ends of the cross belong to the four elements, accordingly. The white Portion belongs to the Holy spirit and the planets. The twenty-two petals of the rose refer to the twenty-two paths. It is the cross in Tiphareth, the receptacle and the centre of Upon the white portion of the symbol, below the rose, is placed the hexagram, with the planets in the order which is the key of the Supreme Ritual of the Hexagram.

---

[211]   The rose cross is worn by all Officers present in this ritual and those who are seated and are simply watching the ceremony.

[212]   To be more specific, the Paths of the King Scale.and are coloured the forces of the Sephiroth and the paths. The extreme centre of the rose is white, the reflected spiritual brightness of Kether, bearing upon the red rose of five petals and the Golden cross of six squares; four green rays issuant around the angles of the cross, from which the Second Order takes its name. They are the symbols of the receiving Force.

Around the pentagrams, which are placed one upon each elemental coloured arm, are drawn the symbols of the spirit and the four elements, in the order which is the key to the Supreme Ritual of the Pentagram. Upon each of the floriated ends of the cross are arranged the three alchemical principles, but in a different order for each element, and as showing their occupation therein.

The upmost arm of the cross, allotted to air, is the yellow colour of Tiphareth. In it the flowing philosophical mercurial nature is chief and without hindrance to its mobility; hence the ever moving nature of air. Its sulphuric side is drawn from the part of fire, whence its luminous and electrical qualities. Its saline side in from the water, whence results clouds and rain from the action of the solar forces.

The lowest arm of the cross, allotted to earth, is of the four colours of Malkuth, the earth being of the nature of a container and receiver of the other influences. The citrine answers to its airy part, the Olive to the watery, the russet to the fire, and the black to the lowest part, earth. Here also is the mercurial part chief, but hindered by the compound nature whence its faculty becomes germinative rather than mobile, while the sulphur and salt are respectively from the sides of water and fire, which almost neutralize their natural operation and bring about the fixedness and immobility of earth.

The extremity allotted to fire is of the scarlet colour of Geburah, and in it the sulphuric nature is chief, whence its powers of heat and burning. The salt is from the side of earth, hence the necessity for a constant substantial pabulum whereon to act, and the Mercury is from the side of air, hence the leaping, lambent motion of flame, especially when acted upon the wind.

The extremity allotted to water is of the blue colour of Chesed, and in it the saline side is chief, as exemplified in the salt water of the ocean, to which all waters go; and from hence also is derived the nature of always preserving the horizontal line. The Mercurial part is from earth, hence the weight and force of its flux and reflux. Its sulphuric part is from the air, hence the effect of the waves and storms. So that the disposition of these three principles forms the key of their alchemic operation in the elements.

The white rays issuing from behind the rose at the inner angles between the arms, are the rays of the divine Light issuing and coruscating from the reflected light of Kether in its centre; and the letters and symbols on them refer to the analysis of the key word of the Adeptus Minor, I.N.R.I. by which the opening of the Vault is accomplished.

The 12 letters of the 12 petals follow the order of the signs of the zodiac. Uppermost is Heh, the letter of Aries, followed by Vau, followed by Zain, Cheth, Teth, Yod, while the letter of Libra, which is Lamed is lowermost. Ascending are Nun, Samech, Ayin, Tzaddi, Qoph. The Seven double letters of the middle row are allotted to the planets in the order of their exaltations, the planets being wanderers; the stars are fixed with respect to earth. These letters are Peh, Resh, Beth, with Daleth exactly over Libra, followed by Gimel, Kaph and Tau. The three mother letters are allotted to the elements and are so arranged that the petal of air should be beneath the arm of the cross allotted to air, while those of fire and water are on counter-changed sides, so that the forces of the arms of the cross should not too much over-ride the planetary and zodiacal forces in the rose, which might otherwise be the case were the petal of fire placed on the same side of the arm of fire and that of water on the side of water.

The back of the cross bears the inscription in Latin: "The Master Jesus Christ, God and Man", between four Maltese crosses which represent the four pyramids of the elements opened out. This is placed in the upmost part because therein is affirmed a descent of the divine Force into Tiphareth, which is the central point between supernals and inferiors. But on the lowest part is written the motto of the Zelator Adeptus Minor, because therein is the affirmation of the elevation of human into the divine. But this is impossible without the assistance of the divine spirit from Kether, hence the space above Malkuth is white upon the front aspect of the cross, white being the symbol of the spiritual rescued from the material.

In the centre is written in Latin between the symbols of the alchemical principles, of which the outermost is sulphur, the purgatorial fire of suffering and self sacrifice, 'Blessed be the Lord our God who have given us the Symbol Signum.' And this is a word of six letters, thus representing the six creative periods in the Universe and the regimen of the planets ere the glory of the Sun can be obtained.[213]

Consecration of Rose Cross

1. Arrange a central altar draped in black.
2. Place the triangle and cross as in the Neophyte Grade.
3. Place on it rose, cup, salt and fire; cup between cross and triangle in Neophyte.
4. Place new rose cross upon triangle.
5. Take up lotus wand, by black part.
6. Stand at West of altar, facing east.
7. Say: *Hekas Hekas Este Bebeloi*
8. Take cup and purify with water, sprinkling to all four quarters.
9. Say:

   And first the Priest who governeth the works of fire must sprinkle with the lustral waters of the loud resounding sea.

10. Put down cup on altar.
11. Take up incense and wave it as you pass round the four quarters.
12. Say:

   And when after all the phantoms have vanished thou shalt see the Holy and formless fire, that fire which darts and flashes through the hidden depth of the Universe, hear thou the voice of fire.

13. Put down incense and take up lotus wand by the white band.
14. Circumambulate three times with Sol then return to West, facing East, say ADORATION:

   Holy art thou Lord of the Universe!

---

[213]   At Whare Ra, all the rose crosses were pre cut and given to the new Z.A.M. to paint. These were made from Copies of Dr. Felkin's. It was eight and a half inches in length from the tip of the air arm to the tip of Malkuth below it, 7 inches from the tip of the fire Arm to the tip of the water arm. The width of each was one and three

Holy art thou whom nature hath not Formed!
Holy Art thou the Vast and the Mighty One!
Lord of the Light and of the Darkness!

15. Perform Supreme Invoking Ritual of the Pentagram at four quarters.
16. Return to West of altar, facing East, hold the lotus wand by the white part.
17. Make over the rose cross, in the air with the lotus wand and as if standing in the centre of the rose, the symbol, and invoke all divine and angelic names by a special form as follows:

Thou most sublime Majesty on High, who art at certain seasons worthily represented by the glorious Sun of Tiphareth, I beseech thee to bestow upon this symbol of the rose and cross, which I have formed to thy honour, and for the furtherance of the Great Work, in a spirit of purity and love, the most excellent virtuous, by the divine name YHVH ELOAH VE DAATH. Deign I beseech thee to grant that the great Archangel RAPHAEL, and the mighty Angel MICHAEL may strengthen this emblem, and through the sphere of the splendid orb of SHEMESH may confer upon it such power and virtue, as to lead me by it towards the solution of the Great Secret.

(Raise the eyes and hands to heaven during prayer and covering them as you finish.)

18. *And a River Nahar went forth from Eden to water the Garden, and from thence it was parted and came into four heads.*[214] .

19. Describe over the white portion the invoking hexagrams of he planets, as if standing upon it, repeating the necessary names while holding the wand by the white part.
20. Describe the equilibrating pentagrams of spirit and the words EXARP, BITOM, HCOMA, NANTA

---

quarter inches. The three bubbles at the end of each arm made it a two inch width. The diameter of the painted rose was thee and one quarter inches.

[214]   From Genesis.

21. Then over the four coloured portions (arms) in turn describe the invoking pentagrams of each element, using the words and the grade signs and repeating the verse of Genesis II verses 11-15 (Over the fire Arm)

> *And the name of the first river is Pishon; it is that which encompasseth the whole land of Havilah[215] where there is gold, and the gold of that land is good; there is bdellium and the onyx stone.*

Make invoking pentagram of fire while holding the lotus wand by the Leo band (do sign of fire grade).
(Over the water arm)

> *And the name of the second river is Gihon, the same as that which encompasseth the whole land of Ethiopia.*

Make invoking pentagram of water while holding lotus wand with the Scorpio band (do sign of water grade).
(Over air arm)

> *And the name of third river is Hiddekel, that is it which goeth towards the East of Assyria.*

Make invoking pentagram of fire while holding the lotus wand by the Aquarius band (do sign of air grade).
(Over earth arm)

> *And the fourth river is Euphrates.*

Make invoking pentagram of earth while holding lotus wand by the Taurus band (do sign of earth grade).

22. Holding the Lotus wand by the white part, describe a circle from left to right over the outermost 12 Petals of the rose, pronouncing the name

> *ADONI*   (vibrating it as taught).

---

[215]   Eden.

23. Describe a similar circle over the seven middle petals while vibrating the word

   ARARITA.

24. Then describe a circle over the three innermost petals and vibrate
   YHVH.

25. Trace a perpendicular line (from the air arm to the earth arm) and vibrate

   EHEIEH

26. Trace a horizontal line (from the water arm to the fire Arm) and vibrate

   ELOHIM.

27. Wrap up cross in white silk or linen.
28. Purify with water and fire (as in opening).
29. Stand West of altar, face east and say:

   In the name of YESHESHUAH, I now set free any spirits that may have been imprisoned by this ceremony.

30. Do Lesser Banishing Ritual of the Pentagram.

THE MAGICAL IMPLEMENTS[216]
by MacGregor Mathers.

These are the Tarot symbols of the divine name YHVH and of the elements, and have a certain bond and sympathy between them. So that if even one only is to be used, the others should also be present, even as each of the four elemental tablets is divided in itself into four lesser angles, representing the other three elements bound together therewith in the same tablet. Therefore the Zelator Adeptus Minor remember that when he works with these forces, he is, as it were, dealing with the forces of the letters of the divine name, YHVH. Each implement must be consecrated, and when this has been done by an Adeptus, no one else may touch it.

Addendum

Like the Tarot, each elemental weapon is analogous to a Tree of Life in each of the four worlds. The fire wand is linked to Atziluth and world of archetypes, the initial impetus that leads to creation which the water cup is linked to, and the world of Briah. The air dagger is allied to the Yetzirah, the world of Formation. Lastly the earth disk is linked to Assiah the Material world of the elements. Each elemental weapon represents the forces of each of these worlds and this should be considered carefully before their use. For example, a fire wand is used not only to instigate something into action but also for quick results. The cup on the other hand should never be used with active gestures, such as a pentagram or hexagram, for its passive nature will not allow it for active situations so all the gestures with the cup are passive ones.

The actual construction and consecration time of these weapons should be timed astrologically. The ideal times would be to make and consecrate the weapons during the Fixed signs for greater durability: fire wand in Leo, water cup in Scorpio, air dagger in Aquarius, and earth Disk in Taurus. The actual day of construction should start at New Moon and the consecration should be a day chosen between first quarter and full Moon. The hour will be of the

---

[216]   Every Addendum listed in this section comes from the Thoth-Hermes temple notes.

planet representing the element of the weapon. For example Mars for the wand, Moon for the cup, Mercury for the dagger and Saturn for the Disk. The planet also represents the day concerned when to construct and consecrate the weapons.

Apart from the four elemental weapons there were also numerous other items utilised by some adepts within the Golden Dawn.

Both a sickle and additional knife were used for collecting herbs for ritual. These days some form of pruning device could be used equally as well. Also a knife could be used specifically for drawing a circle into the earth (using a long rope and small pole so that a circle may be drawn accurately.) Some form of sharp instrument for drawing on metal or slate surfaces (such as a modern engraving tool). A bell or gong for summoning entities. A brazier for incense. Writing material, such as paper, pen, chalk and tape (all of which are to be consecrated) before use.

ELEMENTAL FIRE WAND[217]

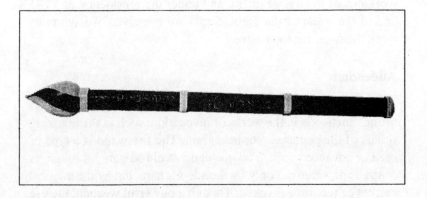

The staff of the fire wand should be of wood, rounded and smooth, and perforated from end to end, and within it should be placed a

---

[217]   The actual design of the fire wand is based on the wand of the Supreme Magus of the 'Societas Rosicruciana in Anglia'.

steel rod, just so long as to project and inch beyond each end of the wooden rod. It is often convenient to form the wand from cane which has a natural hollow to follow through it. If of cane, there should be three natural lengths according to the knots, so these knots may be placed similarly to the manner in which they are placed in the figure which is such as a turner would produce. Eighteen inches is an extreme length.[218]The magnet should be a strong one.

One end of the wooden rod should be cone shaped. The North end of the magnet (known by its repelling the so-called North Pole of a compass needle) should be placed at the end of the wand, which is plain.

The whole is coloured flame scarlet, and divided into three parts by yellow bands. The cone shaped end has also painted upon its red surface three wavy flame shaped YODS; they are painted in bright yellow. The divine and angelic names of the fire element, should be written in green paint along the shaft along with their sigils and the motto of the adept. The green should be bright emerald. The wand must be consecrated. The wand is to be used in all workings of the nature of fire and under the presidency of YOD and of the wand of the Tarot. Sigils are not given. Adepts must work them out for themselves.

Addendum

The fire wand is the most used of all the elemental weapons. Its prime function is in the works of invocation, such as the invoking rituals of the pentagram or hexagram. The fire wand is a type of seed or advance guard. The magnetic steel rod going through its centre is powered not only by the adept's aura, but by the magical current of the force invoked. Though a powerful weapon, the use of the wand is only for invocation, not evocation.

The use of the fire wand is limited compared to the lotus wand. The magnetic steel rod that acts as a condenser which draws off

---

[218]   At Whare Ra Temple in New Zealand, wands were specially constructed and given to the new Adeptus Minors to paint and consecrate. The length of these wands were based on Dr. Felkin's, which was only 7 inches in length.

the energy of the adept and stores it. This type of energy can be classed into three levels. The first is magnetic and is directly from the emanation of the bodies auric fluid. This fluid is the substance that separates the subtle bodies, but works more on the fluid that separates the etheric and physical bodies. When the wand was consecrated, part of this energy was left impregnated into the wand's magnetic field. The second level is the energy from the fire element. This is a limiter or holding factor that separates that part of the etherial fluid from its general magnetic influence. It will only draw a certain type of energy from the operator and acts as a filtration system preventing anything negative or too powerful from coming through. The third is the energy of the different levels (whether etheric, astral, or mental) as this will come through as a type of magnetism and have to adapt to the energy of the wand itself. Adepts will find the fire wand is lightening quick to use as the will directs the energy to wand which is part of the self (via the magnetised rod). Unfortunately it is limited to the type of power it can hold.

Grip Positions[219]

During any type of invocation with the wand, as in the hexagram ritual, the central grip is the one to use for this places things in the hand of the Ruach (even though it is directed from yet a higher level). In the elemental rituals of the pentagram the lower grip is used which relates to the lower or elemental forces being utilised. When blind symbols such as a cross and a circle are traced with the wand, the lower grip position is used. In works of astral projection the adept will hold the wand by the top grip with the cone of the wand directed towards his or her own head.

---

[219]   This is some of the word of mouth teachings passed on from Whare Ra temple by Jack Taylor, who was a stickler for holding things correctly.

WATER CUP

Any convenient clear glass cup may be adapted for this use.

The bowl should resemble a crocus flower, and must show eight petals. A smooth glass cup is acceptable, though if it has eight cuts or ridges it is preferable. These petals must be coloured bright blue, neither too pale nor too dark. They must be edged with bright orange which must be clear and correct, and exact complement of the blue, to produce a flashing.

The petals may be formed by paint or from coloured paper pasted on glass. The proper divine and angelic names are then to be written upon the petals, in orange colour, together with their sigils from the rose. Then add the motto of the adept. The stem and base may be painted blue.

The cup must be consecrated by the appropriate ceremony. When using the cup, you may sprinkle water from the cup in the required direction.

It is to be used in all workings of the nature of water, under the presidency of the letter HEH and the cup of the tarot.

Addendum

The cup, being analogous with water, forces a receptive link to the operator's sphere of sensation and to the forces that one aligns oneself. The key word associated to the use of the cup is 'Receptivity,' and it is a tool to establish such a rapport. Through the faculty of communication, the cup actually attracts the astral forces to oneself. Attraction with a cup is different from invoking, for attracting brings an empathy with the spiritual hierarchies where invoking involves command. The cup attracts willing forces which are then invoked through another medium (there are some exceptions to this). The presence of a cup during ritual, even without active use, will attract certain forces to it.

AIR DAGGER

Any convenient dagger, knife or short sword may be adapted to this use, the shorter the better. The hilt pommel and guard are to be coloured bright yellow.

The divine and angelic names are to be written upon the yellow background in purple or violet colour together with their sigils from the rose cross, and the motto of the adeptus[220].

---

[220]   On the wings of the guard of the sagger, the Hebrew Letter Vau is imprinted with the name of the Archangel of air, Raphael, on the hilt.

EARTH PENTACLE

The pantacle, or pentacle, is formed of a round disk of wood of about six inches in diameter and from half to one inch in thickness, nicely polished, and circular and of an even thickness.

There should be a circular white border, with a white hexagram upon each face of the disk. The space within the white ring should be divided into four compartments by two diameters at right angles. The four compartments are to be coloured:

Upper	Citrine	for the airy part of earth.
Right	Olive Green	for the watery part of earth.
Left	Russet Brown	for the fiery part earth.
Lower	Black	for the earthy part of earth.

The divine and angelic names should be written in black within the white border, each name followed by their sigil taken from the rose cross. Crosses may be placed after each sigil. The motto of the adept is to be added.

The pentacle should be the same on both sides and should be held in the hand with the citrine part uppermost, unless there is some special reason for using one or other of the compartments.

The pentacle must be consecrated by the appropriate ceremony.

It is to be used in all workings of the nature of earth, and under the presidency of HEH and of the Pentacle of the Tarot.

Addendum

When used in conjunction with other elemental weapons the pentacle is always held around the rim. In solo works with the pentacle, pick out what elemental segment the ceremony relates to. Another quick method of identification using the Sephirotic method of identification. Select the kabbalistic Sephiroth that governs the workings, such as:

Airy part of earth	Chesed, Tiphareth and Geburah.
Watery part of earth	Chesed, Tiphareth and Netzach.
Fiery part of earth	Geburah, Hod and Yesod.
Earthy part of earth	elemental.

Once the element the working requires is selected, the pentacle is held with that segment upright. For example, when doing a working regarding love and emotion, the watery part of the earth section would be held upright. This relates to Chesed, Tiphareth and Netzach. By using the Middle Pillar, all or one of these Sephiroth can be activated in one's own aura, then the pentacle. When doing a working for love, most people would consider that the cup be used, but this mainly relates to spiritual love. Love in human terms is the pentacle for it relates directly with the physical body and body chemistry. The pentacle can be used in invocations such as pentagram or hexagram but it is better used conjunction with sword; the pentacle is a blunt weapon and must be used to consolidate once the main invocation has taken place.

The pentacle is useful in works of evocation, for it is able to ground other elemental weapons. It is also helpful in alchemical workings and for workings of a materialistic nature. In cases of illness the and hold fast the spirit, but in these instances it is still used with the pentacle, when placed alongside a sick person helps the aura and gives it additional strength. Though not as long lasting as a talisman, it is quicker acting.

Consecration of the Four Implements[221]

1. The adept is to be robed in white, wear his white sash, and rose cross.
2. Have on hand the lotus wand, magic sword and prepare chamber as for sword.
3. All four weapons should be present at once, on the altar, with all four symbols of the elements.
4. Lay the fire wand near the lamp, The cup near the water, the dagger near the incense and the pentacle near the salt.
5. Each elemental weapon must be consecrated at a time (24min) when the Tattva of the element concerned is in course.
6. The consecration of each weapon is a separate ceremony although they may be done successively.[222] The opening and closing ceremony will suffice for one or all, however and need not be repeated if all are consecrated on one occasion.
7. The Tattva period is found in practice to suffice for the special portion of the ceremony.[223]
8. Prepare each element by invocation to the King and Six Seniors from the elemental Tablets according to instructions laid down in the 'Concourse of Forces' book.
9. After consecration, each implement is to be wrapped up either in white silk or in silk of the colour proper to the element.

---

[221] In the Llewellyn publication of Regardie's Golden Dawn rituals, this section usually contained the Stella Matutina version of the consecration of the elemental weapons, which many have considered far superior to the Golden Dawn notes given below. At Whare Ra, it was done the Golden Dawn way, and not the elaborate Stella Matutina ritual published by Regardie. While this ritual is a good one it is up to the operator as to how effective it is. Taylor used a simple ritual and his Implements are the most powerful I have felt, where some done by the elaborate Stella Matutina ritual are barely 'warm'. It all depends on the operator's abilities. Over the years I have come to the conclusion that for consecration rituals of the elemental weapons, that Adepts should write their own.

[222] I do not agree, as the consecration of each weapon should be timed astrologically. The use of the Tattvas is too slap dash. The Golden Dawn paper on the planetary angels is completely ignored here.

[223] The Golden Dawn used a special Tattva Wheel to find what Tattva governed what portion of the day.

CIRCLE OF PROTECTION

Within the Golden Dawn, the circle of protection that was the most frequently taught was taken from the paper 'Polygons and Polygrams'. Since we have given an example that incorporated these figures from the Sephirah of Hod (Mercury) it would be a good idea to explain the principles behind the construction of this figure.

The circle of Hod is made up of three geometrical figures. One of these figures is an octagon while the next two are two versions of the octagram.

Octagon

First version - reflected from every second point. Mathers says of this:

> The octangle naturally represents the power of the ogdoad, and the octagon showeth the ogdoad operating in nature by the dispersal of the rays of the elements in their dual aspect under the presidency of the eight letters of the name YHVHADNI. The numbers of degrees of the Great circle cut off between its angles is 45; forming the astrological weak semi-square aspect, evil in nature and operation.

If this figure represents evil, then why use it as part of a circle of protection? Mathers clearly relates this figure with the astrological semi-square and a closer study of this shows that YHVH relates to the four fixed signs (and four elements) of the zodiac circle. The semi-Square is considered negative due to its stubbornness and refusal to adapt[224]. There a strength of purpose that can be tapped for our main purpose, to protect anything negative from attacking. The semi-square can direct and channel its stubbornness to a constructive purpose because of the letters of the holy name ADNI influences it. At each point of 45 degrees the letters of the Holy name YHVHADNI also reinforce the ogdoad to a more spiritual purpose.

---

[224] Rael and Rudhyar in their book *Astrological Aspects*, consider the Semi-Square as a level of consciousness and activity that must integrate into the wholeness of the situation to become a reality. This concept, when reduced to its basic fundamentalism is in line with the theory that a Semi-Square is of no real use until it integrates with a fuller pattern that can give it a more focused direction.

Octagon

Second version - reflected from every third Point.

Mathers goes on to say:

> The octagram... yieldeth eight triangles at the apices thereof;
> representing the triad operating in each element in its dual form,
> i.e. of positive and negative, under the powers of the name YHVH
> ADNI but as it is written bound together YAHDVNHY. It is not so
> consonant with the nature of Mercury as the next form, and it is
> composed of two squares united within a circle.

In astrological terms this represents two grand squares, a powerful
symbol when shown on an astrological chart. It not only shows
difficulty (because of focusing on many different levels at once)
but also shows a tremendous source of strength. Here the need is
for spirit and matter to co-exist on more than one level and this is
difficult to control. Once it is controlled on the etheric, the astral
level may waver so this is a powerful symbol. It is best suited
when integrated with the previous symbol which makes it less
volatile and more focused. A combination of the two octagrams
show a willingness to merge and harmonise for each other's sake.
On their on this could not be correctly achieved.

Octagram - Third form - reflected from every forth point.
Quoting Mathers again:

> This Octagram is the Star of Mercury, and is especially applicable
> to his nature. It is a further potent symbol, representing the binding
> together of the concentrated positive and negative forces of the
> elements under the name of YHVH ADNI and forget not that ADNI
> is the key of YHVH.

What Mathers is saying is that this symbol is the crowning point
and dominates the other two previous symbols by letting them
integrate into it. The point of fusion is the Holy name, for ADNI is
a personalisation of YHVH. It is the word needed before any
form of integration can occur.

The methodology of forming a circle from the *Key of Solomon
the King* manuscript was adapted by many Golden Dawn members.
This concept is interesting for it shows the use of additional
implements in the construction of the circle, many of

which are shown in the *Key of Solomon* with no indication as to their use. The following quotes from the Mathers translation of *Key of Solomon* was passed to Golden Dawn and members of the Stella Matutina to study:

First version:

> Take thou the knife, the sickle, or the sword of magical art consecrated after the manner and order which we shall deliver unto thee in the Second Book. With this knife or with the sickle of art thou shalt describe, beyond the inner circle which thou shalt have already formed, a second circle, encompassing the other at the distance of one foot therefrom and having the same centre[225]. Within this space of a foot in breadth the first and second circumferential[226] line, thou shalt trace towards the four quarters of the earth[227], the sacred and venerable symbols of the holy letters Tau[228]. And between the first and second circle[229], which thou shalt thyself have drawn with the instrument of magical art, thou shalt make four hexagonal pentacles[230] and between these thou shalt write four terrible and tremendous names of God, Viz. ;-
>
> Between the East and the South, the supreme name YHVH, Tetragrammaton:-
>
> Between the South and the West, the essential Tetragrammatic name AHIH, Eheieh.
>
> Between the West and the North, the name of the Power ALIVN, Elion:-
>
> And between the North and the East, the great name ALH, Eloah:-
>
> Which names are of supreme importance in the list of the Sephiroth, and their sovereign equivalents.'
>
> At the West, IH, Yah;
>
> At the South, AGLA, Agla:
>
> At North ADNI, Adonai.
>
> Between the two squares, the name Tetragrammaton is to be written in the same way as is shown in the diagram.

---

[225]   i.e. two circles between three circumferential lines. M.Mathers.

[226]   i.e. within the first circle. M.Mathers

[227]   i.e. the four Cardinal points of the compass. M.Mathers.

[228]   The Letter tau represents the cross, and in 10862 Add.Mss. in the drawing of the circle, the Hebrew letter is replaced by the cross; and in 1307 Sloane Mss. by the 'T' or Tau-cross (PZ)

[229]   i.e. the Outer circle, bounded by the second and third circumferential lines. M.Mathers

While constructing the circle, the Master should recite the following Psalms:ii.; liv,; cxiii., lxvii.; lxviii. to be drawn with the knife or consecrated instrument of art. And within these four circles thou must write these four names of God the Most Holy One, in this order:-

At the East, Al, EL;

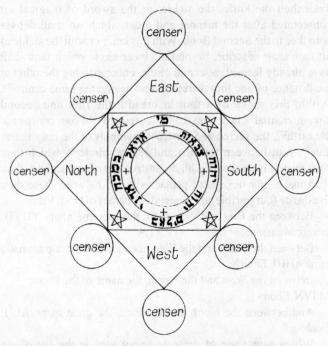

The use of the Psalms is important for they were actually used as magical writings. An examination of each Psalm helps explains their use. Take for example Psalm 2. The text tells us, in verses one to four, that all the different levels of spirits created are all subjected to their maker YHVH. Verse five shows that his power will be directed against them if he is displeased. Verse six implies that the place for the circle is analogous with a holy place. Verses seven to eight take this further, and tells us that the YHVH gives the operator the power to control the spirits. Verse nine tells us to

---

230   10862 Add. Mss. is the only copy which uses the word 'hexagonal', but the others show four hexagrams in the drawing; in the drawing, however, 10862 gives the hexagrams formed by various differing interlacements of two triangles, as shown figure two (the diagram of the circle below P.Z.) M.Mathers.

break the spirit's will with a rod of iron, much like the influence of the sword and wand of the Magus. Verses 10-12 are part of a conjuration. There are a number of methods where words of power are taken from the Temurah of these verses. The other Psalms cited go further than the one above it. Their combined usage produces a cone of power that is imprinted in the Etheric energy of the construction of the circle.

The use of the Psalms is important for they were actually used as magical writings. An examination of each Psalm helps explains their use. Take for example Psalm 2. The text tells us, in verses one to four, that all the different levels of spirits created are all subjected to their maker YHVH. Verse five shows that his power will be directed against them if he is displeased. Verse six implies that the place for the circle is analogous with a holy place. Verses seven to eight take this further, and tells us that the YHVH gives the operator the power to control the spirits. Verse nine tells us to break the spirit's will with a rod of iron, much like the influence of the sword and wand of the Magus. Verses 10-12 are part of a conjuration.

There are a number of methods where words of power are taken from the Temurah of these verses. The other Psalms cited go further than the one above it. Their combined usage produces a cone of power that is imprinted in the Etheric energy of the construction of the circle.

Second version:[231]

> Having chosen a place for preparing and constructing the circle, and all things necessary being prepared for the perfection of the operations, take thou the sickle or scimitar of the art, and stick it into the centre of the place where the circle is to be made; than take a cord of nine feet in length, fasten one end thereof unto the sickle with the other end trace out the circumference of the circle, which may be marked either with sword or with the knife with black hilt. Then within the circle mark out four regions, namely towards the, East, West, South and North, wherein place symbols; and beyond the limits of this circle describe with the consecrated knife or sword another circle, but leaving an open space towards the North

---

[231] Taken from Additional Mss 10862.

whereby instrument, yet leaving therein an open space for entrance and egress corresponding to the open space left in any other. Beyond this again make another circle at another foot distance, and beyond these two circles, which are beyond the circle of art yet upon the same centre, thou shalt describe pentagrams with the Symbols and names of the Creator therein so that they may surround the circle already described. Without these circles shalt thou circumscribe a square, and beyond that another square, so that the angles of the former may touch the centres of the sides of the latter, and that the angles of the latter may stretch towards the four quarters of the Universe, East, West, North and South; and at the four Angles of each square, and touching them, thou shalt describe lesser circles wherein let there be placed standing censers with lighted charcoal and sweet odours....

Both examples of the circles from the *Key of Solomon* manuscripts can be utilised effectively and they were favourites of the adepts of the Golden Dawn.

Those who wish to use the Enochian Tablets they were placed outside the circle in their usual positions. Their presence added power to the ritual and also additional protection. Regardie, in his brilliant *Tree of Life*, said he thought the circle represented the enclosed sphere of the magician - the holy name being equated with the positive aspects of the mind. But I also equate the circle with a certain vibrational level of the subtle bodies. The magician attunes himself to each of these layers and reinforces them. To do this he must produce a state of temporary alignment of the subtle body. During this period he has access to a great deal of power. Regardie said that one should build up a cone of power in the circle by tracing it over many days.

The first trace relates to the etheric power and subsequent tracings of the circle should be attributed to the astral and mental planes. The other three planes above this one are not in our sphere of competence to control.

THE TRIANGLE

The use of the magic triangle is to call the spirit into the sphere of operation, but outside the circle. The triangle becomes a portal or trapped, confined space, where the spirit exists and communicate.

The magic triangle faces towards the relevant planet and a knowledge of where a planet's location is essential. In Bennett's 'Ritual for the Evocation of the spirit of Mercury', a circle was drawn around the triangle. This is to give additional protection if the trapped force breaks out of the triangle. If this happens then the circle traps the entity's energies forcing them to spiral.

There are limitless types of triangles (and circles for that matter) to trap a spirit for the evocation. One variation I have used with success is the following;

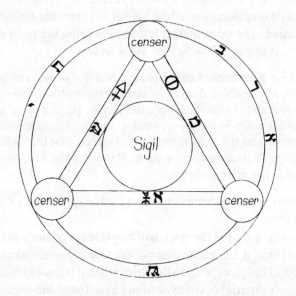

In the outer rim of the circle which surrounds the triangle the Hebrew letters of the words BRASHITh are written. These are the first letters of the Bible and stand for GENESIS - a beginning. The Golden Dawn interpreted this word to mean:

B   This is the magical history
R   Of the dawning of the Light.
A   Begun are the whirling motions;
Sh   Formulated is the primal fire;
Y   Proclaimed is the reign of the Gods of Light
Th   At the threshold of the infinite worlds!

This formulae was adapted to the Z3 document which is called the 'Formulae of the Enterer' where the Magus identified with THOTH to bring the power through.

The black background is like the lamen of the Hiereus and stands for the darkness and the alchemical state of putrefaction with the white triangle trapping and focusing the power. The white triangle is also binding factor and the symbols of sulphur, salt and mercury are the basic building blocks of life in any kingdom. These focus the spirit and give it body and substance and maintain it in the triangle. The three mother letters of Aleph, Mem and Shin are the three main manifestations of the Sepher Yetzirah, the Hebrew book of Creation. The three mother letters help bring the spirit through and give it impetus. The Sepher Yetzirah says:

> ...These three mothers he did produce and design, and combined them; and he sealed them as the three mothers in the Universe, in the year and in Man- both male and female. He caused the letter Aleph to reign in air and crowned it, and combining it with the others he sealed it, as air in the world...He caused the letter Mem to reign in the water and crowned it...He caused the letter Shin to reign in fire, and crowned it...

All of this produces a mini-universe for the spirit being evoked to exist within.

Usually, a sigil of the spirit will be placed in triangle in order to trap and bind it. On each corner of the triangle some adepts place a brazier. This gives body to the spirit when it is visibly appearing. In my own experiences of evocation I have found the energy in the triangle does not relate to that of a circle, in many respects it is the exact opposite. The circle of protection has energy flowing from the centre outwards while the Triangle focuses inwards. As one adept said it is like a localised and controlled black hole.

Magic Censer

The censer brings the use of aromatics into magic. It will come in any shape or size and many adepts use religious ones, such as those used in the Catholic Church.

The censer can be large and immobile or small with a chain attached so that it can be swung or moved around the room. In ritual, the censer has a dual role for any ingredient placed can be seen as a sacrifice. Sometimes small amounts or drops of blood are placed in the censer. This raises the level of etheric density around the circle to a high degree and controls the energy of the circle. When the fire of the censer is lit while reciting Psalms cli; cii; cvii.

Any incense used in the censer must also be consecrated. It is up to the adept to decide what incense to use. Crowley's 777, the works of the late Scott Cunningham, and *Herbs in Magic and Alchemy* by Chris Zalewski will help.

Sign	Holy name	Letter	Tribe	Angel	Colour
Aries	YHVH	Heh	Gad	Melchidael	Red
Taurus	YHHV	Vau	Ephraim	Asmodel	Red-Orange
Gemini	YVHH	Zain	Manasseh	Ambriel	Orange
Cancer	HVHY	Cheth	Issachar	Muriel	Amber
Leo	HVYH	Teth	Judah	Verchiel	Lemon-Yellow
Virgo	HHVY	Yod	Naphthali	Hamaliel	Yellow-Green
Libra	VHYH	Lamed	Asshur	Zuriel	Emerald
Scorpio	VHHY	Nun	Dan	Barchiel	Green-Blue
Sagit.	VYHH	Samech	Benjamin	Advachiel	Blue
Capricorn	HYHV	Ayin	Zebulun	Hanael	Indigo
Aquarius	HYVH	Tzaddai	Reuben	Cambriel	Violet
Pisces	HHYV	Qoph	Simeon	Amnitzel	Crimson

BOOK TWO

hEh
TALISMANS

Chapter 6

Talismans of the Golden Dawn

Talismans come in all shapes and sizes, ranging from flat multicoloured figures on paper or wood to rough cut wax dolls. The word *talisman*,[1] has its roots in the Arabic *talsam* which means a magical figure and the Greek *telesma* which is an incantation or invocation. Where possible, the Golden Dawn used more complex hermetic talismans where kabbalistic symbols rubbed shoulders with other traditional and obscure techniques from Christian magical texts.

Golden Dawn members were widely read. They copied and distributed a number of old magical texts that included detailed talismans. Most popular was the *Key of Solomon* manuscripts already mentioned in the first part of this book. However one of the most feared systems of talismanic symbols were drawn from the book *Sacred Magic of Abramelin the Mage*, which were translated and edited by Mathers. At the Whare Ra temple, this book was looked upon with awe and adepts were advised to stay clear of it. Crowley took a similar viewpoint and kept his edition under lock and key. At the Thoth-Hermes temple we experimented with both seals from the *Key of Solomon* and *Abramelin* and have managed to amalgamate them. The only difficulty comes during consecration, as you effectively have to draw together two different magical systems. In some instances, one could end up using an angelic and a demonic force joined together to achieve the same goal.

---

[1] I draw no distinction between an amulet and talisman. The word amulet comes from the French word *amulette* and the Spanish word *amuletum*, both mean *charm*. Pliny says that an amulet is an object of protection, which I disagree with. The Latin derivative of word amulet was first coined after the Greek and Arabic roots of the word talisman.

We came to the conclusion that a force or energy form that existed outside our current solar system was needed to achieve this. After some trial and error, we used the first Enochian call with remarkable success.

Golden Dawn adepts worked with magic squares (or kamea) of the planets which were first published by Henry Cornelius Agrippa of Nettesheim (1486-1535) in 1531. The origins of these magic squares is obscure. Some think Agrippa's mentor, Abbot Johannes Trithemius (1462-1516), may have invented the technique. However there is some evidence to suggest that if Agrippa learnt it from Trithemius, then the Abbot must have been using an Arabic source. A careful study of these squares and sigils shows that a number of them copied by the Golden Dawn contained a few errors which were mostly compounded mistakes taken from the originals. I have mentioned the structure of these magical squares in my previous books.

Another method of sigil construction is through the rose cross which is the lamen of the Adeptus Minor. The Golden Dawn employed a method where they created an artificial elemental come talisman by certain association to the letters of the Hebrew alphabet.

Another unique Golden Dawn method of talisman use featured the lamen of the Theoricus Adeptus Minor grade. The adepti constructed figures of the godforms Horus, Isis, Aroueris and Nephthys which were worn as a lamen during any business in the Theoricus Adeptus Minor grade. Each of these godforms governed a particular temple function, for example Horus ruled over discord and planning. The adepts were told to use these lamen when:

> "...the member is question is exercising his or her authority or judgement in the matter pertaining to the god or goddess, let him or her, keeping the mind as pure as possible, assume the colossal form of the god or goddess, as taught in the Ritual Z and vibrate its name.
>
> Let him or her judge the question as detached form his ordinary personality. To this end let him be sure to formulate himself as the figure of the god as colossal and not simply as an ordinary size figure... .These symbols are given to us so that you may have greater wisdom and power in the resolution of difficult matters, than the symbols of the theoricus grade could give you."

These lamen, acting as a focus were used as a springboard for astral work. They were unconsecrated, but blessed with holy water and allowed to develop their own power through frequent use.

When impregnating a talisman with the desired force there were many ways to achieve the desired effect and many different levels to choose from; a point many tend to ignore. During a ritual these various levels of energy should be recognised by an adept and be acted upon. Calling upon an angelic or archangelic name does not automatically give access to the august being itself, nor does it help us reach the spiritual state we are targeting. Angels work in a hierarchy of power and like working with a bureaucracy, it is important that you speak to the right chief in the right department. In the Golden Dawn and its later off shoots, there was a real interest in the more obscure names of gods and angels. These lesser names caused a few problems, as many were uncertain of these beings' position in the divine hierarchy.

During an invocation rite within the Golden Dawn, the rule was that the highest names were always called first, then if the occasion required it, the lesser names afterwards. In my view there is a little too much influence on the minor names in modern talismanic work and this results in a loss of power.

Common-sense dictates that the adept should be aware of the power around the ritual and be aware on what exactly he or she is invoking, and whether the invocation is successful or not. An adept can only be aware of this by painful experience.

When I was training under Taylor in the late 1970's, I had made what I considered to be a perfect Jupiter talisman and written an elaborate ritual to consecrate it. While Taylor had approved of the ritual, which was also performed without any errors, he considered the talisman was not powerful enough to have a significant effect. Some months later and two fruitless rituals later, Taylor finally approved the talisman.

"What were the differences between the three rituals?" he asked me.

After thinking about it, I realised that it was not until the second time that I performed the ritual that I started to feel the different power levels involved in creating the talisman. By the third time I had worked out how to harness those energies properly.

Testing a talisman is important, for it is not simply a matter of placing one's hand over it and feeling the magnetic energy. It must be correctly ascertained exactly how powerful it is.

I have adopted a method used in radionic analysis in which the pendulum (or the ring and disk as it is called in the Golden Dawn) plays an important part. Place a sheet of paper with the numbers 0-100, in sets of ten, in a half circle with a series of lines dividing each portion starting from a central point underneath. Put the talisman on the bottom of the paper. Ask the question, 'What percentage of power is the talisman charged to?' The pendulum will then either stay at 100 — which is the best you can hope for, or deviate to a lesser degree.

This method can be used by anyone to test a talisman and I feel should be employed by those giving instruction to others. If the talisman is charged below 50 percent then the ritual should be repeated. The average though seems to be 80-85 percent. Anyone who tests a talisman this way should be experienced with the pendulum, as they take some getting used to. If you wish to get real picky, you can test the power of each name on the talisman by simply using a pencil[2] to point to the name required and it will tell you (if there is more than one name) if the invocations were successful or not.

The following papers on talismans are taken from the Golden Dawn corpus of material and I have taken the liberty of adding additional footnotes that may perhaps amplify certain obscure comments made by the various authors.

---

[2] The pencil is held in one hand and the pendulum in the other. This method is effective dowsing with maps or locating missing items.

TALISMANS AND FLASHING TABLETS[3]
By MacGregor Mathers

A talisman is a magical figure charged with the force that it is intended to represent. In the construction of a talisman, care should be taken to make it, as far as possible, so as to represent the universal forces that it should be in exact harmony with those you wish to attract, and the more exact the symbolism, the more easier it is to attract the force - other things coinciding, such as consecration at the right time.

A *symbol* should be correct in its symbolism, but it is not necessarily the same as a talisman.

A *flashing tablet* is one made in the complementary colours. A flashing colour, then, is the complementary colour which, if joined to the original, enables it to attract, to a certain extent, the akasic current from the atmosphere, and to a certain extent from yourself, thus forming a vortex which can attract its flashing light, from the atmosphere[4].

Colour	Complementary[5]
White	Black or Grey
Red	Green
Blue	Orange

---

[3] This is Flying Roll 14, by Mathers.

[4] If a talisman is made correctly (astrologically speaking) and it has the right symbolism and colour, it attracts the pulse of the time of its creation and that is a powerful magnetic charge. Although it is weaker than a consecration it still have some energy. Complementary colours act as a doorway, for a force to flow through and empower the talisman. The symbol on the talisman is a restrictive force and to prevent just the energy leaking. I have found that by using colour for healing in radionics that colours can be used on almost any level, and not just the astral. Complementary colours bring forces attract forces to the talisman from deeper spiritual or etheric levels. By using the complementary, this prevents more powerful forces coming through and overpowering the talisman without the safeguards.

[5] By studying the *Minutum Mundum*, one will see which paths and Sepheroth are repelling, or opposite, to each other, by cross referencing them with the complementary colour formula. Some colours listed as complementary in Mathers' paper are a little inaccurate. The simplest way to discover a complementary colour is to gaze at the colour with the vision slightly out of focus for a few minutes. The complementary colour will appear as a hue around the one you are staring at.

Yellow	Violet
Olive	Red-Orange
Blue-Green	Russet
Violet	Citrine
Reddish-Orange	Green-Blue
Deep Amber	Indigo
Lemon Yellow	Red Violet
Yellow Green	Crimson

The other complementaries of mixed colours can be found by using this scale.

Coming now to the nature and method of formation of the talisman, firstly is not always just and right to form a talisman with the idea of completely changing the current of another person's karma. In any case you could only do this in a certain sense. It will be remembered that in the words of the Christ, which preceded his cures, were 'Thy sins be forgiven thee,' which meant that the karmic action was exhausted. Only an adept who is of the nature of God can have the power, even if he has the right, to take upon himself the karma of another. That is to say, that if you endeavour to change completely (I am not now speaking of adapting and making the best of a person's karma) the life current, you must be of so great a force that you can take this karma from them by right of divine power to which you have attained, in which case you will only do it in so far as it does not hinder their spiritual development.

If, however, this is attempted on a lower plane, it will usually be found that what you are endeavouring to bring about is in direct opposition to the karma of the person concerned. It will not work the required effect and will probably bring a current of exhaustion and trouble on yourself. These remarks only apply to an attempted radical change in the karma of another, which is a thing you have nor right to do until you have attained the highest adeptship.

The formation or adaptation of talismans in ordinary matters should be employed with great discernment. What may assist in material things is often a hindrance spiritually, seeing that for a force to work, it must attract elemental forces of the proper description, which may thus, to an extent, endanger your spiritual nature. Also, in making a talisman for a person, you must endeavour to isolate yourself entirely from him. You must banish from your mind any feeling of love or hate, irritation, for all these feelings operate against your power. It is but rarely that a talisman for the love of a person is a right and justifiable thing to construct[6]. Pure love links us to the nature of the gods. There is perfect love between between the angels and the gods because there is perfect harmony among them, but that is not the lower and earthly love. Thus a talisman made for terrestrial love would be sealed with the impress of your own weakness, and even if successful, would react on you in other ways. The only way in which real power can be gained, is by transcending the material plane and trying to link your self to the Divine and Higher Soul. That is why trouble is so great an initiator, because trouble brings you nearer spiritual things when material things fail. Therefore a talisman, a rule, is better made for one in whom you have not interest.

In the work of actual consecration, it is always a good thing to purify the room and use the banishing ritual of the pentagram. All these are aids, which the adept, when sufficiently advanced, will know when to use and when not to do so. It is better, if possible, to finish a talisman at one sitting, because it has begun under certain conditions and it may be difficult to put yourself in the same frame of mind at another time.

Another point that beginners are apt to run away with, is that talismans can be made wholesale. Suppose a dozen talismans were made to do good to as many different people, a ray from yourself must charge each talisman. You have sent out a sort of spiral from your aura, which goes on to the talisman and attracts a like force from the atmosphere, that is if you have learned to excite the force in yourself at the moment of consecration. So that, in the case supposed, you would have a dozen links connecting with you, like so many wires in a telegraph office, and when ever the force which any of these talismans was designed to combat becomes too strong for the force centred therein, there is an instantaneous communication with you, so that the loss of force to which you

---

[6] I disagree. I cannot imagine anyone going through the complicated process of making a talisman for someone they did not like. If one loves someone, then that emotional energy could be channelled into the talisman giving it more power. A lot depends on whether one can put enough energy into the talisman and every little bit helps. I have found good feelings work for the talisman's recipient.

would be continually liable might be such as to deplete you of vitality and cause you to faint.[7]

In cases where talismans and symbols have done their work, they should be carefully decharged, then destroyed. If this is not done, and you take a symbol, say of water, still charged and throw away later. Also, if you throw away a still charged talisman, thus it in the fire to get rid of it you are inflicting intense torment on the elemental you have attracted and it will react on you sooner or desecrating it, it will become the property of other things, which, through it, will be enabled to get at you. It is for these reasons that the talisman should be de-charged with the pentagram and hexagram according as it partakes of the planetary or zodiacal nature, and these remarks apply equally to flashing tablets. If a talisman is given to a person who goes away, and does not return it, you can render it inoperative by invoking it astrally and decharging it with great care and force.[8]

Any flashing tablet of two colours should be as nearly balanced in proportion of the extent of colour as possible, the ground one colour, and the charge another. There is a mode in which three colours can be used in a planetary talisman. This is done by placing the seven colours on the heptagram, and drawing two lines to the point exactly opposite, which will thus yield two flashing colours. Thus properly drawn, will give the effect of a flashing light playing on the symbol, partly visible physically and partly clairvoyantly, i.e., if properly charged. An advanced adept should properly charge his tablet to a certain extent as he constructs it.

---

[7] Energy is directed from your subtle bodies, and then through a certain chakra or combination of chakras, depending on the type of talisman. While it is true that a link is formed, the result is not quite like Mathers' description. I disagree with his following comments — using Radionics I have sent vital force to a person, in an object or medicine, to heal them and my vital force is undepleted. It depends entirely on your makeup and, if it does, there gem elixirs and flower essences to fix the problem.

[8] A talisman is not something that takes energy from someone and uses it to combat anything negative. The talisman actually takes part of the godform or force invoked and uses its force to combat anything negative. Our link with the talisman is to *control that force* invoked. I know of one where a health talisman was made and it worked for more than twenty years. When the talisman's creator died, the illness returned. The creator's subtle bodies did not enforce the control and direction after his death, and the force withdrew its protective energy.

A flashing tablet should be made, charged and consecrated[9], and then each morning the adeptus should sit before it and clairvoyance, endeavouring to go through to it to the plane it represents, and then to invoke the power and ask for strength to accomplish the matter desired, which will be granted if it were a lawful and laudable operation.[10] But a talisman for harmony of an idea say, could well be represented by the Tiphareth of Venus, a beautiful yellow-green.[11]

The lion kerub of Venus would represent spiritual fire and thus symbolises the inspiration of the poet, the colour being soft and a beautiful pearl grey, and the charges should be white. The watery part of Venus would reflect the reflective faculty and answer to spiritual beauty, colour a bluish-green. The vault contains a perfect scale of talismans of every description of planet (sign, element, alchemical and kerubic symbol) and shows how a planetary man will look at everything according to the colour of his aura, due to the planet under which he is born. The real adept comes forth from the sides to the centre. He is no longer under the dominion of the stars.[12]

Having made a magical talisman, you should use some form of charging and consecrating it, which is suitable to the operation. There are certain words and letters that are to be invoked at the charging of a tablet, the letters governing the sign under which the operation falls, together with the planet associated therewith (if a planetary talisman). Thus in elemental operations, you take the letters of the appropriate zodiacal triplicity, adding AL thereto, thus forming an angelic name which is the expression of the force'. Hebrew

---

[9] The type of consecrating here is very much in line with the 'blessing' of Christian doctrine. This is done by doing the kabbalistic cross over the flashing tablet and sprinkling it with holy water. It is not usually done with full ceremony.

[10] Golden Dawn adepts often disagree about the difference between flashing tablets and talismans. Taylor told me that a talisman traps a force while a flashing tablet attracts an empathy with the energy — drawing it to a particular location. Flashing tablets tune an individual directly to the plane they or wish to work. They are more flexible than a talisman. Flashing tablets and figures are the primal influence of Enochian chess, giving its powerful effect. I have known people with no magical inclination 'trip out' while playing Enochian chess merely because of the manipulation and effect of the flashing colours of the Enochian chess pieces and boards. The magical weapons used by the adepti in ritual become flashing implements because of their colours as do the squares in the Vault of the Adepts.

names as a rule, represent the operation of certain general forces while the names on the Enochian angelic tablets represent a species of more particular ideas. Both classes of names should be used in these operations.

After repairing the room in the way laid down for the consecration of lesser magical implements, supposing this to be an elemental talisman, first formulate towards the four quarters the supreme ritual of the pentagram as taught. Then invoke the divine names, turning towards the quarter of the element. Let the adeptus then, being seated or standing before the tablet, and looking at the requisite direction of the force which he wishes to invoke, take several deep inspirations, close the eyes, and holding the breath, mentally pronounce the forces of the letters invoked. Let this be done several times, as if you have breathed upon the tablet, pronouncing them in a vibratory manner. Then, rising, make the sign of the rose and cross over the tablet, and repeating the requisite formula, first in your heart, which answers to Tiphareth. (Having first, as already said, ascended to your Kether, you should endeavour to bring down the White Brilliance into your heart, prior to centring your consciousness there.) Then formulate the letters of the name required in your heart, in white, and feel them written there. Be sure to formulate the letters in brilliant white light, not merely in dull whiteness as the colour of the Apas tattva.

> For Fire, put Shin first, then the three fiery signs, then AL. So far for elementary ones. For planetary ones you may add AL to the planet and its houses, the letters of them; and the planet and triplicity, use the hexagram made six times. For zodiacal ones add AL to the letters of the sign and use the pentagram five times. When you use the three letters of the three signs of a triplicity, for an elemental working, you should put as the initial letter of the sign principally invoked as most useful to you -- (Wynn Westcott)

---

[11] The colour of the individual's aura, (which changes constantly) will match the flashing colours empathise with it. At Whare Ra this was interpreted in the light of the Doctrine of the Seven Rays, a view favoured by Mrs. Felkin. The Doctrine of the Seven Rays was a Theosophical teaching that many in the Golden Dawn adapted.

[12] Edgar Cayce said that a person is born through the rays of influence of one or more planets. A quick method to work out which planet this is to take the nearest to the mid-heaven — ignoring the Sun and Moon.

Emitting the breath, slowly pronounce the letters so that the sound
vibrates within you, and imagine that the breath, while quitting the
body, swells you so as to fill up space. Pronounce the name as if
you were vibrating it through the whole universe, and as if it did
not stop until it reached the further limits... (M.Mathers)

In vibrating the divine names, the operator should first of all rise as
high as possible towards the idea of the divine white brilliance in
Kether, keeping the mind raised to the plane of loftiest aspiration.
Unless this is done, it is dangerous to vibrate only with the astral
forces, because the vibration attracts a certain force to the operator,
and the nature of the force attracted rests largely on the condition
of mind in which the operator is in.

The ordinary mode of vibrating is as follows: Take a deep full
breath and concentrate your consciousness and describe around
the talisman, a circle, with the appropriate magical implement, and
then make the invoking pentagrams five times over it, as if the
pentagram stood upright upon it, repeating the letters of the triplicity
involved with AL then solemnly read any invocation required, making
the proper sigils from the rose as you pronounce the names.

The first operation is to initiate a whirl from yourself. The
second, to attract the force in the atmosphere into the vortex you
have formed. Then read the elemental prayer as in the rituals, and
close with the signs of the circle and the cross after performing the
necessary banishing. Be careful, however, not to banish over the
newly consecrated talisman, as that would simply decharge it again
and render it useless. Before any banishing, you should wrap the
charged talisman in clean white silk or linen.

FLASHING SOUNDS[13]

Chromatic Scales[14]

Aries	C[15]	Red
Taurus	c#	Red Orange
Gemini	D	Orange
Cancer	D#	Amber
Leo	E	Yellow
Virgo	F	Green Yellow
Libra	F#	Green
Scorpio	G	Blue-Green
Sagittarius	G#	Blue
Capricorn	A	Indigo
Aquarius	A#	Violet
Pisces	B	Magenta

Mother Letters		Sound	Flash
Shin C	Red	F#	Green
Aleph E	Yellow	A#	Violet
Mem G#	Blue	D	Orange

Note to Planets and their Flashing Opposites

Mars	C	Red	Venus	F#	Green
Sun	D	Orange	Moon	G#	Blue
Mercury	E	Yellow	Jupiter	A#	Violet

Bennett had the following note: 'Try constructing a wand on this principle, a steel tube of one sound resonance and its flashing sound, produced by a fine steel wire string...[16]

---

[13] The following table and contents are taken from Alan Bennett's notebook.

[14] " I have left the colours as Bennett has written them, but I would refer the readers to the *Kabbalah of the Golden Dawn* where more detail colour descriptions are given, and which can be applied to the colour scale of the King (Pages 76—77).

[15] The procedure is simple and is explained in the previous section only instead of colour sound is used.

[16] I would suggest a clear quartz crystal shaped in the Tree of Life form to head the top of the wand.

SIGILS OF THE ROSE[17]
by MacGregor Mathers

In the opening ceremony of the grade of 5=6 adeptus minor, the complete symbol of the rose and cross is called the 'key of sigils and of rituals', and it is further said that it represents the forces of the 22 letters in nature, as divided into a three, seven and a twelve.

The inner three petals of the rose symbolise active elements of air, fire and water, operating in the Earth, which is as it were the recipient of them, their container and ground of operation. They are coloured, as are all the other petals according to the hues of the rainbow in the masculine (positive) scale. The seven next petals answer to the letters of the seven planets and the twelve outer to the twelve signs of the Zodiac.

The Rose of the Rose Cross

---

[17] This is a unique method of obtaining a sigil that originated within the Golden Dawn. Drawing this sigil while wearing the rose cross produces a link between you, the entity invoked or evoked and the power of the rose cross — the symbol of the second order of the power of the rose cross — the symbol of the second order of the Golden Dawn. A vital piece of invocation that is often neglected when using this sigil is to invoke by the power of the R.R.et A.C. For this will bring the power through the rose cross and subtly control the entity. Jack Taylor insisted that one identify and invoke the power of the order as a type of command. When sigil is drawn from the rose it is then under the control and power of the rose, for it exists through that framework. The order has a vast power base and should be used to tap into.

Now if thou wilt trace the sigil of any word or name either in the air, or written upon paper, thou shalt commence with a circle at the point of the initial letter of the rose, and draw with thy magical weapon, a line from this circle unto the place of the next letter of the name. Continue this, until thou hast finished the word that the letters compose. If two letters of the same sort, such as two Beths or Gimels, come together, thou shalt represent the same by a crook or wave in the line at that point. And if there be a letter, as Resh in Metatron, through which a line passeth to another letter and which yet formeth part of the name, thou shalt make a noose in the line at the point to make the same. If thou art drawing the sigil thou mayest work in the respective colours of the letters and add these together to form a synthesis of colour. Thus the Sigil of Metatron shall be: blue, greenish-yellow, orange, red-orange, and greenish blue: the synthesis shall be reddish-citron. [18]

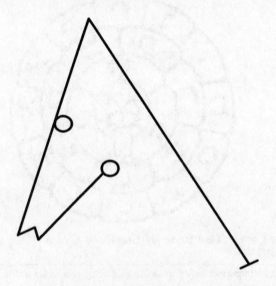

Sigil of Metatron using the Rose

---

[18] The use of a multicoloured sigil like this is good in theory but terrible to utilise in practice. It will be up to the reader to experiment with this formula to see if it works.

Now we will discuss, for example, the sigils of the forces under Binah, the third Sephirah. The sigils for the plane of a Sephiroth are always worked out on this system and in this Order:

1. Sephiroth   BINAH
2. Divine Name in Atziluth: YHVH ELOHIM
3. Divine Name in Briah: TZAPHQIEL (Archangel)
4. Divine Name in Yetzirah: ARALIM (Angelic Choir)
5. Divine Name in Assiah: SHABBATHAI (Sphere of Planet)

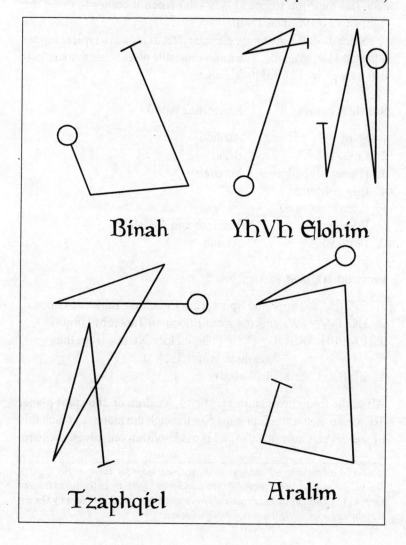

Binah

YhVh Elohim

Tzaphqiel

Aralim

Finally an sigils of any other names whose numbers have some relation to the powers of the Sephirah or its Planet. Yet these latter (the sigils of the intelligence and spirit) are more usually taken from the magical kamea or square of the planets according to a slightly different system hereafter.

TALISMAN, ANGELS AND SUBTLE ANATOMY

We have already pointed out that angels work in a hierarchy and each has their job to do. This is vital when it comes to using the right angel on your talisman.[19]

Since most talismans are planetary, let us look at a typical Jupiter talisman as an example. The following table gives some associations that may prove helpful in this area:

Subtle Anatomy	KabbalisticWorld
1. Spirit	Atziluth
2. Causal	Briah
3. Higher Mental	Yetzirah
4. Lower Mental	"
5. Astral\Emotional	"
6. Etheric	Yetzirah and Assiah
7. Physical	Assiah "

First or Highest invocation

1. EHNB   (Supreme Spirit from Enochian Tablet of Union)
2. HCOMA   (Water King from Enochian Tablet of Union)
3. EMPEH ARSL GAOIL   (Three Holy Names from the
                    Enochian Water Tablet)
4. EL (God Name of Chesed)

All of the four above names relate to Atziluth or the spirit plane. To invoke them the adept must rise through the planes to reach this higher level. Once this contact is made within ourselves, we then

---

[19] For the functions of these associations see *Magical Tarot of the Golden Dawn* by Pat and Chris Zalewski: see *Ladder of Lights* by Bill Gray: *Mystical Qabalah* by Dion Fortune; *Practical Guide to Qabalistic Symbolism* by Gareth Knight and *Making Talismans*, by Nick Farrell.

go to the appropriate level invoked from the Enochian tablets, and the Sephiroth.

4. TZADQIEL (Archangel of Chesed)
5. RA AGIOSEL (Elemental King of the Water Tablet).
6. TZEDEK (Hebrew name for Jupiter)

With the above three Names we invoke the our causal body and our Briatic nature. Once this level is reached it is directed by our causal body to the Briatic world of the invoked entities. Now because our first invocation is in Atziluth, the which is senior to the Briatic, the way has now been paved and the three entities have now been instructed by their seniors to assist us in our invocation.

7. CHASMALIM (Angelic Choir of Chesed)
8. LSRAHPM, SLAIOL, SAIINOR, SONIZNT, LAOAXRP, LIGDSA

(These names are from the seniors of the Enochian water tablet)

9. IOPHIEL (intelligence of planet)[20]
10. HISMAEL (spirit of planet)

The above four names relate to the World of Yetzirah and the higher mental body astral/emotional body and their respective planes.

The symbols that come into play on the etheric level and the world of Assiah, is the planetary seal (usually present during a planetary ritual) and the sigil of the talisman. For these take their energy directly from the astral. The seal of the planet is the modifier at the astral level and helps pour the vital astral fluid into the talisman. The flashing colours work mainly from the etheric level.

The whole process of invocation, is extremely complex, for what I have presented here is only a brief summary of the major considerations.

---

[20] Both the intelligence and spirit of planet have been allocated to the World of Yetzirah, because the influence of this world on us is vast. The intelligence is ranked higher than the spirit.

Above all, the invocations, there is one that is fundamental - the Formula of the Enterer. This is the invocation of Thoth where the adept forges a magical link between his or herself and the godform. Thoth is the link to our spirit consciousness and the adept must assume his form at the start of any of the Z2 rituals, as dictated in the Exordium.

By drawing upon the power of Thoth we can draw from a type of spiritual gene pool of everything that Thoth represents, that in turn gives us the power to command any entity invoked through him. Thoth gives us order in chaos, and he has the power of 'accumulation' (for Thoth has recorded everything since the dawning of time) and it is that is what we draw upon in our ritual. In psychological terms, Thoth becomes the archetypal doorway to Jung's concept of the 'Collective Unconscious'. Within the Golden Dawn his power is almost unlimited and transcends that of Osiris.

The most difficult part of any invocation is to recognise the magical currents of the plane being invoked, and this is done through archetypal imagery. However this is not enough though, as the adept must recognise the currents by the 'feel' of them. This can be accomplished by a combination of scrying and invoking from a particular plane until it is second nature. A simple way to do this is to invoke the deity of the day daily to help with a spiritual task. Over a period of time the energy patterns of each of the seven main deities - whether they be Greco-Roman or Egyptian, will be familiar enough to tap into easily.

ADDITIONAL NOTES ON TALISMANS AND FLASHING TABLETS

Part One

There is some confusion as to the colouring scheme of a flashing tablet or talisman. When using a planetary talisman, the background colour is the colour of the planet and the sigil is the complementary colour and not the other way around. The highest degree of force is focused when the background is the colour of the planet, for this is the main point of concentration that provides the complementary colour of the sigil. The complementary colour represents the higher force of spirit that is produced by the original planetary colour. It must be remembered that the colours of the elemental weapons and that of the Enochian tablets work on this principle. When the colours are reversed then a lower level of planetary power is used. The essence of a flashing tablet does not require it to be consecrated to produce the desired effect for form and colour are the main point of attraction. A talisman, by its makeup needs energy poured into it because the major part of it is planetary.

A flashing tablet will only attract a limited field of force where a talisman is more wide ranging. A flashing tablet can be extended to a talisman only if the invoked force and the sigil are compatible and it is consecrated like an ordinary talisman. Flashing tablets appear in some of the squares of the vault but it must remembered that this is consecrated at least once a year to maintain the power.

A talisman will collect and tap into the energy pattern of the entity or entities invoked. When this energy enters the portal of the ritual it is directed at the talisman and hovers over it. The adept then calls on his power in what is akin to copying the power frequency of the entity invoked. What is created is something like a homeopathic miasm, which is absorbed by the sigils and colours of the talisman. A talisman does not trap an entity but absorbs a copy of its power source and for the brief period of the ritual's duration it acts like a battery for the magnetic power around it.

When the copying is complete, and the talisman is full of energy, the adept then directs it to aid the person it is to help. This comes about through an energy pattern or field created by the adept who then opens a type of doorway (astral and otherwise) to the recipient. Once this doorway is opened the talisman will then send its own link to its master and which will remain in effect until the person either dies or the talisman has been destroyed or deactivated.

The talisman sends out this energy in what some clairvoyants see as a pulse. This low pulse progressively builds up energy over a period of time. It is self-renewing and is transmitted to the target person's spleen chakra (which is the entry point for most talismans that aid individuals).

Negative astrological effects and imbalances in the system of the person it is directed towards can influence a talisman's power. These have to be rectified before the talisman can work properly. In the case of a chronic disease, it may take quite some time for the talisman to work, and once this is done, the effect may not be as strong as the person had hoped.

Flashing tablets are open conductors with non-stop energy producing a magnetic effect to their surroundings. Their energy pattern relates to the form and action of their purpose and can be seen as a shower clairvoyantly. It takes energy of white light and rearranges it by its shape, size and colour into a magnetic field. Tarot cards, especially the 22 trumps, are flashing tablets - for they have the colours of the four worlds and their complementaries on each trump. This gives them a powerful magnetic force that aids the adept by supplementing his or her energy space when using the cards in the search for knowledge. Flashing tablets are used in alchemical working. When an elixir is placed on or near one flashing tablets gently alter the elixir's magnetic field to the desired pitch and changes some aspects of the its nature.

BRIEF NOTES ON TALISMANS AND GEMSTONES

With the popular revival of the use and properties of gemstones in healing, it will be of no surprise to find that they can be used by for talismanic purposes. Certain gemstones can be programmed to perform as effectively as any painted talisman. Marcel Vogel, the pioneer in the development of quartz crystals, used a crystal shaped like a Tree of Life, other have preferred to leave the gem stone in its natural state and have a special sigil carved upon its surface.

The use of different artificial shapes can change the vibration pitch of the crystal, in the same way as tuning into a radio station, to archive a different effect. The trick is to know which shape is ideal for which gemstone.

If we used a gemstone in a protection talisman, it would not deflect a physical attack, but make the wearer more aware of situations that might be dangerous and enable us to take precautions. However when words of power and symbols are utilised the talisman becomes more than a mere amplification device and produces an identical pattern or signature of the force invoked. The amplification pattern synchronises with the crystalline cell structure within the body to become a conductor for the protective force invoked.

Birthstones for each month

Spessartine Garnet	January
Amethyst	February
Red Jasper	March
White Diamond	April
Emerald	May
Pearl	June
Ruby	July
Moonstone	August
Opal	September
Aquamarine	October
Topaz	November
Bloodstone	December

One of the ways we could use a stone of a certain month would be to use a birthstone to amplify the level of consciousness to fine-tune the individual's awareness.

Now if we use a gemstone for protection, we can tune the birthstone to the external astrological influence that would be helpful in our cause. Simply simply wearing the correct stone can change the body and psychic network of subtle anatomy and a sigil draws forth the energy pattern to help us further.

There are many tales associated to certain gemstones and having tested some of these I would say that a quite a few of them have no basis in fact. To give an example, in the works of Albertus Magnus, we are told that the stone called Esmundus or Atasmundus will overcome beasts. A simple way to prove this, would be to take such a stone to see the neighbour's Pit Bull and put it to the test. I would say in 99.9 percent of cases the Pit Bull would win. In areas like this you can only trust your own observations and this requires good occult work of trial and error. It is not wise to take many of these old texts as gospel.

But it has been my observation that gemstones enhance and amplify, and if anything weird and wonderful happens, it is the product of the Self with the gemstone being a focal point. Each person reacts differently.

However in some cases there seems to be some truth behind tradition uses of stones. Take (red) agate as an example. In folklore it is protection against spiders and scorpions, giving the favour of God, and guarding against evil. Now if we look at the actual effect of agate on the body we find that it works on memory cells and tissue regeneration. It balances the endocrine system, particularly the thyroid glands, and can increase the heart rate if incorrect meditation is administered. On the subtle level it balances the astral\emotional, mental and spiritual bodies and works on stabilising the sex instinct by working on the base and heart chakra. Agate works with the fire elementals on the various planes right to the spiritual levels. For those of you who wish to know more of the functions of gemstones, I suggest *Gem Elixirs and Vibrational Healing Vol. 1 & 2*, by Gurudas and the Edgar Cayce readings. This information can be further expanded by self-experimentation. I have found the Gurudas information extremely accurate and have tested it with hundreds of gemstones and elixirs over the years on patients in my radionics practice with positive results.

MAGIC SQUARES OR KAMEAS

In my commentaries on the elemental grades (see rituals of the
Golden Dawn) I have gone to considerable detail on the numerical
formation of the squares and the planetary names associated to
them. To basically recap — using the Aiq Beker system one can
actually form more than one version of the names traced over
these squares. This has caused a great deal of confusion over the
years as to what is correct. The Golden Dawn used one particular
aspect of a large number of variables available in this system and
I have included the full squares for each planet to show how they
are traced. From this it is possible see how a number of errors
have crept into the system over the years. Some of the problems
or errors occur during the Aiq Beker reduction. There is confusion
as to groupings of one or 10 or 100 and the little used principle of
11 as a justifiable number.

It has always intrigued me that the Golden Dawn never had
kamea for the slower moving planets of Neptune and Uranus,
considering they are more powerful than the 'older' planets.
Regardie told me that he had seen a letter from some of the Senior
Golden Dawn adepti to Mathers, asking the same question. Mathers
replied to the enquirer that they were being designed. However
neither Regardie nor anyone else I have known ever saw the
results.

In trying to solve this problem I have given four examples of
magic squares or kamea, and seals for the planets of Neptune,
Uranus, Pluto and Chiron. They have been worked out following
the same principle as the seven traditional kamea.

I use for Uranus, the archangel Raziel, the angel Malkiel, and
Ausiul for the spirit. For Pluto: the archangel Mesukiel, angel Uriel,
intelligence Abaddon, spirit Arkhas. For Neptune: archangel
Metatron, angel Sephurirons, intelligence Nashire and the spirit
Huznoth. These are my own preferences for these squares at the
time of writing and there is still a great deal of more work to do on
them for example I have not found an appropriate intelligence to
rule Pluto.

Then there is another problem. Forgetting the Sun and Moon
as primary energy forms, we have discovered only nine planets in
our solar system. I believe there will be three more found in the

outer rim and there will be difficulties fitting them into our Kabbalistic systems. If I am right, we will end up with a Tree of 15 Sephiroth.

As far as incorporating Chiron into the Tree, I attribute it to the 'dark' or 'flip side' of Daath producing a 12 'Sephiroth' tree. Pluto is the Sephirah at the bottom of the entranceway to the Abyss and Chiron is the planet above it, on the exit way of the Abyss. If time proves me correct, and three more outer planets are discovered in the future, the only space on the existing Tree is the Three Veils of Negative existence, of which each veil will represent a new planet.

4	9	2
3	5	7
8	1	6

Saturn Square

4	14	15	1
9	7	6	12
5	11	10	8
16	2	3	13

Jupiter Square

11	24	7	20	3
4	12	25	8	16
17	5	13	21	9
10	18	1	14	22
23	6	19	2	15

Mars Square

6	32	3	34	35	1
7	11	27	28	8	30
19	14	16	15	23	24
18	20	22	21	17	13
25	29	10	9	26	12
36	5	33	4	2	31

Sun Square

22	47	16	41	10	35	4
5	23	48	17	42	11	29
30	6	24	49	18	36	12
13	31	7	25	43	19	37
38	14	32	1	26	44	20
21	39	8	33	2	27	45
46	15	40	9	34	3	28

Venus Square

8	58	59	5	4	62	63	1
49	15	14	52	53	11	10	56
41	23	22	44	45	19	18	48
32	34	35	29	28	38	39	25
40	26	27	37	36	30	31	33
17	47	46	20	21	43	42	24
9	55	54	12	13	51	50	16
64	2	3	61	60	6	7	57

Mercury Square

37	78	29	70	21	62	13	54	5
6	38	79	30	71	22	63	14	46
47	7	39	80	31	72	23	55	15
16	48	8	40	81	32	64	24	56
57	17	49	9	41	73	33	65	25
26	58	18	50	1	42	74	34	66
67	27	59	10	51	2	43	75	35
36	68	19	60	11	52	3	44	76
77	28	69	20	61	12	53	4	45

Moon Square

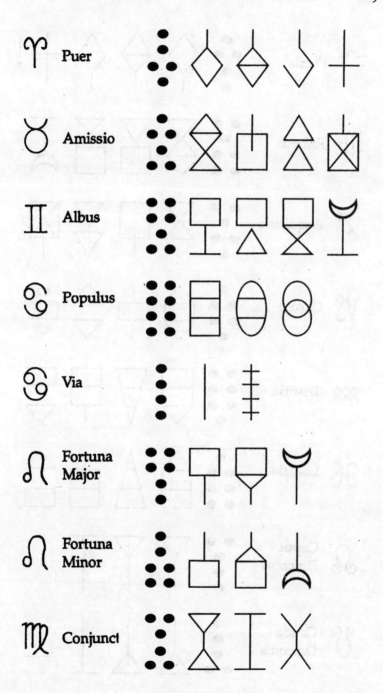

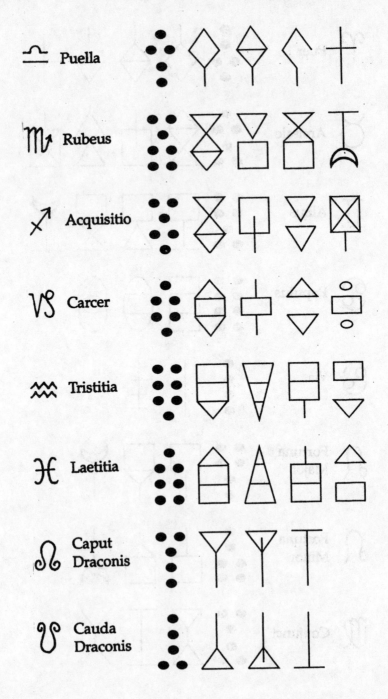

- ♎ Puella
- ♏ Rubeus
- ♐ Acquisitio
- ♑ Carcer
- ♒ Tristitia
- ♓ Laetitia
- ♌ Caput Draconis
- ♋ Cauda Draconis

GEOMANTIC SYMBOLS AND TALISMANS

Within the Golden Dawn, a popular method of adding sigils to a talisman was through the use of geomantic figures (and their associations). Most of these sigils were multiple variations of a single geomantic figure. Numerous examples were given by Agrippa and were later published in Francis Barrett's *Magus* I have come across numerous notes made by Golden Dawn members on the this subject but these were always short and did not provide many clues as to their origin. I have not found any official Golden Dawn lecture them   other than a single page example, published in Regardie's *Golden Dawn* (Vol. 4, page 75 —Llewellyn Publications.) During my training, Taylor gave me a copy of some figures that were taken from Barrett's *Magus* and told me the drawings were self-explanatory.

TELESMATIC FIGURES
by MacGregor Mathers.

PART ONE

There is a mode whereby, combining the letters, the colours and the attributions and their synthesis, thou mayest build up a telesmatic image of a force. The sigil shall then serve thee for a tracing of a current that shall call unto action a certain elemental force. And know thou that is not to be done lightly for thine amusement or experiment, seeing that the forces of nature were not created to be thy plaything or toy. Unless thou doest thy practical magical works with solemnity, ceremony and reverence, thou shalt be like an infant playing with fire and bring destruction upon thyself.

Know, then, that if thou essay in the imagination to form an astral image from the names, the first letter shall be the head of the figure or form, and the final letter shall be its feet. The other letters shall be, and represent in their order, its body and members. AGIEL, for example, shall give thee an angelic form of the following nature and appearance:

ALEPH - AIR

The head is winged, and of a golden colour, with long floating golden hair.[21]

GIMEL - LUNA

Crowned with a bluish silver crescent, and with the face of a grave and beautiful woman, with a bluish halo.

YOD - VIRGO

The body of a maiden clothed in a grass green robe.

---

[21] The process Mathers is describing is designed to create an artificial elemental to do one's bidding. Contrary to what Mathers has said about astral beings, each elemental has a spiritual body. This form, like humanity, changes the higher up the Tree of Life you travel. To limit an elemental to the World of Assiah or Yetzirah is a grave mistake as the roots of all material elements are in the Divine.

ALEPH - AIR

Golden wings of a large size, partly covering the lower part of the figure.

LAMED - LIBRA

Feet and limbs well proportioned and, either in the hand of the figure lying at its feet, the sword and scales of justice bright green. Playing round the figure will be a greenish light, the colour of its synthesis. The Keys of the Tarot may help thee in the form.
See well that thou makest the image as pure and beautiful as possible, for the more impure or common the figure, the more dangerous it is unto thee. Write upon the breast its sigil, upon the girdle its name, and place clouds below the feet. And when thou hast done this with due solemnity and rigid correctness of symbolism, shunning as thou wouldst shun death, any suggestion of coarseness of vulgarity in any angelic symbol, then hear what it shall say unto thee.

SERAPHIM will give thee an angelic figure like a warrioress with flame playing about her, and a countenance glorious like the Sun, and beneath her feet the stormy seas and thunder clouds, and lightning about her, and a glow as of flame. She has a triangular helmet or headdress of flame like the symbol of fire.

GRAPHIEL will give thee a great angel like a female warrior with a most glorious countenance, crowned with the crescent and flashing with light, and surrounded by flame and lightning with four wings.

The termination EL always gives the angelic forms the wings and symbols of Justice. The ending YAH will make the figures like enthroned Kings or Queens, and with flaming glory at their feet.

PART TWO

As mentioned previously, the names of all the angels and angelic forces terminate with few exceptions, in either AL or YAH. The divine name AL belongs to Chesed and it represents a good, powerful and mighty force, but of somewhat milder operation than the name YAH. Since not only the angels but even devils are said to draw their force and power directly from the prolific source of the Divine energies, therefore frequently to the names of evil spirits, is AL added. The Name YAH is added to the name of an Angel or Spirit who exercises only a good[22] and somewhat beneficent office.

These two terminations being rather in the nature of incidental attributions than of essential distinction, they need not be taken too much notice of the construction of a talesmatic image. In building up such an image, you can either imagine it astrally before you, or paint the actual resemblance. Name belonging to the world under which the telesmatic image under the course of construction would fall. Thus to Atziluth are allotted the deific names. To Briah, archangelic and so on. It is useful to employ the Sephirotic names that are comprised in the special world to which the telesmatic image is allotted.

It is well to note that the four worlds formulate the law involved in the building up or expression of any material thing. The world of Atziluth is purely archetypal and primordial, and to it, as before said, deific names are applied. BRIAH is creative and originative, and to certain great gods called archangels are allotted. YETZIRAH is formative and angelic orders are allotted thereunto.

ASSIAH, which is the material world, consists of the great kingdoms of the elementals, human beings, and in some cases the Qlippoth, though these latter really occupy the planes below Assiah.

---

[22] Chiefs of Golden Dawn temples and students should give this paper be given a great deal of consideration. At Whare Ra, some adepts made some beautiful composite coloured drawings of the names in angelic imagery of the whole Tree of Life. An adept will have to design at least 40 drawings and this will take a great deal of time, though it will be worth it (I would suggest that this practice be made mandatory for Golden Dawn adepts). It must be remembered that as one draws these figures, a doorway to their plane leaves a doorway to the adept. A.C.Highfield has in part tried to this by listing some of the names obtained by this method in his book *Book of Celestial Images* Aquarian Press, 1984.

From these remarks it will be seen that a telesmatic image can hardly apply to Atziluth; that to Briah it can[23] do but only in a restricted sense. Thus, a telesmatic image belonging to that world would have to be represented with a type of concealed head, possessing a form shadowy and barely indicated. Telesmatic images, then really belong to YETZIRAH. Therefore it would be impossible to apply the telesmatic image to a divine name in ATZILUTH, for it would not represent that in the world of ATZILUTH, but rather its correlation in YETZIRAH. In Assiah you would get elemental forms.

The sex of a figure depends upon the predominance of the masculine or the feminine or the whole of the letters together, but a jumble of the sexes should be avoided in the same form. The image built up should be divided into as many parts as there are letters, commencing at the upper part and so on in order. In addition to this method of determining the sex of a telesmatic image of a name, certain names are inherently masculine, other feminine, and some epicene, irrespective of the mere testimony of the letters.[24]

SANDALPHON, for instance is thus analysed:

SAMEKH	Male
NUN	Male
DALETH	Female
LAMED	Female
PEH	Female
VAU	Male
NUN	Male

---

[23] Mathers contradicts himself here with statement he made in earlier papers on talismans. for as long as one can use say the rose cross formula to capture the essence of Atziluth then it will work. What he does not say is that there are many levels to Atziluth and although some are inaccessible, others are accessible. The use of analogy can verify this many times. Taking a flower essence can effect the utmost point of our being, the highest subtle body, and spirit. Some crystals can have this effect so why not a talisman?

[24] I disagree with this, consider the Sphinx, a powerful elemental figure that is a composite. My own experience on elemental planes is that the masculine and feminine concepts are rarely important in the scheme of things and make little difference either way. Most elementals are composite figures of either sex.

Therefore masculine predominates, and as it were, an ordinary name you would make a masculine form out of it. But as this name is especially applied to the feminine kerub it is an exception to the rule; it is an archangelic name, belonging to the BRIATIC World and not merely an angelic name relating to YETZIRAH. SANDALPHON is called 'Yetzer' meaning 'left' and its letters are: Female. Female and Male, so that, in this case, it may be any of these.

The seven letters composing the name SANDALPHON are thus adapted to the telesmatic image.

SAMEKH
Head. Would represent a beautiful and attractive face, rather thin than fat.

NUN
Neck, would be admirably full.

DALETH
Shoulders of a beautiful woman.

LAMED
Heart and chest, the latter perfectly proportioned.

PEH
Hips, strong and full.

VAU
Legs, massive.

NUN
Feet, sinewy and perhaps winged. If it be desired to build up an elemental form out of this name a very peculiar figure would be the result.

SAMEKH
Head, fierce but rather beautiful— Blue.

NUN
Neck, with eagle's wings from behind — Blue—Green.

DALETH
Shoulders, feminine and rather beautiful —Green—Blue.

LAMED
Chest, of a woman — Emerald.

PEH
Strong and shaggy hips and thighs — Red.

VAU
Legs of a Bull — Red-Orange.

NUN (Final).
Feet of an Eagle — Green — Blue.

This, it will be seen, is almost a synthetic kerub figure. This figure
may be represented, as it were, with its feet on the earth, and its
head in the clouds. The colours in the paths of the King Scale
would synthesise[25] as a delicate and sparkling green. The
uncovered parts of the body would be blue, the countenance
belonging to Sagittarius would be almost like that of horse. The
whole form would be like that of a Goddess between ATHOR and
NEITH holding a bow and arrows, that as if represented as an
Egyptian symbol. On the tattvic plane we get the following:
SAMEKH comes under Fire
NUN comes under water
DALETH comes under water of Earth
LAMED comes under air
PEH comes under fire
NUN comes under water
If again, we endeavour to translate this Name into symbols on
astral form these would be synthesised thus: A silver crescent on a
red triangle placed over a yellow square. All three would be charged
and enclosed within a large silver crescent.

Now, taking an example, the telesmatic image pertaining to the
letter ALEPH. This is on the Briatic plane, would rather be masculine
than feminine and would be resumed by a spiritual figure hardly
visible at all, the head-dress winged, the body cloud-veiled and

---

[25] The Elemental form for the lower world of Assiah is a composite figure taken
from the lion, bull, eagle and man. As I have mentioned earlier, the above description for the higher worlds could still be classed as an Elemental.

wrapped[26] in mist as if clouds were rolling over and obscuring the outline, and scarcely permitting the legs and feet to be seen. It represents the spirit of ether. In the Yetziratic world, it would be like a warrior with winged helmet, the face angelic but rather fierce, the body and arms mailed, but bearing a child, the legs and feet with mailed buskins and wings attached to them.

In ASSIAH, the same letter ALEPH is terrific energy and represents, as it were, mad force (uncontrolled) . On the human plane, it would represent a person who was lunatic and at times given to frightful, fits of mania. Translated to the elemental plane, it would represent a, form whose body fluctuated between a man and an animal, and indeed, the Assiatic form would be a most evil type with a force something like that compounded of that of a bird and that of a demon, an altogether horrible result. The letter ALEPH represents spirituality in high things, but when translated to the plane contiguous to or below ASSIAH is usually something horrible and unbalanced, because it is so opposed to that the movement is involved therein, there is no harmony between them.

Radiating forces of Divine Light, otherwise called angelic forms, have no gender in the grosser acceptation of the term, though can be classed according to the masculine and feminine sides. As, for example, in the human figure, sex is not strongly marked in the upper part, the head, as in the body, while yet the countenance can be distinctly classed as a masculine or feminine type. So, when quitting the material plane, sex becomes less marked, or rather appreciable in a different manner, though the distinction of masculine and feminine is retained. And herein is a great error of the phallic religions, that they have transferred the material and gross side of sex to the Divine and angelic planes, not understanding that it is the lower that is derived from the higher by correlation in the material development, and not the higher from the lower. Gender, in the usual meaning of the term, belongs to the elemental spirits, kerubic

---

[26] Using tattvic ethers will produce a different type of result than other types of figures. The tattvic relate to the senses and work on the surrounding environment, and their functions are limited to the tattvic tides or currents so the force is inconsistent. Use of the water in the majority will cause contraction in the talisman and make the motion downward and as a result its directive quality would be limited. Its effect is elemental but of a lower type of nature than that utilised for Assiah.

forms, planetary and Olympic spirits, and to the Qlippoth, in the most the exaggerated and bestial aspects, and this is a ratio increasing in proportion to the depths of their descent. Also, in certain of the evil spirits, it would be exaggerated and repulsive.

But, in the higher angelic natures, gender is correlated by forms, either steady and firm, or rushing. Firmness is like that of a rock or pillar and is the nature of the feminine; restlessness and movement —that of the masculine, Therefore, let this be clearly understood in ascribing gender to angelic forms and images. Our tradition classes all forces under the heads [27 & 28] of vehement and rushing force, and firm and steady force. Therefore a figure representing the former would be masculine and that representing the latter, a feminine form.

For convenience in the formation of telesmatic images of ordinary occult names and words, the letters are arranged in masculine and feminine classification. This classification is not intended to affirm that the letters have not in themselves both natures (seeing that in each letter as in each Sephirah is hidden the dual nature of masculine and feminine) but shows more their tendency as regards the distinction of force before mentioned. Those, then, are rather masculine then feminine, to which are allotted forces more rapid in action. And those, again, are rather feminine than masculine which represents a force more firm and steady whence all letters whose sound is prolonged as if moving forward are rather masculine than feminine. Certain others are epicene, yet incline rather to one nature than to another.

---

[27] Everyone has a different concept of this. I have come to the conclusion that the sexual difference between entities is present in the physical, etheric, astral\emotional and lower mental planes. The three planes above this are considered androgynous.

[28] Mathers has this only half right. Tantric godforms came from the mental plane and some devotees mimic their actions. The sexual act as performed on the astral is very different from physical act.

PART THREE

Telesmatic Attributions of the Letters of the Hebrew Alphabet

ALEPH
Spiritual. Wings generally, epicene, rather male than female, rather thin type.

BETH
Active and slight, male.

GIMEL
Grey, beautiful yet changeful. Feminine. Full face and body.

HEH
Fierce, strong, fiery. Feminine.

VAU
Steady and strong. Heavy and clumsy, masculine.

ZAYIN
Thin, intelligent and masculine.

CHETH
Full face, not much expression, and feminine.

TETH
Strong and fiery, feminine.

YOD
White, delicate and feminine.

CAPH
Big, strong and masculine.

LAMED
Well proportioned, feminine.

MEM
Reflective, dreamlike; epicene, but female rather than male.

NUN
Square determined face, masculine, dark.

SAMEKH
Thin expressive face, masculine.

AYIN
Mechanical, masculine

HEH
Fierce, strong resolute and feminine.

TZADDAI
Thoughtful, intellectual, feminine.

QOPH
Full face, masculine.

RESH
Proud, dominant, masculine.

SHIN
Fierce, active, epicene, rather male than female.

TAU
Dark, grey, epicene, male rather than female. Mechanical, masculine

PEH
Fierce, strong resolute and feminine.

TZADDAI
Thoughtful, intellectual, feminine.

QOPH
Full face, masculine.

RESH
Proud, dominant, masculine.

SHIN
Fierce, active, epicene, rather male than female.

TAU
Dark, grey, epicene, male rather than female.

Telesmatic Figures and the Tarot

The Golden Dawn used this principle for some of the designs of
the Tarot Trumps as well, in an unpublished paper *Order of the
Ritual of the Heptagram; part 2*. Mathers gives some further
descriptions of the Tarot Trumps for the grade of Theoricus Adeptus
Minor. Since this paper was undated and written in the hand of
Brodie Innes, I have no way of knowing whether it was designed
for the Golden Dawn or the later Alpha et Omega.

While it is evident that the Mathers designs of the Trumps differed
from those published by Wang it is obvious from this paper that
these designs were never officially issued.

The following paper on the Empress is one of the best described.
The others are vague as to exactly what goes where, and it appears
Mathers had nothing but a generalised concept that never actualised:

'Venus: To her is attributed the Third Key or Trump of the Tarot,
known as the "Empress". The true design and colouring thereof is
as follows. The figure is the Telesmatic Figure of Aniel (in Hebrew)
and is thus constructed:-

Aleph: A winged, white, brilliant, radiant Crown.
Nun: Arms bare and strong: on right, a shield, golden, and charged
with a dove (the eagle on the card in the ordinary pack is a
corruption): in the left hand, three lilies, held like a sceptre, and the
crux ansata or "Nile Key" hanging from the left wrist - the colouring
of bluish green.
Yod: A yellowish green robe, covering a strong breast, in which is
a square golden lamen, in the angles of which are respectively the
crux ansata, the caestus: the conch shell: and the sigil of Venus
traced in scarlet.
Aleph-Lamed: El gives the usual angelic attribution of the
termination - AL or EL: and, in addition, seeing the letter lamed is
referred to Libra, it giveth a balanced and equilibrated figure of
great beauty.
The whole figure, then, is more or less feminine counterpart of
Adonai Ha - Artez - A beautiful female for with pale-golden hair
(for Aleph), wearing a radiant crown of seven points (the number
of Venus) with large golden wings: her robe of brilliant light-spring
green, rayed with darker olive: her feet bare, with golden Sandals:

her shield and lamen have already been described: and about her waist abroad belt of scarlet, bearing the name Aniel (in Hebrew). This card dominateth the entire Heptagram, in as much as it is the signet-star of Venus; and, in the brazen candlestick of seven lights, when set in a straight line, the metal what of Venus, and to her was the central and highest light ascribed, and *Daughter of the Mighty Ones* was her name.'

I would suggest that the reader look at the card of the 'Empress' in the Oswald Wirth deck as if fits very closely with some of Mathers' symbolism. The Empress card has a telesmatic vibration of attraction and in turn attracts that force to it. When the operator meditates on the a card, or uses it for divination the higher forces embedded in that trump, through colour, now come into action and direct the operator closely to Mathers' symbolism. The Empress has a telesmatic vibration of attraction and it attracts forces to it. It is because of this that the cards are required to be kept in a white or black cloth so that the flashing colours lie dormant when not in use.

METHOD OF USE

How to draw the figure

The first step is to select the figure and the purpose of the figures task. Take for example, the name ADONI HA ARETZ, the God-name of Malkuth. A breakdown of the figure will be as follows:

ALEPH
Winged, white, brilliant radiant crown.

DALETH
Head and neck of a woman, beautiful but firm, hair long, dark and waving.

NUN
Arms bare, strong, extended as in a cross. In the right[29] hand are ears of corn, and in the left a golden Cup.

---

[29] The figure's composition is made from just the first word of the name. Broken up, the full name is applied to the figure for the Three words that make up the name relates to Malkuth, matter and zelatorship.

YOD

Deep yellow green robe covering a strong chest on which is a square lamen of gold with a scarlet Greek cross - in the angles, four smaller red crosses. Round her waist is a broad gold belt with the letters written on in scarlet the name ADNI HA ARTZ in the letters of the alphabet of Honorius. Her feet are flesh coloured and she wears golden sandals. Her long yellow-green drapery is rayed with olive, beneath her feet roll black clouds lit with lurid colour patches.

How to bring forth the Image in the Astral

1. Lesser banishing ritual of the pentagram.

2. Trace sigils (from the Rose) of the name in each quarter of the room

3. Bring down the Divine White Brilliance (LVX Signs).

4. Formulate in front of you the cross of Hebrew letters

A

D

ZTRANHINDA

Y

H [30, 31 & 32]

5. Bring down the bright light of your Kether and extend it (by way of Tiphareth) to the letters in front of you until the cross grows brilliant white.

6. Invoke the telesmatic image you have drawn and place exact likeness over the cross of Hebrew letters in front of you.

---

[30] The emblem on the breast of the 14th Key of Temperance, in my copy of the ritual had four crosses in it while the original Mathers version had a rectangle.

[31] Bring the image of the sigil down from the brilliance of Kether, then push it out through your Tiphareth centre.

[32] This cross give the full name of the figure invoked, both vertical and horizontal.

7. The figure will now glow with the brightness of Kether behind it. You have drawn forth and given it life. Now instruct it in the task you wish to do for you.

Rituals

Consecration rituals were developed using the same formula of the enterer described in Part One of this book. Just like the evocations, Mather's broke down the ritual into stages that I have listed below. The 5=6 adept had to write a ritual of their own which used this structure. Later we will look at one of these rituals.

Consecration of Talismans

Part One

Skelatonic Breakdown of Talisman Ritual.

A. The place where the operation is done.

B. The magical operator.

C. The forces of Nature employed and attracted.

D. The telesma or material basis.

E. In telesmata, the selection of the matter to form the telesma; The preparation and arrangement of the place. The drawing and forming of the body of the telesma. In natural phenomena the preparation of the operation; the formation of the circle, and the selection of the material basis, such as a piece of earth, a cup of water, a flame of fire, a pentacle, or the like.

F. The invocation of the highest divine forces, winding a black cord around the telesma or material basis, covering the same with black veil, and the initiating blind force therein. Naming aloud the nature of the telesma or operation.

G. The telesma or material basis is now placed towards the West, and duly consecrated with water and fire. The purpose of the operation, and the effect intended to be produced is then to be rehearsed in a loud and clear voice.

H.   Placing the talisman or material basis at the foot of the altar, state aloud the object to be attained, solemnly asserting that it will be attained, and the reason thereof.

I.   Announce aloud that all is prepared and in readiness, either for charging the telesma, or for the commencement of the operation to induce the natural phenomena. Place a good telesma or material basis within the white triangle on the altar. Place a bad telesma to the West of same, holding the sword erect in the right hand for a good purpose, or its point upon the centre of the triangle for evil.

J.   Now follows the performance of an invocation to attract the desired spirit to the telesma or material basis, describing in the air above it the lineal figures and sigils. etc.., with the appropriate instrument. The, taking the telesma in the left hand, let him smite it thrice with the flat of the blade of the sword of art. Then raise it in the left hand (holding erect and aloft the sword in the right hand stamping thrice upon the earth with the right foot).

K.   The talisman or material basis is to be placed towards the North, and the operator repeats the oration of the hierophant to the candidate. 'The voice of exorcism said unto me, let me shroud myself in darkness, peradventure thus shall I manifest myself in light. I am the only being in the abyss of darkness. From the darkness came I forth ere my birth, from the silence of primal sleep. And the voice of ages answered my soul, creature of talismans, the light shineth in darkness, but the darkness comprehendeth it not. Let the mystic circumambulation take place in the path of darkness with the symbolic light of occult science to lead the way.'

L.   Then, taking up the light (not from the Altar) in right hand, circumambulate. Now take up telesmata or M.B., carry it round the circle, place it on the ground due South, then bar it, purify and consecrate with water and fire afresh, lift it up with left hand, turn and facing West, say: 'Creature of talismans, twice consecrate, thou mayest approach the gate of the West.'

M.   Now pass to the West with telesmata in left hand, face south-east, partly unveils telesmata, smite it with the flat of the blade of the Sword, and pronounces, 'Thou canst not pass from concealment unto manifestation, save by virtue of the Name ELOHIM. Before all things are the chaos and the darkness and the gates of the land of the night. I am he whose name is Darkness. I am the great one of the paths of the shades. I am the exorcist in the midst of the exorcism. Take on therefore the manifestation without fear before me, I am he in whom fear is NOT. Thou hast known me so pass thou on.' This being done he replaces the veil.

N.   Then passes around the circle with telesmata, halt due North, place telesmata on ground, bar purify and consecrate again with water and fire, and say, 'Creature of talismans, thrice consecrate thou mayest approach the Gate of the east.' Hold talisman aloft.

O.   Hold telesmata in left hand, lotus wand in right, assume hierophant's form. Partly unveil telesmata, smite with flat of sword, and say, 'Thou canst not pass from concealment unto manifestation save by virtue of the Name YHVH. After the formless and the void and the darkness, then comes the knowledge of the Light. I am the light which rises in darkness. I am the exorcist in the midst of the exorcism. Take on therefore manifestation before me, for I am the wielder of the forces of balance. Thou hast known me now so pass thou on unto the cubical altar of the universe.'

P.   He then recovers telesmata or M.B., passes on to the top of the Altar, laying it thereon as before shown he then passes to the East of the altar, hold left hand over talisman, and sword over it erect. The doth he rehearse a most potent conjuration and invocation of the spirit to render irresistible this telesmata or M.B., or to render manifest this natural phenomenon of ...., using and reiterating all the Divine, angelic, and magical names appropriate to this end, neither omitting the signs, seals, lineal figures, signatures and the like from the conjuration.

Q.   The magician now elevates the covered telesma or material basis towards Heaven, then removes the veil entirely, yet leaving it corded, crying out with a loud voice 'Creature of talismans (or M.B.) long hast thou dwelt in darkness. Quit the night and seek the day.' He then replaces it on the altar, holds the magical sword erect above it, the pommel immediately above the centre thereof, and says, 'By all the names, powers, rites already rehearsed, I conjure upon thee power and might irresistible.' Then he says the mystic words, Khabs Am Pekht, etc.

He then replaces it on the altar, holds the magical sword erect above it, the pommel ediately above the centre thereof, and says, 'By all the names, powers, rites already reharsed, I conjure upon thee power and might irresistible.' Then he says the mystic words, Khabs Am Pekht, etc.

R.   Saith the magician, 'As the light hidden in darkness can manifest here from, so shalt thou become irresistible.' He then takes up the telesmata, or the M.B. stands to the East of the altar, and faces West. Then shall he rehearse a long conjuration to the powers and spirits immediately superior unto that one which he seeks to Invoke, to make the telesmata powerful. Then he places the telesmata or M.B. between the pillars, himself at the East, facing West, then in the sign of the enterer, doth he project the whole current of his will upon the talisman. Thus he continueth until such time as he shall perceive his will power weakening, he protects himself by the sign of silence, and then drops his hands. He now looks toward the talisman, and a flashing, light or glory, should be seen playing and flickering on the talisman or M.B., and in the natural phenomena should be waited for. If this does not occur, let the magician repeat the conjuration of the superiors from the place of throne of the East.

And this conjuration may be repeated thrice, each time ending a new projection of will in the sign of the enterer, etc.. But is at the third time of repetition of the talisman or M.B. does not flash, then it be known there is an error in the working. So let the master of evocations replace the talisman or M.B. on the altar, holding the sword, and thus doing, let him address a humble prayer unto the great gods of Heaven to grant unto him the force necessary to correctly complete the work. he is then to take back the talisman, to between the pillars, and repeat the former process when assuredly the light will flash.

Now as soon as the magician shall see the light, he shall gait the station of the hierophant and consecrate afresh with water and fire.

S.   This being done, let the talisman or M.B. have the cord removed and smite it with the sword and proclaim: 'By and in the name of.........., I Invoke upon thee the power of ....' He then circumambulates thrice, holding the talisman of M.B. in his right hand.

T.   Then the magician, standing in the place of the hierophant, but fixing his gaze upon the talisman or M.B. should be placed on the ground within the circle, should now read a potent invocation of some length, rehearsing and reiterating the Divine and other names constant with the working. The talisman should now flash visibly, or the natural phenomena should definitely commence. The let the magician proclaim aloud that the talisman has been duly and properly charged, or the natural phenomena induced.

U.   The magician now addresses an invocation unto the lords of the plane of the spirit to compel him to perform that which the magician requires.

V.   The operator now carefully formulates his demands, stating clearly what the talisman is intended to do, or what the natural phenomena he seeks to produce.

W.   The master of evocations now addresses a conjuration unto the spirit, binding him to hurt or injure naught connected with him, or his assistant or the place. He then dismisses the spirits in the name of JEHOVASHAH and JEHESHUA, but wrap up the talisman first, and no banishing ritual shall be performed, so as not to discharge it, and in the case of natural phenomena it will usually be best to state what duration is required. And theM.B. should be preserved wrapped in white linen or silk all the time that the phenomena is intended to act. When it is time to cease, the M.B. - if water, is to be poured away; if earth ground to powder and scattered abroad; if a hard substance such as metal, it must be discharged, banished over and thrown aside; if flame of fire, it shall be extinguished; or if a vial containing air, it shall be opened and after that well rinsed out with pure water.

Ritual

Part Two

One example of a consecration ritual was written by Regardie and published in his *Golden Dawn* book. This previously unpublished talisman ritual comes from the notebook of Alan Bennett, and is dated around 1898. Bennett worked the ritual to help Dr. Felkin guard against obsession. Basically it is a talisman of protection. A comparison with the previously letter section in Part One, shows a couple of omissions.

Bennett was notorious for condensing his written work and possibly where the gaps are in the original ritual, he would have done something there anyway. However, I have taken the liberty of breaking down the ritual according to the Letters, and where he has missed out a section I have included what should have been placed — according to the Z2 skelatonic framework, so to a certain extent there is a little reconstruction. I have cross referenced this talisman ritual with another one written by Bennett for a Jupiter talisman(dated 1899), so essentially, the words are Bennett's, but I have merely inserted the purpose and who the ritual is for. In Bennett's note book the beginning of this ritual says:

> To Open as usual, with Water and Fire, Circumambulate, etc.. Then take the 'T' and say 'O ye Divine powers of the Hall of two fold manifestation of Thmaist.'

The ritual begins from section 'F'. His Jupiter[33] ritual is more explicit and missing section 'E' in this ritual is taken from his Jupiter ritual. Bennett had a habit of condensing at least two sections together and I have broken this up and placed them under the appropriate letter heading. I have added section 'N', which is not in the original Bennett ritual, and is nothing but a set of instructions and small speech.

As you study the ritual, you will note that initially section 'A' is not included and as such we are unsure of the exact location, date and time of the ritual but we do know that Felkin was present

---

[33] I have not included it here as this ritual is incomplete and only goes as far as the beginning of section 'P'.

during it. Unfortunately there are no references as to who else was present.

It was a real pleasure going through this ritual as it gives us a further example of Golden Dawn efforts in the field of talismanic work. I must say however, how much easier it is following the Mathers step-by-step outline where the magician has the part to fill in certain invocations and making the formula work.

Talisman Against Obsession Devised by Alan Bennett for the Protection of Dr.Felkin

The talisman during these operation lies unveiled and outside the circle.

'E'

HEKAS, HEKAS, ESTE BEBELOI!

I, Yehi Aour, a frater of the Golden Dawn in the Outer, and members of the R.R.et A. C., am this day about to consecrate a talisman of Tiphareth, for the protection of against obsession of Frater F.R., and to this end I have formulated thereon the appropriate symbols and words. But inasmuch the beginning of wisdom is the fear of YHVH, let us all kneel down together and say:

From thy hands oh Lord, cometh all good, from thy hands flow down all grace and blessing. The characters of nature with thy fingers hast thou traced, but none can read them, save he has been taught in thy school. Therefore, even as servants look unto the hands of their masters, the handmaidens unto their mistresses: even so do our eyes look up unto thee! For thou art our help! Oh Lord our God! Who should not extol thee, Who should not praise thee, Oh Lord of the Universe!

Perform lesser banishing ritual of the pentagram and hexagram (Sol) over talisman, saying:

I exorcise ye, impure and unclean spirits of the Elements, dwelling in this creature of talismans. By the flaming star of the unconquerable will, by the symbol of the rose and cross, And by the symbol of the divine name YHShVH, I say unto ye: depart!

Lesser banishing ritual of the Hexagram.

I exorcise ye, evil spirits of the planetary spheres dwelling in this creature of talismans.
By the mystical seal of Horus,
By the symbol of life,
And by the divine name ARARITA!
I say unto ye: depart!

Exorcise with water, Consecrate with fire. Invoke the forces of Sol.

'F'

INVOCATION OF THE HIGHER

Thee I invoke, spirit of Osiris triumphant, divine lord and god of dwellers upon the Earth.
Thou, who art known to us by the symbolic name YHShVH as thou manifested glory upon Earth as man, became God through perfected self—sacrifice, Osiris, man almighty, hear and aid!
Thou, whose blood was shed by the Arkhons of the Earth, that through thy suffering all mankind might find thy throne. Osiris, man almighty, hear and aid!
Thou, whose Love and Mercy didst reveal to man the Golden Gateway of the Path of Sacrifice; who did open the way to Immortality to men. Osiris, Man
Almighty hear and Aid!
Glory of aeshoori, lord of life triumphant over death: Glory of the Word incarnate, glory of the Son Divine; Holy aeshoori hear my prayer!
Come unto me, divine soul of my brother Finem Respice'
Osiris suffering for that thou art clothed with one body of flesh. Come thou art unto me to aid me. Vitalise thou

this mine operation of the magic arts that I may bring cure and healing into the body wherein is made thy habitation.

Binding the talisman with a magic cord, say:

Lo, even as I do now physically bind this creature of talismans: so let there be restriction placed upon the larvae of evil. Even as I bind this talisman on Earth, so let the larvae that betime obsesses Frater F.R. be bound and restrained. ELOHIM! let there be unto the void restriction.

Veiling the talisman say:

And even as I do now veil and envelope with blackness, this creature of talismans, so let the larvae that betimes obsesses Frater F.R. be blinded in darkness and in fear. And may the holy names, the standards, and ensigns of the mighty God hereon engraven and depicted, create and institute herein and elemental force, which may become powerful with the help of YHShVH to guard and protect Frater F.R.[34] from the larvae that betimes obsesses him. Even as it is written herein 'ALHIM GBR' Elohim hath protected him.

'G'

Place talisman without the western gate.

So let this creature of talismans become for Finem Respice a powerful and holy guard and protection having two-edged swords turned every way to guard his magic aura or sphere of sensation.

Admit, bar and purify.

Creature of talismans I purify with water.

Consecrate, formulating pillars.

Creature of talismans, I consecrate thee by fire.

---

[34] Felkin.

Now in a loud clear voice recite the following declaration:

Hear me, ye divine lords and forces of the Hall of the Twofold Manifestation of Thmaist: Hear me, divine spirit of my God! Osiris glorified and triumphant; hear Thou me, Oh divine genius of my Frater Finem Respice: Ye all spiritual and holy powers, hear my prayer and aid!

I, Yehi Aour, a brother of the Order of the Golden Dawn in the Outer and an Initiate of the 5=6 Grade thereof; A lord of the paths in the portal of the Vault of the Adepts; A Zelator Adeptus Minor Ordinis R.R.et A.C.: Do at this time propose to constitute and prepare a holy magical talisman of great virtue and efficiency against obsessions; in accordance with the sacred rites and mysteries of our order, and by the knowledge that is mine inheritance from a bygone age.

And I do this thing that I might bring aid unto the soul of my Frater F.R. who betimes is attacked by a terrible obsession which he is unable to resist. For at time there entereth into his Daath an evil and opposing force of the nature of the Qlippoth: causing him to lose control of his thoughts and actions, and establishing itself as the lord and master of his reason for a time.

Hereby cometh woe unto him, and woe to those that love him; woe to his Soul and woe to his mind and body. And of himself he is unable to defy this evil power. And of himself he is unable to defy this evil power.

Wherefore doth it rest alone with God who is father, and the Lord, and the great master of our destinies, to bring him aid. Wherefore is this magical operation is but one prayer to him, the vast one; that he will in his great mercy see fit to grant my supplication: and so to strengthen my will and my power that I may become his minister in this great work. Endowed with a power beyond the power of my own soul:
being able to make magical and perfect this creature of talismans. Mighty in the name of God, in whom is all glory and all compassion.
Oh Lord of Humanity, Oh Osiris, Perfect through

sacrifice — not unto me, but unto thy name be the glory of this work.

'H'

Place the talisman at the foot of the Altar and say:

Now therefore, in the name of Osiris triumphant, do I proclaim that with divine aid I will this night prepare a potent spell, a charm, and a working of magic arts: which shall so operate upon this creature of talismans which now, corded and veiled, lieth at the foot of the altar. Also to make thereof a very potent throne and seal of power so that thereby my Frater Finem Respice may be delivered from his adversary, to the end so that his soul may glorify God the vast one, and his body becomes again a temple of the living God. And I swear by him that sitteth upon the holy throne, and that liveth forever in the glory of the heavens, that this my aim shall be fulfilled, and that this my Frater so shall be delivered, that these powers, larvae or shells which obsess him, be they many or few, weak or mighty shall be so cast out unto the uttermost darkness. And if this thing I lie, then may the evil powers I exorcise fall upon me and destroy even me: for so I will it but that my Frater may be freed.

'I'

Behold, ye sons of the mighty! I have sacrificed unto ye, and have made my oblation: I have moved ye in power and presence: fulfilled are the mystic rites, formulated is the magic chain, declared is the object of mine operation. Wherefore do I say, Move show yourselves, rise and come forth: for that all things are now prepared and made perfect in the great names and powers of God the vast one and mighty; for the commencement of mine invocations.

Wherefore, delay not to come hither and serve me for that in me is the knowledge of the mystic rites that bind thee. Declared in my name, formulated is the object of my working: perfect is the preparations of my charm.

Feel ye and receive then the subtle perfumes and suffumigation of art: accept ye these pleasant sacrifices, and the pure oblation.

Place talisman on Altar (within White Triangle). Left hand on it, right hand holding sword vertically over it.

'J'

Invocation

Hear me then therefore oh ye divine powers and forces whose names and symbols I have placed therein. Hear me, leader of God's hosts, oh Prince Mikhael who art like unto God. Behold herein the symbol of thy power, the magic sword of God wherewith thou did slay the Dragon Apep.

Holy Mikhael, prince of God, consecrate thou the emblem and cidolon of this sword: making therefore a two-edged sword flaming, destroying forever the larvae that obsesses. Hear me! Evil powers of the dragon of evil! Dwellers in the dark path! Larvae that obsesses!

Even into the great symbol of the dragon herein engraved: By and in the name of God, I.A., and of [35 &36] *the Great avenging Angel HUA, do I bind and conjure thee. And even as the sword of Mikhael pieced thrice the coils of the stooping dragon Leviathan; so shall ye be pierced, cut off, and destroyed, except ye depart forever and ever, and strive no more to obsess the body of my Frater Finem Respice.*

Flee then, to the ends of the East: or behold forever the bright glory of the dawn, and inhale forever the sacred perfume of the rose. Flee then to the South: or burn forever in the fire and wrath of God. Flee then to the West: but the great terror of the vast depths of the waters be upon ye.

---

[35] This instruction was left out of the Felkin talisman ritual but I have included it in and taken it from the Jupiter Ritual of Bennett's.

[36] Though there is no instruction to do so in the Bennett manuscript but the sigil of Mikhael (traced from the rose cross) should be traced in the air here.

Above the are the overshadowing wings of the Holy

Flee then to the North: or be cast down forever into the uttermost depths of the Earth. Flee then to the beneath: take again your abodes amongst the beasts of the field; for the name of the Avenger is uttered against ye.

Only flee not above; for there is established one light of the holy three; And the Mount of Abiegnus: and the Fire of the lamb of God. Not thither can ye flee.

For I swear unto ye by the great name of the avenger HUA, that if once again ye seek to attack and obsess him who weareth this holy talisman of art: that ye shall be thrice pierced with the holy sword of him who is like unto God: and that it shall be with thee as with the symbol of the dragon engraven herein: and ye shall be cast down forever unto the abodes of the chained ones and shells: where the worm dieth not and the Fire is never quenched: and ye shall be cut off from God, and from man, and from brute: and ye shall everlastingly endure the most horrible torments; and ye shall never rise no more again! For learn the promise of God which he hath made a covenant unto the Son of Man; which is engraven herein in letters of fire through thrusting. For God hath said:

'Upon the lion and the adder shalt you go, and the young lion and the dragon shalt trample underfoot.' Hear me, lord of the silence, Oh Harpocrates enthroned upon the lotus. Behold, herein the symbol of thy majesty: even the image of the child standing upon the lotus in the sign of silence.

One, and behind thee is the gleaming glory of the dawning sun.

Immortal child of immortal godhead: hear my prayer, and aid thou me in this my magical working. Let a ray of thy presence enter into this magical eidolon, so that this creature of talismans may presently become a sure and certain protection against all obsessions and attacks: so that whosoever weareth it shall be protected, guarded and assisted by the unassailable might of thy purity, that

the power name herein engraven may be manifested in
presence: and that whosoever bears or wears this talisman
may be overshadowed by the protecting wings of the holy
Elohim of Life.

So that the words of God herein declared may be
fulfilled, as it is written:

'He shall chase his angels concerning thee, to guard
thee in all thy ways. They shall bear thee in their hands.'

Take up the talisman in the left hand, smite thrice with the sword,
then hold aloft in the left, with the sword elevated in the right.
Stamp thrice with the left foot.

'K'

Place the talisman towards the North and repeat the Oration:

'The voice of the holy invoked powers said unto me, let
me shroud myself in darkness, peradventure thus shall I
manifest myself in light. I am the only being in an abyss
of darkness. From darkness came I forth ere my birth,
from the silence of a primal sleep. And the voice of ages
answered unto my soul, creature of talismans, the light
shineth in the darkness, but the darkness, comprehendeth
it not. Let the mystic circumambulation takes place in the
path of darkness with the symbolic light of the occult
science to lead the way.

'L'

Take up talisman in the left hand, holding Lamp in [37 & 38] right. Start
the circumambulation. Bar at South after placing it on the ground,
purify and consecrate with water and fire. Formulate Pillars. Lift
talisman with left hand, turn and facing west say,

Creature of talismans, twice consecrate, thou mayest now
approach the gate of the west.

---

[37] Bennet changed these two words from the original and I tend to agree with
his choice, in this respect.

[38] Bennett has left out some instructions in this section. I have added them in
brackets.

'M'

Pass to west, carrying talisman in the left hand. Face southeast, partly unveil talisman, and smite it with the flat of the sword while saying:

> *Thou canst not pass from concealment unto manifestation save by virtue of the name ALHIM. Before all things were the chaos and the darkness and the gates of the night. I am he whose name is darkness. I am the Great One of the Paths of the Shades. Rise, therefore into operation before me, for I am he in whom fear is not. Thou has known me now, so pass thou on.*

'N'

Circumambulate with talisman, halt at north, Place talisman on ground, bar and purify, and consecrate with water and fire and say:[39 & 40]

> *Creature of Talismans, thrice consecrate, Thou mayest approach the Gate of the East.*

Hold talisman aloft.

'O'

Hold telesmata in left hand, lotus wand in right, assume hierophant's form Partly unveil telesmata, smite it with flat of sword, and say:

> *Thou canst not pass from concealment unto manifestation save by virtue of the name YHVH. After the formless and the void and the darkness, then comes the knowledge of the light. I am the light which rises in darkness. I am the exorcist in the midst of the exorcism. Rise therefore into*

---

[39] What Bennett did here is to take the talisman and the Lamp in the same circumambulation, condensing them into one instead of separate operations. The object being that the symbolic light of the kerux (in the neophyte ceremony) leads the way.

[40] Bennett left out the line 'I am the exorcist in the midst of the exorcism' and replaced it with one of this own invention. I agree with him in this instance. For 'N' Bennet only wrote 'circumambulate, purify and consecrate'.

operation for I am the wielder of the forces of balance.
Thou hast known me now so pass thou on unto the cubical
altar of the universe.

'P'

Place talisman on altar, go to the east of altar, hold left hand
over talisman, and sword over it erect and say:

Potent Invocation

I am yesterday, today and tomorrow, for I am born again
and again, I am the guider in the east, the lord of
resurrections who cometh forth from the dark and Whose
birth is from the house of death. Thou art the creature of
talismans whom I have created in my power, Thou art
mighty against [41] *obsessions, Thou art mighty against*
attacks. I am the lord of the shrine which standeth in the
centre of the earth. He is in me and I in him. thou art the
creature of my thought, thou art the manifestation of my
will, thou art a creature of talismans having power; power
against the larvae that obsesses.

I am the radiance in which Ptah floateth over his
firmament, I am he who bursteth the bonds uttermost
extension in my name. I bring to its fullness the force
which is hidden in me.

Thou art fashioned by my hands. I have implanted in
thee my divine spirit, Thou art become powerful,
powerful, powerful against the demons that attack. I
travel upon high, I tread upon the firmament: I raise a
flame with the flashing lightning of mine eye, I fly forward
in the sphere of the daily-glorified Ra.

Thou art myself, mine image, my shadow: I have
fashioned thy form, I have fashioned thy soul, I have
made thee a creature of my thought: powerful art thou
forever thee a creature of my thought: powerful art thou

---

[41] There are some changes by Bennett here to the original Mathers text.

forever against the larvae that obsesses. If I say come upon the mountain, Behold! the celestial waters will flow at my word!

For I am Ra incarnate: I am Khepra in the flesh. I am the living image of my father Toum, lord of the city of the Sun.

Thou art my mind, thou art my thought: In thee I make shine forth my godhead.

In thee I manifest my power: making thee mighty against all spirits, even against the demons and larvae that obsess.

The god who commands is my mouth! The god who commands is in my heart! My tongue is the scantily of truth! A god sitteth upon my Lips!

My words are accomplished every day and the desires of my heart realizeth itself, like that of Ptah when He createth his works.

Thou art the image in my mind, thou art the desire of my heart: There is given unto thee - life, strength, health: Thou rejoiceth in thy life which I have given thee: Thou continually accomplish thy work; Thou draweth power threefold, from the daily-glorified Ra.

Thou art the restriction of evil.

Thou art the dawning of the new light and life. Thou art all-powerful in Earth, in Heaven and in Hell.

Thou destroyeth all that attack thee:

I have given thee power against all spirits in the Universe! Terrible is thy might! restless is thy power! No spirit of the firmament or of the fire: of the water or of the air, of the Earth, or of the Beneath can prevail against thee. Thou protecteth him who shall wear thee, Thou defendest my Frater Finem Respice who is here present before thee: Thy power is for him, Thy aid is his right: Thou goest with him whithersoever he goeth, whether thy body is with him or not. Continually doest thou aid him: drawing ever life and pleasure from the Godhead which is mine. Never can he fall again, for I have formed thee and fashioned thee with my hands as

*a holy talisman of threefold power, protecting as a sun
and as a shield in time of trouble. No temptation can
overcome him; no larvae can ever more obsess: Thou
art unto him forever as a guard holy of two-edged
swords flaming against his adversaries. While he lives
thou livest: when he dieth, Thy spirit is released: having
accomplished thy work when thou shalt flee unto the
gate of the setting sun, Thou shalt pass with him in his
boat of evening, Thou shalt enter him unto the fields of
AHURA (A-hoora)*

*For I have fashioned thee with my hands; I have created
thy life from nothing: Thou livest in me and I in thee. Over
thee has my word and my will, dominion everlasting, none
can dismiss thee, none can disperse thee or destroy. None
can give into thee rest, and glory everlasting in the field
of AHURA. But thither shalt not thy freed spirit flee until
my Frater Finem Respice, unto whom I have appointed
thee as guardian, shall die in peace: Not until thy work
on earth is accomplished can thou gain the immortality of
life.*[42]

Elevate the consecrated sigil toward heaven, remove the veil and
cry in a loud voice:

*Creature of talismans, now and forever all-powerful
.against obsessions. Long hast thou dwelt in darkness;
quit the night and seek the day!*

Place telesmata in the triangle (on the altar). Hold the sword over
it while saying:

*Wherefore by the names, rites, words, thoughts and
powers already rehearsed. By the will of the godhead;
by the aid of the divine Osiris; and of the higher soul of
my Frater F.R., do I conjure upon thee the power of
evermore protecting my Frater F.R., known in the outer
world as Robert W. Felkin, from all obsessions and attacks
of every spirit that lives; and do I seal and bind in thee*

---

[42] Dragon Slayer.

this my will and decree in the mighty words of God the
Vast One!

Khabs am Pekht
Knox Om Pax
Light in Extension

'R'

As the Light hidden in darkness can become manifest
therein so shalt thou become manifest from concealment
into operation.

Take up sigil in the left hand, standing East of altar, facing West,
recite the following invocation:

A Conjuration of Dignitaries

Hear me! Ye lords and rulers of the elemental powers
whom I have invoked; Hear me! for I have moved Thee
in power and presence; Hear me! for I know your
names!
  Come unto me Oh elemental image of Harpocrates;
divine SAH of the lord of the lotus. Come unto me, and
make powerful the dweller in this talisman which I have
fashioned with mine hands, whose soul is the creation of
my will. I am Har-par-kra-tist, lord of silence: I am the
lord of the lotus: I come forth protecting from the gate of
the east. I am encircled with the mist of the morning. I am
the babe in the egg of the blue:
  My mother Nuit hath extended over me her wings.
Thou art the work of my fingers. I have fashioned thy
form, I have created thy soul: I am powerful against all
spirits that attack. I live in thee: I bestow upon thee my
powers. Mighty art thou to protect against obsessions.
YHVH Eloah ve-Daath, and in the name of AGLA do I
Invoke thee!
  I am Mikhael, leader of god's hosts: in my right hand
is the sword and flame. I pierce the coils of the stooping

dragon. I establish in darkness the light of the holy three.[43 & 44]

Thou art the work of my fingers. I have fashioned thy form. I have created thy soul. I destroy the powers of evil, the demons that attack: I live in thee, I bestow upon thee my powers. Mighty art thou to cast out and destroy the evil ones of the earth. Come unto me, light of the dawn overshadowing: Make light and glorious the one dweller in this talisman:

Come unto me, in the great name Elohim Gibor, the name protecting.

I am the dawn, light of the morning: I am the sun in his rising, I have passed through the hour of the cloud and of the night. I am come forth in the splendour of the daily-glorified Ra, and before me the shadows of the night rolled back, and the darkness hasteth away.

Thou art the work of the fingers. I have fashioned thy form: I have created thy soul. I disperse the dark mists of the nighttime. I live in thee. I bestow on thee my powers. Thou art as the dawn:

Mighty art thou as thou banishest the darkness of evil.I will declare the decree: YHVH hath said unto thee:

Thou art my son: this day I have begotten thee. Thou shalt rule them with a rod of iron, Thou shalt break them in pieces like a potter's vessel. Surely shall he deliver Thee from the snare of the Powers of the air: and from the demons of corruption.

He shall cover thee with his feathers: under his wings shall thou trust: His truth shall be thy shield and buckler.

---

[43] Some have equated this Egyptian division of the soul with the etheric body
[44] There are many advantages to the way Bennett has written this ritual. He has invoked the higher powers only, and not every being beneath them. Bennett has skilfully woven the invocation with the *Egyptian Book of the Dead*. He taps into an extra magical formula. If I had any criticism of Regardie's Z2 rituals (which he wrote when he was still a young man) it would be that he invoked too much, and too many hierarchies, which made the ritual little disjointed. As he got older he corrected this point, or possibly even went to the other extreme. One should beware of falling into this trap.

Thou shalt not fear the terror of the night, Nor the arrow which flieth by day, Nor the pestilence that stalketh in the darkness, Nor the destruction that wasteth at noonday.

A thousand shall fall at thy left hand, and tens of thousands at thy right hand. But I shall come not nigh thee. Only with thine eyes shalt (thou) behold and see the reward of the evil ones.

because thou hast the lord my refuge: even the most high; thy habitation. There shall no evil befall thee; neither shall any plague come nigh thy dwelling. For he shall keep his angels charge concerning thee. To keep thee in all thy ways. They shall bear thee up in their hands lest any time thou dash thy foot against a stone.

Thou shalt go upon the lion and the adder: the young lion and the dragon shall thou trample underfoot. Because he has set his love upon me, therefore will I deliver him: I will set him upon high, because he hath known my name.

He shall call upon me, and I will answer him, I will be with him in trouble, I will deliver and honour him. With length of days I will rejoice Him, and will show him my salvation.

Place talisman between pillars and charge it with the enterer Sign. Take it in left hand and repeat foregoing conjuration, charge again till it has now been recited four times and then consecrate finally with water and fire.

'S'

Remove the bind, and smite with sword and proclaim:

By, and in the names, rites, the divine Osiris, words and symbols already rehearsed. I invoke upon thee the power of delivering from obsessions and of casting out demons that obsess.

Circumambulate thrice, holding sigil in right hand. (When arrived at East, facing East) say (while doing appropriate Signs - enterer and silence):

Holy Art Thou Lord of the Universe!
Holy Art Thou whom Nature hath not formed!
Holy Art Thou the Vast and Mighty One!
Lord of Light and of Darkness

'T'

Sigil is given to F.R. to hold the potent invocation is repeated.

Proclamation

And now! in and by the powers whom I have invoked: in
the name of the Lord of the Universe, and by mine own
authority and will: do I declare that this creature of talismans
hath been duly consecrated,[45] formed and prepared; in
accordance with the sacred rites. I declare that it is powerful
against obsessions: I declare that it is a sure defence against
attacks: I declare that as liveth the Lord of the Universe
and mine own higher soul, it shall for ever deliver this my
Frater Finem respite from the demons that have betimes
obsessed him.

'U'

Take talisman back and place between pillars and say:

Herein are engraven and depicted the standards, signs,
seals and powers mighty against attacks and obsessions.
On one side is shown the dragon of evil, even Leviathan
and the crooked serpent, pierced thrice by the sword of
the great Archangel Mikhael, which is Dexter in chief,
held by a hand about which is glory.

Sinister: There is a blazoned star of evil restricted,
the limitation of the rule of the evil ones: therein is the
great name of God the vast one AL: as it is written 'Where
are now their Gods?' About it is written in letters of fire,
in Hebrew, that which signifieth.

---

[45] Bennett did not give a position for Felkin at this point, but I assume he was
in the hierophant's chair on the dais.

'*Upon the lion and the adder shalt thou go and then the young lion and the dragon shalt thou trample underfoot.*

These words are in the Hebrew tongue and are taken[46] from xci.th Psalm, verse 13, and their colours are the colours of fire, because that by fire is the evil purged and cast out.

Upon the other side is the symbol of defence and protection, is that of the child Harpocrates, clothed in white and surrounded by and egg of blue. he is in the sign of silence, and in his right hand is the symbol of immortal life. He standeth upon the lotus of the waters, the flower of the holy Isis: and behind him ariseth the glory of the Golden Dawn, Upon whose golden beams cast athwart the Blue, appear the letters of the holy name ELOHIM GIBOR, which signifieth God hath covered or protected. Dexter, and sinister chief, are the symbols of the holy wings of the chariot of the gods, whereon is formulated the name of strength through sacrifice YHShVH: and in the midst of each is the great symbol of the eye of Horus, showing that the dweller herein shall never sleep, but always live in the light and act.

And from each winged disk there issueth a hand bearing the symbol of Life. And about it is written the versicle in Hebrew from Psalm xci., verses 11 and 12, of which the interpretation is 'He shall charge his angels concerning Thee, To keep Thee in all thy ways, The shall bear Thee in their hands.' Which is the colours symbolic of the divine light from Kether brought down into operation in the ruach in Tiphareth.

'V'

And concerning this holy talisman of art, I charge thee that thou ever keep it as a thing sacred and holy: revere the holy names of God therein inscribed. Revere the

---

[46] See *Kabbalah of the Golden Dawn*, (Thoth Publications) by Pat Zalewski, pages 140-141 which may shed some light upon this Psalm.

symbols of the mighty ones that are thereon; finally treat with love and brotherly and care the elemental magical entity which I have this night invoked and sealed therein. Offering unto it of the water and the scent of fire, and pure oblation, so shall thy love for it at once be thine own safeguard from attack, and thy deliverance from the evil; and shall presently bring the dweller of the talisman unto the glorious light of the freed spirit of God.

All this is brilliant and flashing. Wherefore by God's grace, having come thus far, let us kneel down together and say:

PRAYER UNTO THE HIGHER

Unto thee, sole wise, sole mighty, sole eternal one, be praise and glory forever! Who hast permitted the dweller of this talisman who now kneeleth before thee, to penetrate thus far into the sanctuary of thy mysteries! Not unto me, but unto thy name be the glory. Let the influence of the divine ones descend upon it and teach unto it the mystery of one life. Let it be strong pure and holy, so that it will fail not in the hour of trial; but that it's name may be written upon high, and that its genius may stand in the presence of the holy One, in that hour whence the Son of man is invoked before the Lord of Spirits, and its soul in the presence of the Ancient of Days. Oh Lord of the Universe. Oh spirit of life, Oh Holy who art all hope and truth, let it become indeed mighty against all spirits that attack and would seek to destroy our souls. Amen!

Take from F.P. the Talisman, place it in its cover, with hypericum, incense and the amethyst and say:-

Thus, then, have I completed this mine operation of art: I have made an everlasting protection for thee:

I have delivered thee from the enemy that wrought thee ill . Thou hast no more now to fear from that horror, for the wings of the Godhead overshadow thee in peace.

Take then this creature of talismans in thy care, and

guard it and love it well. Never reveal to any other this operation of mine, never mention that thou bearest this talisman, never show to any but thyself. Never reveal that mystery of the dweller therein, or declare my name as one who wrought thy help. So shall it be well with thee forever, and thou shalt go upon the lion and the adder, and the young lion and the dragon shalt thou trample underfoot. And he shall give his angels charge over thee, to keep thee in all ways. They shall bear thee in their hands.

'W'

Close with the formula of Osiris.

FRATER I. A.'s TALISMAN

Obverse

'Upon the Lion and the Adder shalt thou go
And the young Lion and the Dragon
shalt thou trample underfoot'

FRATER I.A.'s TALISMAN

Reverse

'He shall charge His Angels concerning thee,
to keep thee in all thy ways.
They shall bear thee in their hands'

Other titles from Thoth Publications

APPRENTICED TO MAGIC
By W.E.Butler

This volume is for the true aspirant after magical attainment. In his earlier books the author has defined the real magical art and described the training to be undergone by the serious student. Now he goes a step further, and has written a book which, if properly read, meditated upon, and followed up, will bring those who are ready to the doors of the Mysteries.

This book is not for those who seek sensation. It has been written by one who has himself followed the magical path as a sound and competent guide for all who seek initiation into the Western Mysteries.

Contents include:

Application Accepted
First Exercises
Postures and Breathing
Meditation
The Tree of Life
The Tree as an Indicator
The Contact of Power
Bring Through the Power
The Gates are Open

ISBN 1-870450-41-8

PRACTICAL MAGIC AND THE WESTERN MYSTERY TRADITION
Unpublished Essays and Articles by W. E. Butler.

W. E. Butler, a devoted friend and colleague of the celebrated occultist Dion Fortune, was among those who helped build the Society of the Inner Light into the foremost Mystery School of its day. He then went on to found his own school, the Servants of the Light, which still continues under the guidance of Dolores Ashcroft-Nowicki, herself an occultist and author of note and the editor and compiler of this volume.

PRACTICAL MAGIC AND THE WESTERN TRADITION is a collection of previously unpublished articles, training papers, and lectures covering many aspects of practical magic in the context of western occultism that show W. E. Butler not only as a leading figure in the magical tradition of the West, but also as one of its greatest teachers.

Subjects covered include:

What makes an Occultist
Ritual Training
Inner Plane Contacts and Rays
The Witch Cult
Keys in Practical Magic
Telesmatic Images
Words of Power
An Explanation of Some Psychic Phenomena

ISBN 1-870450-32-9

PRINCIPLES OF HERMETIC PHILOSOPHY
By Dion Fortune & Gareth Knight

Principles of Hermetic Philosophy was the last known work written by Dion Fortune. It appeared in her Monthly letters to members and associates of the Society of the Inner Light between November 1942 and March 1944.

Her intention in this work is summed up in her own words: "The observations in these pages are an attempt to gather together the fragments of a forgotten wisdom and explain and expand them in the light of personal observation."

She was uniquely equipped to make highly significant personal observations in these matters as one of the leading practical occultists of her time. What is more, in these later works she feels less constrained by traditions of occult secrecy and takes an altogether more practical approach than in her earlier, well known textbooks.

Gareth Knight takes the opportunity to amplify her explanations and practical exercises with a series of full page illustrations, and provides a commentary on her work

ISBN 1-870450-34-5

ISBN 1-870450-34-5

*   *   *   *   *

THE STORY OF DION FORTUNE
As told to Charles Fielding and Carr Collins.

Dion Fortune and Aleister Crowley stand as the twentieth century's most influential leaders of the Western Esoteric Tradition. They were very different in their backgrounds, scholarship and style.

But, for many, Dion Fortune is the chosen exemplar of the Tradition - with no drugs, no homosexuality and no kinks. This book tells of her formative years and of her development.

At the end, she remains a complex and enigmatic figure, who can only be understood in the light of the system she evolved and worked to great effect.

There can be no definitive "Story of Dion Fortune". This book must remain incompete and full of errors. However, readers may find themselves led into an experience of initiation as envisaged by this fearless and dedicated woman.

ISBN 1-870450-33-7

THE WESTERN MYSTERY TRADITION
By Christine Hartley

A reissue of a classic work, by a pupil of Dion Fortune, on the mythical and historical roots of Western occultism.

Christine Hartley's aim was to demonstrate that we in the West, far from being dependent upon Eastern esoteric teachings, possess a rich and potent mystery tradition of our own, evoked and defined in myth, legend, folklore and song, and embodied in the legacy of Druidic culture.

More importantly, she provides practical guidelines for modern students of the ancient mysteries, 'The Western Mystery Tradition,' in Christine Hartley's view, 'is the basis of the Western religious feeling, the foundation of our spiritual life, the matrix of our religious formulae, whither we are aware of it or not. To it we owe the life and force of our spiritual life.'

ISBN 1-870450-24-8

A MODERN MAGICIAN'S HANDBOOK
By Marian Green

This book presents the ancient arts of magic, ritual and practical occult arts as used by modern ceremonial magicians and witches in a way that everyone can master, bringing them into the Age of Aquarius. Drawing on over three decades of practical experience, Marian Green offers a simple approach to the various skills and techniques that are needed to turn an interest into a working knowledge of magic.

Each section offers explanations, guidance and practical exercises in meditation, inner journeying, preparation for ritual, the arts of divination and many more of today's esoteric practices. No student is too young or too old to benefit from the material set out for them in this book, and its simple language may help even experienced magicians and witches understand their arts in greater depth.

ISBN 1-870450-43-4